BODY IMAGE

Body Image provides a comprehensive summary of research on body image in men, women and children, drawing together research findings in the fields of psychology, sociology, clothing and gender studies.

This third edition has been thoroughly revised and updated to reflect the significant increase in research on body image since the previous edition, as well as the considerable cultural changes in how men's and women's bodies are viewed. Data are also included from interviews and focus groups with men, women and children who have spoken about their experiences of body image and body dissatisfaction, producing a comprehensive understanding of how men and women construct and understand their bodies in the twenty-first century.

The only sole-authored text to provide a comprehensive view of body image research focusing on men, women and children, *Body Image* will be invaluable to students and researchers, as well as practitioners with an interest in body image and how to reduce body dissatisfaction.

Sarah Grogan is Professor of Psychology Health and Wellbeing at Manchester Metropolitan University, UK. She has been involved in body image research since 1990. She is interested in reducing body dissatisfaction in men, women and children, with a particular focus on the impact of body image and related behaviours on physical health.

"In this revision, Sarah Grogan offers a comprehensive distillation of current knowledge in the field of body image. She skilfully summarises and makes sense of a wide-ranging and ever-expanding body of research in one thoughtful but very readable and accessible volume. The accompanying illustrations and quotations make the material come alive and highlight the human significance of this contemporary concern." *Marika Tiggemann, Matthew Flinders Distinguished Professor, Flinders University, Australia*

"This is an outstanding and stimulating text by Professor Grogan. She uniquely brings together historical, cultural, developmental and contemporary perspectives, and provides a thorough, readable, up-to-date and international coverage of the body image field. This is essential reading for novices and experts, as the book examines both fundamentals and specialized topics." *Lina A. Ricciardelli, School of Psychology, Deakin University, Australia*

"Written in an accessible style, Sarah Grogan's updated book will not disappoint those who want to gain a grounding of key theorists combined with good coverage of contemporary issues and illustrated with recent empirical research. This book should be mandatory for students wishing to study body image." *Sarah Seymour-Smith, Nottingham Trent University, UK*

"Body image scholarship has grown substantially over the past decade. Professor Grogan knowledgably informs us of the foundations, advances, and applications of this fascinating field. Her accessibly written third edition of *Body Image* is the up-to-date and well-told story of how our experiences of embodiment emerge and can powerfully shape our lives." *Thomas F. Cash, PhD, Professor Emeritus of Psychology, Old Dominion University, USA, and Editor-in-Chief of* Body Image: An International Journal of Research

BODY IMAGE

Understanding body dissatisfaction in men,
women and children

Third Edition

Sarah Grogan

Routledge
Taylor & Francis Group

LONDON AND NEW YORK

Third edition published 2017
by Routledge
2 Park Square, Milton Park, Abingdon, Oxon OX14 4RN

and by Routledge
711 Third Avenue, New York, NY 10017

Routledge is an imprint of the Taylor & Francis Group, an informa business

First edition published by Routledge, 1998
Second edition published by Routledge, 2008

British Library Cataloguing in Publication Data
A catalogue record for this book is available from the
British Library

Library of Congress Cataloging in Publication Data
Names: Grogan, Sarah, 1959- author.
Title: Body image : understanding body dissatisfaction
in men, women and children / Sarah Grogan.
Description: Third edition. | Abingdon, Oxon ; New
York, NY : Routledge, 2017. | Includes bibliographical
references.
Identifiers: LCCN 2016014895 (print) | LCCN
2016023987 (ebook) | ISBN 9781138928879 (hardback
: alk. paper) | ISBN 9781138928886 (pbk.) | ISBN
9781315681528 (Ebook)
Subjects: LCSH: Body image--Social aspects--United
States. | Body image--Social aspects--Great Britain.
Classification: LCC BF697.5.B63 G76 2017 (print) |
LCC BF697.5.B63 (ebook) | DDC 306.4/613--dc23
LC record available at https://lccn.loc.gov/2016014895

ISBN: 978-1-138-92887-9 (hbk)
ISBN: 978-1-138-92888-6 (pbk)
ISBN: 978-1-315-68152-8 (ebk)

Typeset in Times New Roman
by Saxon Graphics Ltd, Derby
Printed and bound by CPI Group (UK) Ltd, Croydon, CR0 4YY

FOR EVERYONE INVOLVED IN PROMOTING
POSITIVE BODY IMAGE

CONTENTS

FIGURES

PREFACE TO THE THIRD EDITION

Surveys show that many people are dissatisfied with their appearance. Women generally have higher levels of body dissatisfaction than men, although sexuality and age, as well as psychological factors such as self-esteem and the internalization of body ideals, impact on these gender differences. Women often want to lose weight, whereas men are equally likely to want to be heavier or lighter, and are likely to want to be more muscular at all ages. This third edition of *Body Image: Understanding Body Dissatisfaction in Men, Women and Children* presents updated research literature, and considers what we know about body image in men, women and children in the twenty-first century.

Body dissatisfaction is important in its own right as a threat to well-being, and also because it is associated with various health-related behaviours, some of which present significant health risks. Forty-five million Americans diet each year, and it is estimated that around $33 billion is spent on weight loss products each year in the USA alone. The twenty-first century has also seen a significant increase in men and women having cosmetic surgery; over twenty million cosmetic procedures were performed worldwide in 2014, 87 per cent on women. Incidence of anabolic steroid use is increasing worldwide, with recent studies suggesting that about 2.4 per cent of Australian male adolescents and 6 per cent of US adolescent boys use steroids to bulk up muscle mass in spite of serious health risks associated with their use. Diet pills such as ephedrine are widely available on the internet and are used by both men and women to reduce body fat levels. Site enhancement oils such as synthol are also being used more frequently to create the appearance of trained muscle, and botulinum toxin (botox) is widely used to reduce facial wrinkles.

It has been suggested that media contribute to body dissatisfaction through the portrayal of unrealistic ideals. Television programmes such as *Extreme Makeover* show viewers how their bodies and faces can be reshaped through cosmetic procedures to conform more closely to current beauty ideals, and serve to normalize these practices. Magazines and video games present traditionally "slim and curvy" ideals for women and slender and muscular ideals for men. A US size 0 (UK size 4) has now become the fashion industry standard, causing activists from within the modelling industry to lobby for change because of concerns about models' health. Although there is a higher level of awareness of possible impacts of media idealization of slenderness on women's health, images remain very slender and represent a restricted range of cultural images of attractiveness. Men also report feeling societal pressure to conform to a slender, muscular shape.

The twenty-first century has seen a significant increase in academic research on body image carried out by researchers from a range of disciplines worldwide who are trying to understand these issues. Since the second edition of this book more researchers have focused on body image in children and men, and these studies are explored in this volume. There has also been an increase in the number of new measures to assess dimensions of body image, and these are reviewed. Pressures to be more muscular and toned are explored in terms of the possible impacts on health-related behaviours such as exercise and body-related drug use. The impacts of social media on body image in men and women are investigated, focusing on debates around whether social media promote more positive images through showcasing a wider range of body types, or have a more negative impact in encouraging the objectification of women's and men's bodies. Clothing and fashion and their influences on body image are considered, and new work investigating the impacts of whole-body scanner technology on appearance concern is reviewed. The work of activists and academics who are trying to change how the fashion industry presents women's bodies is also considered.

In this book, data from qualitative and quantitative research in psychology, sociology, women's studies, clothing and textiles research and media studies are integrated to provide a comprehensive summary of what we know about body image in the twenty-first century, and how we might reduce body dissatisfaction and promote positive body image.

This text is intended for students of psychology, sociology, women's studies, men's studies, apparel/clothing and media studies. It will be useful to anyone with an interest in body image.

Sarah Grogan, March 2016

ACKNOWLEDGMENTS

Many thanks to all the people who have given their expertise and their time to make this book possible.

Most importantly, thanks to those who agreed to be interviewed or to complete questionnaires and who shared their experiences of body (dis)satisfaction. This book would not be possible without your input.

Thanks also to ex-students at Manchester Metropolitan University, Manchester, UK (Penny Cortvriend, Lisa Bradley, Helen Richards, Debbie Mee-Perone, Clare Donaldson, Wendy Hodkinson and Nicola Wainwright) and at Santa Fe Community College, Florida, USA (Jacqueline Gardner, Renee Schert, Melissa Warren, Harry Hatcher, Damien Lavalee, Timothy Ford and Rhonda Blackwell) for collecting data for the first edition of this book, some of which appear again in this version. Thank you to ex-MSc students at Staffordshire University (Vivienne Hopkins, Jo Ann Campbell and Beth Rhodes) for allowing me to include excerpts from your dissertations. I am also indebted to Paul Husband, Sarah Shepherd and Ruth Evans for running interviews with steroid users, to Geoff Hunter for advice on anabolic steroids, and to Sam Wright for her work on all aspects of the steroid project. Thanks to Rhona Reardon and Jayne Mechan for discussions about breast surgery, and to Vicky Fern and Emily Buckley for input on body image in post-natal women. Thanks also to Brendan Gough and Matthew Hall for support on men's body image, to the scanner team (Simeon Gill, Kathryn Brownbridge, Amanda Whalley, Sarah Kilgariff, Chris Armitage, Dawn Warnock, Emma Storey and Clair Templeton), and the dance team (Jill Bunce, Johanne Simone Heyland, Wendy Davies, Talia Padilla, Alison Williams, Lisa Cowap and Chloe Woodhouse) – I have learned about body image from you all. Many thanks as well to all colleagues who have provided suggestions and support. In particular, thanks to Lina Ricciardelli, Tracy Tylka, Rachel Calogero, Sarah Seymour-Smith, Emma Halliwell, Sofia Persson, Mark Forshaw, Brendan Gough and an anonymous reviewer. Your support has been invaluable.

Also, many thanks to Caroline Bailey at The Picture Desk, Kristy Cannings at Photoshot and Sara Toso at Mary Evans for advice and help when choosing images for this book. Special thanks to Liz Rankin and Ceri Griffiths at Routledge for all your help.

Thanks to the following for permission to include illustrations: Musée du Louvre for Figures 2.2 (*Bathsheba*) and 2.8 (*Study of Two Nude Figures*); Sterling and Francine Art Institute for Figure 2.3 (*Blonde Bather*); Mary Evans Picture Library for Figure 2.4 (Woman in flapper dress 1923); The Picture Desk for Figures 2.5 (Marilyn Monroe), 2.9 (Marlon Brando) and 2.10 (Dolph Lundgren); Photoshot for Figures 2.1 (Beyoncé), 2.6 (Twiggy), 2.7 (Kate Moss) and 5.1 (Serena Williams); and Simeon Gill and Kathryn Brownbridge for Figure 3.1 (Whole-body scan image).

Thank you to friends who have provided encouragement and support while I have been researching and writing this book. You may not have known it, but each of you said just the right thing at the right time: Rachel Davey, Ruth Evans, Emily Smith, Fiona Tweed and Will Waldron.

Finally, many thanks to Mark Conner for careful proofreading and support while I was researching and writing this book. Thank you.

1

INTRODUCTION

The twenty-first century has seen a significant increase in academic research and popular interest in body image. In academia, researchers from a number of disciplines have become interested in factors that affect people's experiences of embodiment, and the impact of body image on behaviour. The significant rise in referrals for cosmetic surgery, concerns about unhealthy eating and drug use to reduce weight, and an increase in the use of drugs designed to make men and women more muscular have inspired researchers to try to understand the motivations behind these behaviours, and more general experiences of embodiment. Recent theoretical developments have enabled us to understand and predict body image and appearance with greater confidence than previously, and new research into body image is developing in disciplines as varied as medicine and clothing/apparel. This chapter reviews some of the developments that will be addressed in future chapters.

History

Interest in the psychology and sociology of body image originated in the work of Paul Schilder in the 1920s. Prior to Schilder's work, body image research was almost exclusively limited to the study of distorted body perceptions caused by brain damage. Schilder developed this work to consider the wider psychological and sociological frameworks within which perceptions and experiences of body image take place (e.g. Schilder, 1950).

Until the 1980s most psychological investigations of body image were conducted with young women, largely because body image research in psychology had its roots in clinical psychology and psychiatric work focusing on eating disorders. Unfortunately, this reinforced the ideas that the psychology of body image was only relevant to young women, and that the construct only encompassed weight and shape concern. Although these issues are important, body image and its consequences are of relevance to men and women of all ages, and the concept incorporates more than just concern about shape and weight.

Since the 1980s we have seen a significant shift in focus in favour of broadening the participant population in body image studies in psychology to incorporate boys, men, girls, older women and men, and the expansion of "body image" into a multifaceted construct that includes much more than weight and shape concern. There has also been a huge surge of interest in body image research within psychology. In 2004 Thomas Cash noted that there was an escalation of body image and body (dis)satisfaction citations in the PsychINFO database, rising from 726 in the 1970s to 1,428 in the 1980s and 2,477 in the 1990s. This trend has continued, and the success of the research journal *Body Image*, which was first published in 2004, attests to the importance of this area of research within psychology.

In 2012 Thomas Cash edited an *Encylopedia of Body Image and Human Appearance* which provides a summary of research on body image and related areas, mostly written from a psychology perspective (Cash, 2012a). This text, which runs to two volumes and contains 117 in-depth articles, summarizes work published internationally and demonstrates wide-ranging developments in this area. Perhaps most significantly, this *Encyclopedia* shows conclusively that body image research in psychology in the twenty-first century has moved significantly beyond its original foundations in studies of young white women who had problematic relationships with food to encompass men and women of all ages with a range of views and understandings of their bodies.

The sociology of the body became an established discipline in the 1990s, when Bryan Turner (1992) coined the term "somatic society" to describe the newfound importance of the body in contemporary sociology. The success of the UK-based journal *Body and Society*, set up in the mid-1990s, demonstrates the high level of interest in the role of the body in sociology and related disciplines, and the journal continues to publish research focusing on embodiment and critical approaches to the body. More recently, work in Fat Studies has focused in particular on fat embodiment and obesity politics. In Australia, sociologist Deborah Lupton has investigated the sociocultural bases for revulsion towards and the unacceptability of heavier bodies in Western cultures, and in her 2013 book *Fat* she challenges negative ideologies around shape and weight and discusses fat activism and the size acceptance movement. More recently, Samantha Murray (2016) has explored the moral panic over the "obesity epidemic", and the intersection of medicine and morality in stigmatizing heavier bodies, investigating the politics of embodiment and the social construction of "fat" bodies. The launch of the new US-based journal entitled *Fat Studies* in 2015, edited by Esther Rothblum, evidences the surge of interest in this research area.

There has also been a significant increase in popular interest in body image in the twenty-first century. Articles on the dangers of dieting, and critiques of the use of skinny models in advertising, are more common now than in the twentieth century. There have also been high-profile international initiatives on promoting positive body image, such as the *Dove® Movement for Self-Esteem* in 2010, and the recent development of an All-Party Parliamentary Group on Body Image in the UK to explore how to improve body confidence in collaboration with advertisers, the fashion industry and the media. However, fashion and lifestyle magazines continue to carry airbrushed images of young men and women with slender, toned bodies, and popular media such as tabloid newspapers continue to run articles critiquing the bodies of celebrities, which somewhat calls into question the suggestion of any significant change in cultural pressure to be slender.

A key change in our understanding of body image has been the development of work on positive body image. Historically, research on body image had been largely skewed towards a focus on negative body image, but the last ten years have seen a surge of interest in understanding a range of positive body image constructs including body appreciation, body acceptance, and the broad conceptualization of beauty (Tylka and Wood-Barcalow, 2015). These new developments have enabled a more complete and holistic understanding of body image, including the development of additional scales to measure positive aspects of body image.

Another notable change in the twenty-first century has been an increased academic interest in factors influencing the desire for muscularity and muscle tone in men, women and children. Researchers based in the USA, Canada, Australia, Britain and China have developed an understanding of the motivations for, and experiences of, increased muscularity for men, women and children, including drug use in children and women as well as in men. This work has involved the development of measurement scales that can be used to assess drive for muscularity in women and children. Research on body image in children, especially boys, has also been an area of significant growth in the twenty-first century with a focus on developing ways of trying to help children become resistant to the internalization of thin/muscular cultural ideals. Various researchers have also engaged in interesting debates around the potential positive and negative effects of sport and exercise on body image, and particularly on gender differences in these effects. This book reviews all these areas and presents an account of what we know about body image in the twenty-first century.

Definitions

In *The Image and Appearance of the Human Body*, Schilder (1950) argued that body image is not just a perceptual construct but also a reflection of attitudes and interactions with others. He was interested in the "elasticity" of body image, the reasons for fluctuations in perceived body size, feelings of lightness and heaviness, and the effects of body image on interactions with others. He defined body image as:

> The picture of our own body which we form in our mind, that is to say, the way in which the body appears to ourselves.
>
> (Schilder, 1950: 11)

Since 1950 researchers have taken "body image" to mean many different things, and have moved beyond Schilder's primarily perceptual definition to focus on weight satisfaction, size perception accuracy, appearance satisfaction, body satisfaction, appearance evaluation, appearance orientation, body concern, body esteem, body schema, body percept, body appreciation, body acceptance and more. In an attempt to incorporate the key elements, the definition of body image that will be used in this book is:

A person's perceptions, thoughts, and feelings about his or her body.

This definition can be taken to include psychological concepts, such as perception and attitudes towards the body, as well as experiences of embodiment. It can also be taken to encompass both positive and negative aspects of body image. Perceptual body image is usually measured by investigating the accuracy of body size estimation relative to actual size. Attitudinal body image is assessed by measures of four components: global subjective satisfaction (evaluation of the body); affect (feelings associated with the body); cognitions (investment in appearance, beliefs about the body); and behaviours (such as avoidance of situations where the body will be exposed). Psychological measures of body image tend to assess one or more of these components, or measure global or site-specific satisfaction/dissatisfaction (Thompson et al., 2012).

Although all aspects of body image will be discussed in this book, there is a focus on trying to understand the factors that influence body dissatisfaction in men, women, and children. Body dissatisfaction is defined here as:

A person's negative thoughts and feelings about his or her body.

Body dissatisfaction relates to negative evaluations of body size, shape, muscularity/muscle tone and weight, and it usually involves a perceived discrepancy between a person's evaluation of his or her body and his or her ideal body.

Theoretical perspectives

Although much early work on the psychology of body image was largely atheoretical, there are now several established theoretical perspectives that aim to assist our understanding of the various influences on body image. These will be reviewed briefly below to contextualize the remainder of this book.

Sociocultural perspectives

Sociocultural theories of body image propose that societies have body shape ideals which are communicated (though media, family and peers) to individuals, who internalize them resulting in body (dis)satisfaction (see Tiggemann, 2011). Perhaps the best known of these models is the Tripartite Influence Model (van den Berg et al., 2002) which proposes that media, peers and family are all key sociocultural channels for the transmission of body ideals. This model assumes that body ideals tend to emphasize the desirability of slenderness and muscularity for women and men respectively, meaning that the reference point for judging attractiveness becomes unrealistic, leading to perceptions of relative unattractiveness and body dissatisfaction. Systematic studies using complex statistical modelling support the validity of these theories for both women and men (Tiggemann, 2012).

Cognitive-behavioural perspectives

One of the most influential paradigms within body image research has been the cognitive-behavioural perspective espoused by authors such as Thomas Cash (e.g. Cash, 2011). In 2002, Thomas Cash presented a cognitive-behavioural model of body image development and experiences which emphasized the importance of cultural socialization, interpersonal characteristics, physical characteristics and personality attributes in body image evaluation and investment (Cash, 2002). This model recognizes the reciprocal relationship between environmental events, cognitive, affective and physical processes, and the individual's behaviours in determining body image. Cash differentiates between two kinds of body image attitudes: body image evaluation (body (dis)satisfaction), and body image investment (the cognitive, behavioural and emotional importance of the body). Cash (2011; 2012b) notes that cognitive-behavioural models are well-supported in terms of validity of concepts, and have also been shown to be useful in guiding body image measurement and generating interventions.

Objectification Theory

Objectification Theory (Fredrickson and Roberts, 1997) focuses on the impact on women of existing in a culture that objectifies women's bodies. It suggests that existing in a sexually objectifying culture means that women may experience self-objectification at two levels: state self-objectification, which is where attention is drawn to women's bodies in particular contexts (such as when others comment on how they look or when they see their bodies in photographs), and trait self-objectification, which is where some women develop a chronic view of their bodies as objects, leading to habitual body monitoring, shame and anxiety about their bodies. Trait self-objectification has been linked with body dissatisfaction in women of all ages (Grippo and Hill, 2008). This theory, along with other feminist perspectives on body image such as Nita Mary McKinley's Objectified Body Consciousness Theory (which links body surveillance, the internalization of cultural body standards, and appearance control beliefs; see McKinley, 2011), has been useful in understanding the social construction of women's body image and in developing interventions to improve women's body image.

Positive body image

This perspective has emerged in the last decade, and has its roots in positive psychology. It aims to enable people to recognize their strengths and nurture them

(Tylka and Wood-Barcalow, 2015). Proponents of positive body image tend to take the view that positive body image is not just the inverse of negative body image but has unique elements that require understanding (Tylka, 2011). These elements are: having a favourable opinion of the body irrespective of its actual appearance; acceptance of the body in spite of weight, imperfections and body shape; respect for the body involving engaging in healthy behaviours and responding to its needs; and rejection of media imagery, which helps to protect the body. These elements have been incorporated into a Body Appreciation Scale which has been found to be reliable and valid (Avalos, Tylka and Wood-Barcalow, 2005).

Positive body image has been shown to be multifaceted, holistic, stable though malleable in interventions, and shaped by social identities (Tylka and Wood-Barcalow, 2015). Proponents are clear that positive body image does not mean complete satisfaction with all aspects of the body and does not protect against all body image-related threats. This perspective is a flourishing area within body image research, and presents clear and original suggestions for promoting more positive views of the body. These will be investigated later, and implications for interventions will be reviewed in Chapter 7.

This book

In this book body image will be investigated from both psychological and sociological viewpoints, because body image is a psychological phenomenon that is significantly affected by social factors. To understand it fully, we need to look not only at the experiences of individuals in relation to their bodies, but also at the cultural milieu in which the individual operates. Only by investigating social context will it be possible to produce an explanation of body image that recognizes the interactions between individual and societal factors.

Body image is conceptualized here as subjective. There is no simple link between people's subjective experience of their bodies and what is perceived by the outside observer. This is obvious in distortion of body size (e.g. many young women who experience *anorexia nervosa* believe they are much heavier than they appear, and some highly muscled bodybuilders believe that they are less muscular than they are in reality), and in cases of "phantom limb" phenomena (in which people who have had limbs amputated report still feeling the missing limb). It is also relevant (though less obvious) to the large number of women and girls who "feel fat" although they are objectively of average (or below average) weight for their height, and to men who feel too thin or too fat although they are objectively of average size.

The image that an individual has of his or her body is largely determined by social experience. Body image is elastic and open to change through new information. Media imagery may be particularly important in producing changes in the ways that the body is experienced and evaluated, depending on the viewer's perception of the importance of those cues (Diedrichs, 2012; Levine, 2012). It is likely that some people are more sensitive to such cues than others. For instance, it has been suggested that adolescents are especially vulnerable because body image is particularly salient while they undergo the significant physical and psychological changes of puberty (Ricciardelli and Yager, 2015). Other groups who attach particular importance to body-related imagery (e.g. people with eating disorders, bodybuilders) may also be sensitized to media cues. Research has suggested that most people have key reference groups that furnish social information relevant to body image (friends, family, media). Since body image is socially constructed, it must be investigated and analysed within its cultural context.

In this book, theory and data from psychology, sociology, women's studies, media studies and clothing/apparel are integrated to address the question of how men and women experience body image and embodiment. Recent conceptual frameworks that have been designed to understand body image will be critiqued. It will be argued that some degree of body dissatisfaction is normative in women in the Western world from eight years of age and possibly earlier, and that this has a significant impact on behaviour such that many women try to change their shape and weight and/or avoid activities that would involve exposing their bodies. Body image in men and boys will also be investigated. Data show that boys show concern over being acceptably V-shaped with a well-developed upper body and slim hips, and that adult men's self-esteem is related to how good they feel about their body shape and weight. There is an emphasis in this book on understanding factors that might reduce dissatisfaction in women and men. Understanding how some people manage to resist social pressure to conform to the cultural ideal may also be helpful in promoting positive body image in those who are less satisfied.

Chapter 2 reviews current research on culture and body image. It is argued that Western cultures in the twenty-first century prescribe a narrow range of body shapes as acceptable for men and women, and that those whose body shape and size fall outside this range may encounter prejudice, especially if they are heavier than is culturally acceptable. The debate as to the basis for current Western cultural ideals is reviewed. Arguments from a biological perspective (suggesting a biological basis for weight preferences) and from social psychology and sociology (stressing cultural relativity) are evaluated. An historical review of trends during the twentieth and twenty-first centuries shows how cultural ideas of acceptable body shape have changed radically over the years, particularly for women. Myths about weight and health are questioned, and the impact of the dieting industry on the lives of men and women is examined. Pressures from the dieting industry, and resistance to these pressures, are discussed. Chapter 2 provides a backdrop for the data on body image presented in subsequent chapters.

Chapter 3 looks specifically at body dissatisfaction in women. Different techniques that have been used to assess body image are evaluated, along with findings based on each technique, to determine the extent of body dissatisfaction and the reasons why women are dissatisfied. Women's attempts to modify their bodies through cosmetic surgery, dieting, exercise, bodybuilding and anabolic steroid use are investigated, reflecting data from psychology, sociology, and women's studies. Interview data are presented from women who have had cosmetic surgery, who engage in bodybuilding, and who use anabolic steroids. Body scanning is investigated as a possible technique to improve body image. The chapter ends with a review of cultural pressures on women to conform to the socially acceptable "slim but shapely" body shape, drawing mostly on work from contemporary feminist writers on the social construction of the feminine body.

Chapter 4 focuses on body satisfaction in men. Work conducted prior to the late 1980s tended to focus on body image in women. A review of men's body satisfaction is timely in the light of recent arguments that there has been a cultural shift in the twenty-first century such that men are under increased social pressure to be slender and muscular, and because more and more research on body image and the experience of embodiment is being conducted on men. Men's satisfaction is evaluated, using work from sociology and psychology and introducing new data from interviews with young men, to determine whether men are aware of societal pressures, and whether these pressures affect their body satisfaction. Recent work on bodybuilding and anabolic steroid use is reviewed, including data from interviews involving male bodybuilders, to understand the psychological and social effects of becoming more muscular and the motivations behind using anabolic steroids and other muscle-enlargement substances such as synthol. Work on the social construction of the masculine body is also reviewed to produce a picture of social pressures on men, and to evaluate the extent of recent cultural changes on men's acceptance of their body shape and size.

Chapter 5 looks directly at studies of the effects of media pressure. Theory and data from psychology, sociology and media studies are discussed in relation to the effects of exposure to idealized media images of attractive photographic models. Content analyses of media portrayals of the male and female body are reviewed. Empirical evidence from studies linking media exposure to body dissatisfaction is reviewed and evaluated, including work on the impacts of social media on body image. Theories of media influence are reviewed, along with their implications for observing body-related media imagery. Data from surveys and laboratory experiments are complemented by data from interviews to evaluate the mechanisms through which media role models, including images shown in video games, may affect body satisfaction in men and women. The trend in the twenty-first century for mainstream magazine and newspaper journalists and models and fashion designers to critique the use of extremely thin models in the media is discussed, along with a consideration of the possible effects of these social changes.

Chapter 6 investigates the effects of age, ethnicity, social class and sexuality, and the intersections between these variables, on body satisfaction. Questionnaire studies that have charted changes in satisfaction throughout the life span are discussed, along with relevant data from interviews with children and adolescents. Dissatisfaction is identified in the accounts provided by children as young as eight years old, and the reasons for this dissatisfaction are discussed. There is discussion of ethnicity and body dissatisfaction, evaluating claims that black women and men are more satisfied with their body shapes and sizes in the context of a subculture where plumpness may be perceived as attractive and erotic. Social class differences in body satisfaction are discussed within a social context that associates slenderness with the middle and upper socioeconomic classes, especially for women. Finally, differences in body satisfaction among heterosexual men and women, gay men and lesbians are investigated, including an evaluation of evidence suggesting that lesbian subculture protects against body dissatisfaction and that gay male subculture promotes dissatisfaction. The importance of considering intersections between these sociocultural factors when understanding social support and social pressure in relation to body image is also discussed.

In the concluding chapter the preceding arguments are summarized, with an exploration of their implications for men's and women's health and well-being. This chapter summarizes factors that seem to predict body dissatisfaction, and focuses in particular on strategies for raising self-esteem, enabling people to resist the internalization of a slender/muscular ideal and tendencies to make upward social comparisons with media-ideal models, increasing physical self-efficacy (including through exercise programmes), reducing body objectification, and increasing body appreciation through promoting body functionality, embodiment and body acceptance.

This book presents a comprehensive and up-to-date review of the variety of influences on men's, women's and children's body image and the possible behaviours associated with body image, including original data on body image in men, women and children. It provides an evaluation of what we know about body image in the twenty-first century, and makes concrete suggestions for how we might go about trying to promote body satisfaction at individual and societal levels.

Bibliography

Avalos, L., Tylka, T.L. and Wood-Barcalow, N. (2005) 'The Body Appreciation Scale: Development and psychometric evaluation', *Body Image*, 2 (3), 285–97.

Cash, T.F. (2002) 'Cognitive-behavioral perspectives on body image', in T.F. Cash and T. Pruzinsky (Eds) *Body image: A handbook of theory, research, and clinical practice* (pp. 38–46), New York: Guilford.

Cash, T.F. (2004) 'Body image: Past, present and future', *Body Image*, 1 (1), 1–5.

Cash, T.F. (2011) 'Cognitive-behavioral perspectives on body image', in T.F. Cash and L. Smolak (Eds) *Body image: A handbook of science, practice and prevention*, 2nd edition (pp. 39–48), New York: Guilford.

Cash, T.F. (Ed.) (2012a) *Encyclopedia of body image and human appearance*, London: Elsevier.

Cash, T.F. (2012b) 'Cognitive-behavioral perspectives on body image', in T.F. Cash (Ed.) *Encyclopedia of body image and human appearance* (pp. 334–42), London: Elsevier.

Diedrichs, P.C. (2012) 'Media influences on male body image', in T.F. Cash (Ed.) *Encyclopedia of body image and human appearance* (pp. 547–53), London: Elsevier.

Fredrickson, B.L. and Roberts, T. (1997) 'Objectification theory: Towards understanding women's lived experience and mental health risks', *Psychology of Women Quarterly*, 21 (2), 173–206.

Grippo, K.P. and Hill, M.S. (2008) 'Self-objectification, habitual body monitoring, and body dissatisfaction in older European American women: Exploring age and feminism as moderators', *Body Image*, 5 (2), 173–82.

Levine, M.P. (2012) 'Media influences on female body image', in T.F. Cash (Ed.) *Encyclopedia of body Image and human appearance* (pp. 540–6), London: Elsevier.

Lupton, D. (2013) *Fat,* London: Routledge.

McKinley, N. (2011) 'Feminist perspectives on body image', in T.F. Cash and L. Smolak (Eds) *Body image: A handbook of science, practice and prevention*, 2nd edition (pp. 48–65), New York: Guilford.

Murray, S. (2016) *The 'fat' female body*, London: Palgrave.

Ricciardelli, L.A. and Yager, Z. (2015) *Adolescence and body image: From development to preventing dissatisfaction*, London: Routledge.

Schilder, P. (1950) *The image and appearance of the human body*, New York: International Universities Press.

Thompson, J.K., Burke, N.L. and Krawczyk, R. (2012) 'Measurement of body image in adolescence and adulthood', in T.F. Cash (Ed.) *Encyclopedia of body image and human appearance* (pp. 512–20), London: Elsevier.

Tiggemann, M. (2011) 'Sociocultural perspectives on human appearance and body image', in T.F. Cash and L. Smolak (Eds) *Body image: A handbook of science, practice and prevention*, 2nd edition (pp. 12–20), New York: Guilford.

Tiggemann, M. (2012) 'Sociocultural perspectives on body image', in T.F. Cash (Ed.) *Encyclopedia of body image and human appearance* (pp. 758–65), London: Elsevier.

Turner, B.S. (1992) *Regulating bodies: Essays in medical sociology*, London: Routledge.

Tylka, T.L. (2011) 'Positive psychology perspectives on body image', in T.F. Cash and L. Smolak (Eds) *Body image: A handbook of science, practice and prevention*, 2nd edition (pp. 56–67), New York: Guilford.

Tylka, T. and Wood-Barcalow, N. (2015) 'A positive complement', *Body Image*, 14, 115–17.

van den Berg, P., Thompson, J.K., Brandon, K.O. and Coovert, M. (2002) 'The tripartite influence model of body image and eating disturbance: A covariance structure modeling investigation testing the mediational role of appearance comparison', *Journal of Psychosomatic Research*, 53: 1007–20.

2

CULTURE AND BODY IMAGE

This chapter explores the effects of cultural influences on body image. Cultural prejudice in favour of slenderness and against overweight is placed in its psychological and sociological context, with a critical evaluation of the roles of biology and culture in promoting the slim ideal.

The idealization of slenderness

In affluent Western societies in the twenty-first century, slenderness is generally associated with happiness, success, youthfulness and social acceptability. Being overweight is linked to laziness, lack of willpower and being out of control. For women, the ideal body is slim. For men, the ideal is slenderness and moderate muscularity. Nonconformity to this ideal has a variety of negative social consequences. Overweight (for both men and women) is seen as physically unattractive and is also associated with other negative characteristics.

Tracing the social meanings attached to slimness over the years, Susan Bordo (2003) shows how, starting at the end of the last century, excess flesh (for men and women) came to be linked with low morality, reflecting personal inadequacy or lack of will. This has continued into the twenty-first century, where the outward appearance of the body is seen as a symbol of personal order or disorder. Slenderness symbolizes being in control. The muscled and toned body has become another symbol of willpower, energy and control. The firm, toned body is seen as representing success. Most people do not have slim, toned bodies naturally, so they have to be constantly vigilant (through exercise and diet) so as to conform to current ideals. Bordo argues that the key issue in the current idealization of slenderness is that the body is kept under control:

> The ideal here is of a body that is absolutely tight, contained, bolted down, firm.
>
> (Bordo, 2003: 190)

More recently, Deborah Lupton (2013) also talks about societal idealization of the "tightly controlled, hard, impermeable body" (p. 105). These authors link the spare, thin, feminine ideal with the solid, muscular, masculine ideal, since both require the eradication of loose flesh and both emphasize firmness. In the preface to the 2003 edition of *Unbearable Weight*, and reflecting on the lack of significant change since the 1990s, Bordo notes that the pressure to have a spare, hard body is still intense in the twenty-first century despite cultural discourses suggesting that variety in body shapes is a positive thing. Noting that Beyoncé Knowles (Figure 2.1) and Jennifer Lopez dwell on how happy they are with their "bodacious bottoms", she suggests that having a body that is not thin is acceptable only if it is worked out and firm:

> Sexy booty is OK, apparently, only if it's high and hard, and if other body-parts are kept firmly in check. Beyoncé is comfortable with her body because she works on it constantly. On the road she does five hundred sit-ups a night.
>
> (Bordo, 2003: xxii)

Others have commented on the shift in ideals represented in social media towards a more muscular and fitter-looking body. The recent rise of social media sites devoted to "Fitspiration" (combining the words "fit" and "inspiration" and presenting images designed to promote health, fitness and empowerment) reflects this increased

Figure 2.1 Beyoncé Knowles.

pressure to have a body that looks worked out and muscular as well as slender. Fitspiration sites have been seen as a more healthy alternative to "Thinspiration" sites (a combination of "thin" and "inspiration" and mainly consisting of images of very thin women and text promoting weight loss), and it is possible that their rise in popularity in the last few years represents a move in favour of a strong rather than thin body for women. However, Leah Boepple and Kevin Thompson (2015) have noted that these kinds of images can carry negative meanings as well as inspiring women to exercise and eat healthily. Comparing Fitspiration and Thinspiration sites using content analysis, Boepple and Thompson (2015) conclude:

> Thinspiration sites featured more content related to losing weight or fat, praising thinness, showing a thin pose, and providing food guilt messages than Fitspiration sites. However, sites did not differ on guilt-inducing messages regarding weight or the body, fat/weight stigmatization, the presence of objectifying phrases, and dieting/restraint messages. Overall, 88% of Thinspiration sites and 80% of Fitspiration sites contained one or more of the coded variables.
>
> (Boepple and Thompson, 2015: 1)

So, even sites designed to promote a strong rather than thin ideal may be promoting messages that stigmatize heavier bodies. Research on weight stigmatization has a long history, and there is good evidence that people (both men and women) who do not conform to the slender ideal may face prejudice throughout their life span. In 1990 Thomas Cash argued that overweight people are treated differently from childhood. Children prefer not to play with their overweight peers, and assign negative adjectives to drawings of overweight people. This prejudice continues into adulthood, when overweight people tend to be rated as less active, intelligent, hardworking, successful, athletic, and popular than slim people. People who are overweight are likely to find more difficulty in renting property, being accepted by "good" US colleges, and getting jobs than their slimmer peers (Latner, 2012). Rebecca Puhl and Jamie Lee Peterson (2012) note that overweight men and women are vulnerable to stigmatization in the workplace and may be stereotyped by health professionals as lazy, dishonest, and lacking in self-control. Stigmatization may be even more marked for those who fall into the "obese" category, as Janet Latner (2012) notes:

> Obese individuals are subjected to widespread stigma and discrimination across interpersonal, educational, employment and medical settings. In both adults and children, those who are more obese are more likely to be stigmatized and teased for their weight.
>
> (Latner, 2012: 267)

In an early study of stereotypes assigned to different body types, Marika Tiggemann and Esther Rothblum (1988) asked large groups of American and Australian college students about their stereotypes of fat and thin men and women. They were asked to rate the extent to which eight qualities were typical of thin men and women and fat men and women. Men and women in both cultures reported negative stereotypes of fat people. Although fat people were seen as warmer and friendlier, confirming the traditional stereotype of the fat and jolly person, they were also viewed as less happy, more self-indulgent, less self-confident, less self-disciplined, lazier and less attractive than thin people. These differences were more marked for judgements of fat women than fat men. The results indicate negative stereotyping of heavier people, especially women, among these college students (Tiggemann and Rothblum, 1988). What was particularly interesting was that there were no differences in stereotyping between students who were fat and those who were thin. Even those who were overweight had negative stereotypes of fat people. This finding has been replicated more recently in other studies showing that individuals perceived to be overweight are rated as lazy, unhealthy, and deserving of teasing and ridicule. Christy Greenleaf and colleagues (2004) found that their participants associated terms describing the heavier weight body (such as "fat" and "obese") with negative personal characteristics such as "lazy", "gross", "slow" and "disgusting".

The tendency to link physical attractiveness with positive personal qualities has been documented since the 1970s, when Karen Dion and colleagues coined the saying "What is beautiful is good" (Dion et al., 1972: 285). They suggested that people tend to assign more favourable personality traits and life outcomes to those they perceive as attractive. In a review of research in this area carried out almost two decades later, Alice Eagley and colleagues (1991) suggested that the effects of the physical attractiveness stereotype are strongest for perceptions of social competence (sociability and popularity). Negative stereotyping of overweight people may be a specific aspect of the physical attractiveness stereotype that refers specifically to the assignment of negative traits to those who have a body size and shape that is not considered attractive by dominant groups in Western culture. Jennifer Rennels (2012) suggests that the "beautiful is good" stereotype continues to affect people's interactions in "significant and meaningful ways" (p. 643), but she also notes that the effects of the stereotype on job-related outcomes seem to be decreasing relative to previous decades, possibly because people making personnel decisions are now better informed about research on the possible impacts of attractiveness stereotypes than previously.

It is likely that causal attributions also affect responses to overweight people; if overweight is seen as being within the individual's control (through overeating and lack of exercise), then overweight people are more likely to be stigmatized. For many people in the USA and other Western countries, being perceived as overweight is the ultimate failure and represents a public demonstration of weakness of will. Christian Crandall and Rebecca Martinez (1996) argue that anti-fat attitudes are part of an individualistic Western ideology that holds individuals responsible for their life outcomes, stressing that prejudice against overweight is culturally bound and depends on attribution of blame. Within Western ideology, being overweight is perceived to violate the cultural ideal of self-denial and

14

self-control. Rebecca Puhl and Jamie Lee Peterson (2012) propose that weight stigmatization can be predicted by cultural beliefs that people are responsible for their own life outcomes and societal values that stigmatize fatness and idealize thinness, and that obese people are less likely to be stigmatized if their weight is seen to be outside their control (such as due to a medical condition). In fact, there is a growing body of evidence that overweight results, at least in part, from genetic factors (Lupton, 2013; Monaghan, 2005a). However, people in Western cultures still tend to hold the erroneous belief that the individual is "to blame" for increased body weight, because it fits ideological beliefs of personal responsibility. This can result in prejudice against people who do not conform to the slender cultural ideal.

The basis of body shape ideals

The debate continues on why Western cultures in particular show a preference for slenderness. On the one hand, biologists and some psychologists have suggested that these body shape preferences derive from biology. They argue that these ideals are based on the fact that slenderness is more healthy than overweight. On the other hand, theorists who have looked at cultural differences in body shape preferences at different times and in different cultures have tended to suggest that biology plays only a minor role in the idealization of slenderness, and that it is largely learned. These two views will be evaluated here.

Body weight and health

Biological arguments stress the importance of slenderness for health (and the unhealthiness of overweight). Slenderness has not always been linked with health. At the start of the twentieth century thinness was associated with illness in the USA and in Britain, because of its link with tuberculosis (Bennett and Gurin, 1982), and in the 1980s extreme thinness came to be associated with illness through links with AIDS (Yingling, 1991). However, in the twenty-first century there is a general belief that to be plump is unhealthy, and that thinness is an indicator of good health (Lupton, 2013; Murray, 2016). In fact, this link is a matter of significant debate in the literature on weight and health.

In order to determine the health risks of overweight, it is first necessary to draw a distinction between mild to moderate overweight and obesity. Internationally, the most widely used measure to determine degree of overweight is body mass index (BMI), obtained by dividing weight in kilograms by squared height in metres. The normal range of BMI is 18.5–24.9. Those with a BMI of 25–29.9 may be classified as overweight, and those over 30 as obese (World Health Organization, 2015). The advantage of using BMI as an indicator of overweight is that it controls for a person's height. However, BMI does not take into account body composition, and highly muscular individuals (such as bodybuilders and some other sports people) may fall into the overweight or obese category because their high levels of muscularity mean that they weigh heavily in spite of having very low levels of body fat (Bee, 2006).

Other measures are available and may be used in conjunction with BMI. Standard weight tables based on frame size (small, medium or large) were popular in the 1980s and 1990s and are sometimes still used, but have been criticized for their inability to take account of age and cultural differences, causing some commentators to dismiss them as "arbitrary, random and meaningless" (Gaesser, 2002: 106). Measuring skin-fold thickness by applying calipers to various target areas of the body is another measure that gives a direct measure of body fat, but it tends to have low interrater reliability (i.e. different raters produce varying estimates) and is uncomfortable for the person being assessed. Also, skin-fold thickness measures assess subcutaneous fat and use this to infer total body fat, which may lead to error due to individual differences in fat distribution (Tovee, 2012).

Another measure that is becoming more widely used is waist circumference. This is easy to measure, and many health problems seem to correlate with fat collected in the abdominal region (Bee, 2006; Lee et al., 2008). Public Health England (2015a) notes that for men a waist size of 94cm (37 inches) may indicate increased risk of health problems, and 102cm (40.2 inches) a greatly increased risk of health problems; for women the criterion waist sizes are 80cm (31.5 inches) and 88cm (34.6 inches). Unfortunately, the measure does not take account of height (which may correlate with healthy waist measurement) or age, so it may overestimate likely health risks in older and taller people if used as a sole measure.

Recently, measures of bioelectric impedance have been used in clinical practice to determine fat levels. These measures provide an indication of body fat percentage and fat-free mass by passing a safe electrical current through the body. This method is fast and easy to use, but is affected by dehydration and can be hard to calibrate, particularly among those with BMIs over 35, decreasing accuracy. Measures are also influenced by ethnicity, phase of the menstrual cycle and underlying medical conditions (Dehghan and Merchant, 2008).

Clearly there are challenges associated with each of these measures, and it has been suggested that measures such as waist circumference do not add benefits in predicting health outcomes relative to BMI alone (Huxley and Jacobs, 2011), so studies linking health with body weight tend to use BMI as the preferred measure. Higher levels of overweight (BMI > 30) have generally been seen as harmful to health and have been associated with heart disease, hypertension and diabetes. According to Kelly Brownell and Judith Rodin in the 1990s:

> Obesity is a major cause of morbidity and mortality. To argue that greater levels of excess weight are not associated with increased risk is to dismiss an abundant and consistent literature.
>
> (Brownell and Rodin, 1994: 783)

This was supported by the World Health Organization in 2015:

Risks of coronary heart disease, ischemic stroke and type 2 diabetes mellitus increase steadily with increasing body mass index (BMI), a measure of weight relative to height. Raised body mass index also increases the risk of cancer of the breast, colon, prostate, endometrium, kidney and gall bladder. Mortality rates increase with increasing degrees of overweight, as measured by body mass index.

(World Health Organization, 2015)

However, evaluation of research is difficult because of reliance on correlational data. Most studies have looked at mortality and health in a sample of people (usually men) of different weights. It is obvious that extraneous variables may operate to confound the relationship between weight and health, such as the frequency of stringent dieting in the obese, which may itself be deleterious to health. Lee Monaghan (2005a) critiques the link between obesity and health, suggesting that cardiorespiratory fitness, not fatness, is important in predicting mortality rates. He shows that obese men who were fit had similar mortality rates to lean men who were fit, and that active obese individuals had lower morbidity and mortality rates than normal-weight people who were sedentary. He argues that the case for a link between obesity and health is far from proven and suggests:

The highly publicized war against fat is about moral judgements and panic (manufactured fear and loathing). It is about social inequality (class, gender, generational and racial bias), political expediency and organizational and economic interests.

(Monaghan, 2005a: 309)

Similar arguments are presented by Deborah Lupton (2013) who argues that evidence from "obesity science" is weak.

The health risks posed by moderate overweight are the subject of even greater debate than those related to obesity. Many authors have argued that moderate overweight represents no significant health risk (Flegal et al., 2005) and that medical concern with overweight is grounded on cultural prejudice rather than on realistic health risks. Authors taking this position have suggested that overweight has become a visible marker of poverty and inferior social status (Campos, 2004), and that "fat bigotry" in the medical profession may lead doctors to focus on weight loss and ignore more important health risks, thereby compromising patient health (Monaghan, 2005a). However, other authors have argued that even moderate overweight may present some health risks. Amy Berrington de Gonzalez and colleagues (2010) present evidence from pooling data from longitudinal studies (where people are tested at multiple time points) investigating BMI and mortality in white men and women aged 19 to 84. They found that women who had never smoked and who were overweight (BMI 25–29.9) were 13 per cent more likely to die during the study follow-up period than those with a BMI between 22.5 and 24.9. In women who were classified as obese, there was a 44 per cent to 250 per cent higher risk of death than among those in the 22.5–24.9 range. Results were similar for men and for men and women combined, and the authors concluded that a five unit increase in BMI translated into a 31 per cent increase in risk of death. As the data came from white groups, implications for other ethnicities are unclear. Also, the study focused on mortality rather than health or quality of life, so links with specific illnesses are also unclear. However, studies where measures are taken at multiple time points are useful in enabling us to review the impacts of overweight on health and mortality, rather than relying on correlational data.

Clearly, this issue has generated controversy. The most parsimonious explanation of the data as they stand at present is that obesity may represent a health risk to some individuals, but links between moderate overweight (BMI of 25–29.9) and health are unclear. The belief that slenderness is healthier than moderate overweight is not borne out by medical research (Lupton, 2013; Monaghan, 2005a; Rich, 2005). This suggests that social pressures to be slender are based more on cultural aesthetic preferences than on health concerns.

Culture and body shape preferences

Many authors have argued that cultural differences are primarily responsible for body shape ideals. Data mostly derive from studies of historical differences in body shape preferences, and from studies of differences between different cultural groups. Evidence for historical changes in body shape fashions in the Western world will be reviewed, followed by some evidence of cultural variation in body shape preferences.

Historical trends: portrayal of the female body

There is general agreement that social pressure to conform to the slender ideal is greater on women than on men. The idealization of slenderness in women is often viewed as the product of an historical evolution that occurred in the twentieth century. Within Western industrialized cultures, there have been many changes over the years in the body shape and size that is considered attractive and healthy, especially for women. It is possible to trace a cultural change in the ideal body, from the voluptuous figures favoured from the Middle Ages until the turn of the twentieth century, to the thin body types favoured by the fashion magazines of today.

A heavier body size was considered fashionable and erotic until relatively recently. From the Middle Ages the "reproductive figure" was idealized by artists. Fleshiness and a full, rounded stomach were emphasized as a symbol of fertility (Fallon, 1990). The female body was frequently represented with full, rounded hips and breasts. This trend is represented in Rembrandt van Rijn's *Bathsheba* (1654), which portrays a woman with a plump body and which represented the aesthetic ideal of its time (Figure 2.2).

This trend is also evident in the fleshy bodies painted by Rubens in the 1600s and by Renoir in the 1880s. Renoir's *Blonde Bather* (1881; Figure 2.3) portrays a

18

Figure 2.2 Rembrandt van Rijn, *Bathsheba* (1654).

Figure 2.3 Pierre-Auguste Renoir, *Blonde Bather* (1881).

healthy-looking plump figure, idealized as the antithesis to the taut male body portrayed around this time.

Slender figures were not seen as attractive until the twentieth century. In fact, Manet's *Olympia* (1863) (which he considered his masterpiece) was denounced when it was shown in 1865 because the subject was not considered sufficiently plump to be erotic (Myers and Copplestone, 1985). Various authors have dated the origin of the idealization of slimness in Western culture to the 1920s, and it is argued that the thin ideal is the outcome of successful marketing by the fashion industry, which became the standard of cultural beauty in the affluent industrialized societies of the twentieth century (Gordon, 1990). Clothes fashions were represented by hand-drawn illustrations until the 1920s, when images started to be photographed and widely distributed in mass-market fashion magazines. These magazines presented a fantasy image of how women should look. The fashions themselves demanded a remoulding of the female body, because each look suited a particular body shape (Orbach, 1993). Flapper fashion, which originated after the First World War, demanded a boy-like, flat-chested figure to show off the straight, low-waisted dresses to advantage (Figure 2.4).

Figure 2.4 Woman in flapper dress, 1923.

In the 1920s middle- and upper-class women began binding their breasts with foundation garments to flatten their silhouettes (Caldwell, 1981). They used starvation diets and vigorous exercise to try to get their bodies to the preadolescent, breastless, hipless ideal (Silverstein et al., 1986; LaFrance et al., 2000), and in 1920 a conference of the New York Academy of Science was convened to study the new phenomena of eating disorders. Winners of the Miss America beauty contest at this time had average bust-waist-hip measurements of 32-25-35. In the 1930s and 1940s ideals moved toward a more shapely figure, epitomized by Jean Harlow and Mae West in the 1930s and Jane Russell in the 1940s. The mean measurements of Miss America winners changed to 34-25-35 (an increase of 2 inches in bust size from the previous decade) in the 1930s, and to 35-25-35 in the 1940s. Breasts became fashionable, along with the clothes that emphasized them. Lana Turner and Jane Russell became famous as "sweater girls". In the 1950s this trend continued, when the Hollywood movie industry and the fashion industries promoted large breasts (along with tiny waists and slim legs). Marilyn Monroe personified this trend (Figure 2.5) and was the first *Playboy* centrefold.

Figure 2.5 Marilyn Monroe.

Miss America winners increased in bust and hip measurements in the 1950s and reduced in waist measurement, so that the body was (on average) an exaggerated hourglass shape of 36-23-36.

In the 1950s there was also a significant move toward slimness. Grace Kelly and Audrey Hepburn were slim (rather than buxom) and were portrayed to movie-goers as symbolizing sophistication (rather than sensuality). They became role models for some young women, and slimness became associated with the upper classes (Mazur, 1986). The trend for slimness became particularly acute in the 1960s when the fashion model Twiggy became the role model for a generation of young women (Figure 2.6). She had a flat-chested, boyish figure, and weighed 96 lb (Freedman, 1986).

Slimness came to exemplify unconventionality, freedom, youthfulness, and a ticket to the "Jet-Set" life in 1960s Britain, and was adopted as the ideal by women of all social classes (Orbach, 1993). Miss America winners also were slimmer and taller in the 1960s than in the previous decade, with an increase of about an inch in height and a weight loss of about 5 lb by 1969 (Mazur, 1986). This trend

Figure 2.6 Twiggy.

occurred across Europe and the USA. Studies of the portrayal of the female body in the media have reliably found that models became thinner and thinner between the 1960s and the 1980s. For example, models in *Vogue* magazine became gradually thinner, and even *Playboy* centrefolds became taller and leaner so that, although their breasts remained large, Playmates became slim and nearly hipless in the 1980s (Fallon, 1990). This trend for thinness as a standard of beauty became even more marked in the 1990s than it had been in the 1980s. In the 1980s models were slim and looked physically fit, with lithe, toned bodies. In August 1982 *Time* magazine argued that the new ideal of beauty was slim and strong, citing Jane Fonda and Victoria Principal as examples of the new ideal of beauty. In Britain and the USA the slim, toned figure of Jerry Hall epitomized this ideal. The 1990s saw a departure from this trend with the emergence of "waif" models with very thin body types, perhaps the most famous of these being Kate Moss (Figure 2.7) who has a similar body shape to Twiggy from the 1960s.

Although the three most highly paid supermodels of the mid-1990s were not "waifs" (Cindy Crawford, Claudia Schiffer and Christy Turlington), designers and

Figure 2.7 Kate Moss.

magazine editors often chose to use extremely thin models such as Kate Moss to advertise their clothes and beauty products. The late 1990s saw the rise of "heroin chic"; that is, fashion houses made very thin models up to look like stereotypical heroin users, with black eye make-up, blue lips and matted hair. In a *Newsweek* article from August 1996 Zoe Fleischauer, a model who was recovering from heroin addiction, told the interviewer that models are encouraged to look thin and exhausted:

> They [the fashion industry] wanted models that looked like junkies. The more skinny and f****d up you look, the more everyone thinks you're fabulous.
>
> (Schoemer, 1996: 51)

In the late 1990s the model Emma Balfour condemned the fashion industry for encouraging young models to take stimulants to stay thin and for ignoring signs of heroin addiction (Frankel, 1998), and US President Clinton denounced "heroin chic" in the wake of fashion photographer Davide Sorrenti's death from a heroin overdose. In 2000 the Women's Unit of the British Labour government were so concerned about the potential effects on young women's health of representations of "waif" models in magazines and other media that they convened a meeting to discuss the potential links between eating problems and these media images. This Body Summit prompted a flurry of articles discussing the potential link between thin images and young women's body image and eating, most of which suggested that magazines and newspapers needed to review their practices (e.g. Reid, 2000).

Irrespective of the moral panic in the early 2000s, the extremely thin Western ideal has been maintained. Scarlett Grey, a successful 17-year-old UK model, quit modelling in 2015 after allegedly being told to lose weight by her modelling agency, even though she was only a UK size 8 (US size 4) and 5 feet 10 inches tall, prompting a UK parliamentary enquiry (Calderwood, 2015). In the USA, models such as Crystal Renn who were a US size 12 (UK size 16) modelled for brands such as Chanel and Dolce and Gabbana, drawing media attention (e.g. Winter, 2014). In addition, digital modification of images in magazines now means that virtually every fashion image is digitally modified. Susan Bordo (2003) notes that digital modification of images means that we are being educated to shift our perception of what a normal woman's body looks like, so that we see our own bodies as wanting because they do not match an unrealistic, polished, slimmed and smoothed ideal. Unfortunately, labelling these kinds of idealized images as "retouched" does not seem to prevent them from producing increased body dissatisfaction when viewed by young women (Tiggemann et al., 2014).

Historical trends: portrayal of the male body

Representation of the male body also has an interesting history. Myers and Copplestone (1985) note that sculptors in ancient Greece were keenly interested in the problems of representing the anatomy of the human figure in a realistic form, and that it was at this stage that lifelike male nudes started to appear. Men were often presented nude, whereas women were represented clothed in cloaks and undergarments. The male body was revered and considered more attractive than the female body. In the seventh century BC a trend developed for a broad-shouldered, narrow-hipped ideal that has become known as the "Daedalic" style after the mythical Daedalus, who, according to legend, was the first Greek sculptor. At this stage the male body was idealized and presented in a strictly stylized way, with emphasis on clearly defined muscles that were carved into a surface pattern on the marble.

Idealization of the male body can also be found in the art of the Roman Empire, where the epitome of physical beauty for the Romans, who hated obesity and idealized slenderness in their paintings and sculpture, was the slim, muscular warrior. In Renaissance art, too, the male body was traditionally presented nude, emulating the physique represented in classical Greek sculpture. The naked, muscular male body which represented this aesthetic ideal can be seen in Signorelli's *Study of Two Nude Figures* (1503; Figure 2.8).

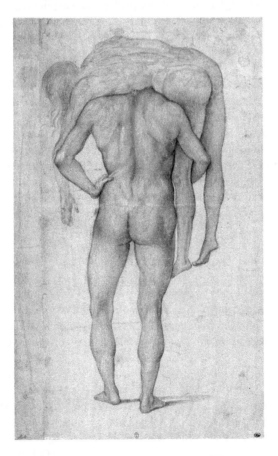

Figure 2.8 Luca Signorelli, *Study of Two Nude Figures* (1503).

The male body continued to dominate art until the mid-nineteenth century, when artists such as Courbet shifted the erotic focus from the male body to the female body. From then until the 1980s the male body was rarely idealized in art, except in paintings and photography aimed at a gay male audience. However, there were exceptions. In the late nineteenth century Thomas Eakins photographed his own nude body in the series *Thomas Eakins at 45 to 50*, in defiance of the convention that male bodies should not be shown to a heterosexual audience. However, his body is not presented in an idealized form. On the contrary, it is seen as mature and fleshy, without the firm muscles usually portrayed in pictures of the male body. Another notable exception to this general trend was the idealization of the male body in Nazi propaganda. Leni Riefenstahl's photographs of the 1936 Olympic Games (*Schönheit im olympischen Kampf*) were modelled on classical Greek poses, and were used by the Nazi propaganda machine to represent the Teutonic ideal. This ideal (highly muscled and engaged in athletic pursuits) is echoed in images in the specialist bodybuilding magazines that emerged in Europe in the 1940s (Ewing, 1994). In publicity photographs explicitly aimed at a female audience, the Hollywood idols Rock Hudson, Kirk Douglas, Marlon Brando and James Dean were also portrayed semiclothed, in poses designed to flatter their muscularity (Meyer, 1991; see Figure 2.9).

It was not until the 1980s that idealized images of the naked (or semi-naked) male body started to become common in mainstream Western media. The 1980s and 1990s saw an increase in the objectification of the nude male body in photographs that follow the conventions of photographing the female nude (eyes or face averted or not visible). Some of these photographs were specifically aimed at gay men, such as those by Robert Mapplethorpe, but entered the mainstream market (Pultz, 1995). The advent of the magazine *For Women* and the appearance of male strippers and dancers such as the Chippendales in the 1990s blurred the traditional boundaries between men as the viewers and women as the viewed. Muscular actors such as Dolph Lundgren exemplified the well-muscled male ideal as portrayed in the popular media in the 1990s (Figure 2.10).

The 1990s were an important turning point as the male body lost its originally homoerotic connotations, and advertisers felt happy to use the naked male torso in mainstream advertising to sell everything from ice cream to perfume and orange juice. Lisa O'Kelly (1994) discusses the influence of gay culture in making men's bodies more visible, showing that the iconography of gay culture had moved into the mainstream, blurring the edges of men and women's sexual identities, and extending the range of images that are considered acceptable for men:

> Once advertisers would have been fearful of linking their products with images that might have been thought homoerotic. Now even Marks and Spencer advertises its socks with pictures of hunky men. ... Mainstream women's publications such as *Marie Claire* regularly feature articles on men and their bodies and have no qualms about including revealing pictures.
>
> (O'Kelly, 1994: 32)

Figure 2.9 Marlon Brando.

Figure 2.10 Dolph Lundgren.

Peter Baker (1994) argued that there were sound commercial reasons for this increase in the visual portrayal of the male body in the media. Cosmetics companies came to realize that there was a gap in the market for male cosmetics, and that men need to be persuaded to buy them.

> They had to find a way of persuading men that it's actually macho to use a moisturiser and not fey to have a facial, hence the pictures of hunks splashing on the perfume.
>
> (Baker, 1994: 132)

More recently, Brendan Gough and colleagues (2014) have noted that men are becoming even more interested in appearance in the twenty-first century, including spending more time and money on grooming products while maintaining traditionally masculine ways of accounting for these practices:

> Our research suggests a positive engagement with once feminized ideas and practices in the arena of appearance and embodiment; however, this engagement is still circumscribed by investments in orthodox markers of masculinity. So while men can wear make-up, they do it discreetly, talk about it online only, and emphasize their heterosexuality, and men who attempt to lose weight may well distance themselves from the female world of 'diets' and instead talk of desired body shape where muscularity, rationality and autonomy may be foregrounded.
>
> (Gough et al., 2014: 10)

It might be expected that the portrayal of idealized images of men's bodies in the media is likely to lead to increasing problems with self-image and body satisfaction in men. Karen Henwood and colleagues (2002) have argued that men are increasingly defined by their bodies, and that media representations of male bodies present a slender and muscular ideal linked with aspirational consumer goods aimed at men:

> Media advertising routinely depicts in positive ways youthful toned muscular male bodies or focuses on style in men's clothing and physical appearance.
>
> (Henwood et al., 2002: 183)

In fact there has been a growing preoccupation with weight and body image in men, which parallels this increased "visibility" of the male body. In *The Adonis Complex*, Harrison Pope and colleagues (Pope et al., 2000) noted that contemporary actors dwarf Hollywood icons of the 1950s and 1960s, and cite evidence that the average *Playgirl* centrefold man lost 12 lb of fat while gaining approximately 27 lb of muscle in the twenty-five years leading up to the turn of the century. Roberto Olivardia (2002) suggests that this is paralleled in men's dissatisfaction with the ways that they look, especially with their chests and muscle tone.

Don McCreary and colleagues have carried out extensive work on men's drive for muscularity (e.g. McCreary et al., 2006; McCreary, 2012), showing the importance of the muscular ideal for men and demonstrating links between desire for muscles and low self-esteem, depression and psychological distress (see also Thompson and Cafri, 2007). Work on substances designed to increase muscularity has also suggested that men are under pressure to become more muscular, and this may be becoming even more extreme in the twenty-first century. In a recent review of factors predicting anabolic steroid use, overcoming negative body image was a key motivator (Sagoe et al., 2014), and Matthew Hall and colleagues (2015) have shown that increasing numbers of men are risking their health by injecting synthol (an oil-based substance) into their muscles to increase their size.

It is likely that appearance-related social pressures on men are different and less extreme than those on women (Gough et al., 2014). However, men are under increased social pressure to conform to the muscular, well-toned, mesomorphic (medium-sized) shape, and increases in cosmetic surgery and the use of substances designed to increase muscularity among men in the twenty-first century suggest that pressure on men to attain a slender but muscular physique should be a matter of concern.

Cultural variations in body shape preferences

Work on body image in non-Western cultures has suggested significant cultural differences in the meanings associated with thinness and plumpness, although recent work suggested that these differences may be decreasing due to the influence of Western media. In poorer cultures thinness has historically been seen as a sign of malnutrition, poverty and infectious disease, and increased weight has been viewed positively as an indication of health, wealth and prosperity. Research in Latin America, Puerto Rico, India, China and the Philippines in the 1980s showed that in these cultures increased body weight was linked with wealth and health (Rothblum, 1990), and Iwawaki and Lerner (1974) found that Japanese college students tended to assign more negative stereotypes to thin bodies than to fatter body types. Various authors have reported that a large body size has been regarded positively among Pacific populations, such as on Fiji, as late as the 1990s, reflecting agricultural expertise, community commitment and high quality of care, and that in women, big hips were associated with the ability to bear children, and large size indicated health, nurturance and attractiveness (Becker, 1995). Other work conducted in the 1980s showed that moving from a culture where plumpness is valued to one where slenderness is the cultural ideal may lead to a shift in body weight preference (Furnham and Alibhai, 1983).

More recent work suggests that a desire to be slender is becoming more and more common across cultures, particularly in individuals who have a lot of contact with Western media. In one British study, white and Asian women living in London and women living in Pakistan who were recruited from slimming clubs and gyms scored similarly on body esteem and attitudes to eating (Bardwell and

Choudury, 2000). Another study (Swami et al., 2006) found that Japanese men prefer pictures of women with significantly lower BMI than British men, suggesting that the Japanese preference for larger BMIs observed in the 1970s by Iwawaki and Lerner (1974) has undergone a significant change in favour of the Western ideal of thinness.

Ye Luo and colleagues (2005) present evidence that urban Chinese women, who had been generally reported to have fewer body image concerns than Western women, now have significant body image concerns and desire to lose weight at modest BMI levels. They conclude:

> The findings suggest that China has joined the worldwide diffusion of the thin ideal, with negative consequences for women.
>
> (Luo et al., 2005: 333)

It has been suggested that Western media are responsible for the development of body dissatisfaction and eating problems in cultures where such concerns had previously been rare. In a study reporting data from semi-structured interviews with adolescent women in a rural community in western Fiji three years after Western television became available, Becker (2004) found that women reported explicit modelling of Western media models. They also reported developing weight and shape preoccupation, and purging behaviour to control weight. A similar pattern of results was found by Lauren Williams and colleagues (2006) in interviews with sixteen Fijian and European Australian 13- to 18-year-old girls. They found that both groups of girls experienced body concerns including body dissatisfaction and a preference for thinness. Viren Swami (2015) argues that a slender ideal is now evidenced in individuals across a variety of cultures:

> Evidence is presented to indicate that the largest differences in body size ideals are no longer found between Western and non-Western cultures, but between sites differing in socioeconomic status. It is further argued that a thin ideal is now prevalent in most socioeconomically developed, urban sites. In explanation, it has been suggested that both Westernization and modernization bring cultural changes that promote a thin ideal.
>
> (Swami, 2015: 44)

There can be no doubt that the idealization of slenderness depends on cultural factors. Historically, poorer cultures (where thinness may signify negative factors such as poverty and/or disease) have been more likely to value plumpness, whereas affluent cultures (where thinness may be associated with self-control and self-denial in the face of plenty) have valued slenderness. However, promotion of the "culture of slenderness" through mass media may be reducing this gap, and globalization may be reducing regional differences in the understandings of body image across the world (Edmonds, 2012).

The dieting industry

One of the most powerful social forces in the promotion of thinness in Western society is the dieting industry. Books, slimming plans and diet foods are all sold to a public that "feels fat". Of course, a proportion of that public is overweight to a degree that may affect their health. However, many more people diet than need to do so for health, and most do so for aesthetic reasons. Kay Uzoma (2015) notes:

> Dieting is a national pastime. While the number of Americans who diet varies, depending on the source, the Boston Medical Center indicates that approximately 45 million Americans diet each year and spend $33 billion on weight-loss products in their pursuit of a trimmer, fitter body.
>
> (Uzoma, 2015: 1)

"Dieting" means different things to different people. It usually means a reduction in the intake of calories for the purpose of weight loss; however, approaches differ in numerous ways, from drastic weight-reduction programmes such as *SlimFast* (low-calorie meal-replacement drinks) and *Beverly Hills* (fruit) diets to the relatively less radical approaches such as the *Hip and Thigh* (low-fat diet with exercise), *Atkins* (low carbohydrate) and *F-Plan* (high-fibre, low-fat) diets. Commercial weight loss programmes such as *Weight Watchers* typically support clients through weekly meetings or provide online support and aim to help clients lose around 1 to 2 lb a week through adherence to target meal-plans (Webb et al., 2012).

There has been a well-publicized debate about the long-term efficacy of dieting. Pro-dieting lobbyists argue that dieting leads to weight loss, and that weight loss improves health. In support, randomized controlled trials (where people are allocated at random to different diet plans) have shown that diets such as the *Weight Watchers* and *Atkins* diets can enable weight loss (Webb et al., 2012). However, these kinds of studies tend to focus on those who are obese and who have medical problems such as hypertension or diabetes rather than people who are overweight and want to lose weight for aesthetic reasons. The former group is likely to be better motivated and better supported (clinically and socially) than the latter, and diets that work with obese people will not necessarily be effective (or appropriate) for those who are not obese. Generalizing from these kinds of randomized controlled trials may also be problematic as they tend to involve additional assessments and meetings that are not normally available to dieters (which might increase motivation to adhere to the diet). They also tend to lack long-term follow-up measures, so that long-term effects are unclear.

The anti-dieting movement is helping to make people aware of the potential dangers of dieting, and is starting to reduce the power of the dieting industry. Most research suggests that dieting works in the long term for only around 5 per cent of non-obese dieters, so the other 95 per cent are likely to feel that they have failed (Freedhoff, 2014). Anti-dieting lobbyists argue that dieting may actually lead to an increase in weight. The tendency to gain weight after successful dieting is well established in the medical and psychological literature. It is suggested that the body interprets dieting as a period of starvation and slows the metabolic rate to make more efficient use of the calories that are eaten. When dieters come off the diet, the body sends signals to store extra fat that can be used in the next famine. So they put on the weight that they lost and some extra, because the body is now more efficient at storing calories. They then go on another diet and lose the weight that they put on, and the whole cycle starts again. In the 1980s Kelly Brownell and colleagues used the term "weight cycling" to describe this phenomenon (Brownell et al., 1986), and it has become known colloquially as "yo-yo dieting".

In the 1990s, campaigns by groups such as Diet Breakers in the UK (Evans-Young, 1995) worked to raise public awareness of the dangers of dieting and the importance of healthy eating, and the popular press carried articles warning of the dangers of crash dieting ("Breaking the Diet Habit" in the *Daily Mail*, May 1992; "Diet Addiction: Your Ten Point Recovery Plan" in *Options*, January 1993). In the twenty-first century the pressure to be slim is still apparent. Models are as thin as they were in the 1990s, and the cultural preoccupation with weight and body shape is as strong as ever, although the new cultural trend is to attain the perfect body through exercise rather than diet, and to achieve a slender, toned, hard-looking body (Lupton, 2013). For instance, *Eve* magazine in February 2006 carried the front-page headline "I jogged off 9 stone [126 lb]" alongside the traditional dieting message "Exclusive Food Doctor Diet: Lose 7 lbs in 7 Days", and *Cosmopolitan* magazine in February 2016 announced "So, you want abs? OK... we found the 5-minute plan". Celebrities today promote exercise DVDs and exercise plans rather than diet books, selling the promise of a similarly slender body to the body-aware consumer (Freeman, 2007). In 2015 Kourtney Kardashian was quoted as using exercise as well as a healthy diet to lose 45 lb after childbirth:

> Kourtney attributes her weight loss by rigidly following an organic diet and regularly working out. "I've been working out with a trainer, and having somebody else to work out with really helps motivate me. Some days Khloe will join me. I also try to eat really clean and at home as much as I can," revealed the 36-year-old reality star.
>
> (Antonio, 2015: 1)

Overweight is still linked culturally to lack of willpower and laziness, but in the twenty-first century this relates to lack of exercise rather than diet-breaking. This may be a generally positive move in terms of encouraging a healthy lifestyle for people who are within the normal range of weight through encouraging them to exercise, especially given the relatively low numbers of women and men in Western countries such as the UK who take regular exercise (Public Health England, 2015b). Exercise has many benefits, including toning the body by strengthening muscle, and can lead to increased feelings of well-being, increased energy levels and benefits for cardiovascular health, and may be particularly beneficial for women in terms of raising self-esteem and mood (Choi, 2000). However, for people who are significantly overweight (and particularly those who are obese), exercise can be difficult because of social stigma in the sports/exercise culture against overweight (Monaghan, 2005b). So, although this trend may be generally positive for people who just "feel fat", it may be unlikely to benefit those who are obese.

Summary

- Western societies promote slenderness for men and women. Women are expected to be slim and shapely, men to be slender and muscular.
- There is some disagreement among theorists as to the basis for these cultural ideals. Psychologists working within a biological framework have stressed the healthiness of the slender ideal.
- Social psychologists have emphasized the importance of cultural factors in determining what is attractive, demonstrating that the slender ideal is relatively recent and has become thinner over the last few years with the emergence of the (male and female) "waif' model in the 1990s and its continuation into the twenty-first century, in spite of some challenge to this ideal.
- The dieting industry promotes a very thin ideal, although dieting may lead to health problems and is only likely to lead to long-term weight loss in a small percentage of non-obese dieters.
- The anti-dieting lobby is actively involved in promoting the dangers of dieting and is reducing the power of the diet industry.
- Pressure to exercise is replacing pressure to diet as the socially acceptable means to the slender and toned body ideal.

Bibliography

Antonio, M. (2015) *Kourtney Kardashian weight loss tips and tricks: How did the celebrity mom lose 45 pounds for hot swimsuit body?* Available online at: www. latinoshealth.com/articles/14281/20151222/kourtney-kardashian-weight-loss-tips-tricks-how-did-the-celebrity-mom-loose-45-pounds-for-hot-swimsuit-body.htm [accessed 23 December 2015].

Armstrong, M.L. and Fell, P.R. (2000) 'Body art: Regulatory issues and the NEHA body art model code', *Environmental Health*, 62 (9), 25–30.

Atkinson, M. (2004) 'Tattooing and civilizing processes: Body modification as self-control', *Canadian Review of Sociology and Anthropology*, 41 (2), 125–46.

Baker, P. (1994) 'Under pressure: What the media is doing to men', *Cosmopolitan*, November, 129–32.

Bardwell, M.D. and Choudury, I.Y. (2000) 'Body dissatisfaction and eating attitudes in slimming and fitness gyms in London and Lahore: A cross-cultural study', *European Eating Disorders Review*, 8 (3), 217–24.

Becker, A.E. (Ed.) (1995) *Body, self, and society*, Philadelphia: University of Philadelphia Press.

Becker, A. (2004) 'Television, disordered eating, and young women in Fiji: Negotiating body image and identity during rapid social change', *Culture Medicine and Psychiatry*, 28 (4), 533–59.

Bee, P. (2006) 'The BMI myth', *The Guardian*, 28 November, 18.

Bennett, W. and Gurin, J. (1982) *The dieter's dilemma*, New York: Basic Books.

Berrington de Gonzalez, B., Hartge, P., Cerhan, J.R., Flint, A.J. et al. (2010) 'Body-Mass Index and mortality: Prospective analysis of 1.46 million white adults', *New England Journal of Medicine*, 363 (23), 2211–19.

Boepple, L. and Thompson, J.K. (2015) 'A content analytic comparison of fitspiration and thinspiration websites', *International Journal of Eating Disorders*, 49 (1), 98–101.

Bordo, S. (2003) *Unbearable weight: Feminism, Western culture, and the body*, 10th anniversary edition, Berkeley, CA: University of California Press.

Brownell, K.D. and Rodin, J.R. (1994) 'The dieting maelstrom: Is it possible and advisable to lose weight?' *American Psychologist*, 49 (9), 781–91.

Brownell, K.D., Greenwood, M., Stellar, E. and Shrager, E. (1986) 'The effects of repeated cycles of weight loss and regain in rats', *Physiology and Behaviour*, 38, 459–64.

Calderwood, I. (2015) *Teenage size eight catwalk model quit one of the world's biggest agencies after it 'told her to lose weight to get more work'*, available online at www.dailymail.co.uk/news/article-3319240/Teenage-size-eight-catwalk-model-quit-one-world-s-biggest-agencies-told-lose-weight-work.html#ixzz3u1DxblgC [accessed 15 November 2015].

Caldwell, D. (1981) *And all was revealed: Ladies' underwear 1907–1980*, New York: St. Martin's Press.

Campos, P. (2004) *The obesity myth: Why America's obsession with weight is hazardous to your health*, New York: Gotham Books.

Cash, T.F. (1990) 'The psychology of physical appearance: Aesthetics, attributes, and images', in T. Cash and T. Pruzinsky (Eds) *Body images: Development, deviance and change* (pp. 51–79), New York: Guilford Press.

Choi, P.Y.L. (2000b) *Femininity and the physically active woman*, London: Routledge.

Crandall, C. and Martinez, R. (1996) 'Culture, ideology, and anti-fat attitudes', *Personality and Social Psychology Bulletin*, 22, 1165–76.

Dehghan, M. and Merchant, A.T. (2008) 'Is bioelectrical impedance accurate for use in large epidemiological studies?' *Nutrition Journal*, 7, 26.

Dion, K., Berscheid, E. and Walster, E. (1972) 'What is beautiful is good', *Journal of Personality and Social Psychology*, 24, 285–90.

Eagley, A., Ashmore, R., Makhijani, M. and Longo, L. (1991) 'What is beautiful is good but...: A meta-analytic review of research on the physical attractiveness stereotype', *Psychological Bulletin*, 110 (1), 109–28.

Edmonds, A. (2012) 'Body image in non-Western societies', in T.F. Cash (Ed.) *Encylopedia of body image and human appearance* (pp. 238–242), London: Elsevier.

Evans-Young, M. (1995) *Diet breaking: Having it all without having to die*, London: Hodder and Stoughton.

Ewing, W.A. (1994) *The body: Photoworks of the human form*, London: Thames and Hudson.

Fallon, A. (1990) 'Culture in the mirror: Sociocultural determinants of body image', in T. Cash and T. Pruzinsky (Eds) *Body images: Development, deviance and change* (pp. 80–109), New York: Guilford Press.

Flegal, K.M., Graubard, B.I., Williamson, D.F. and Gail, M.H. (2005) 'Excess deaths associated with underweight, overweight, and obesity', *Journal of the American Medical Association*, 293 (15), 1861–7.

Frankel, S. (1998) 'The fashion of destruction', *The Guardian*, 7 February, 5.

Freedhoff, Y. (2014) *The diet fix: Why diets fail and how to make yours work*, Toronto, Canada: Random House of Canada.

Freedman, R. (1986) *Beauty bound*, Lexington, MA: Lexington Books.

Freeman, H. (2007) 'Celebrity fit club', *The Guardian*, 23 January, 17–19.

Furnham, A. and Alibhai, N. (1983) 'Cross cultural differences in the perception of male and female body shapes', *Psychological Medicine*, 13 (4), 829–37.

Gaesser, G. (2002) *Big fat lies: The truth about your weight and your health*, Carlsbad, CA: Gurze Books.

Gordon, R. (1990) *Anorexia and bulimia: Anatomy of a social epidemic*, Oxford: Blackwell.

Gough, B., Hall, M. and Seymour-Smith, S. (2014) 'Straight guys do wear make-up: Contemporary masculinities and investment in appearance', in S. Robertson (Ed.) *Debating modern masculinities: Change, continuity, crisis?* (pp. 106–24), Basingstoke: Palgrave Macmillan.

Greenleaf, C., Starks, M., Gomez, L., Chambliss, H. and Martin, S. (2004) 'Weight-related words associated with figure silhouettes', *Body Image*, 1 (4), 373–85.

Hall, M., Grogan, S. and Gough, B. (2015) 'Bodybuilders' accounts of synthol use: The construction of lay expertise', *Journal of Health Psychology* [E-pub ahead of print DOI: 10.1177/1359105314568579].

Henwood, K., Gill, R. and McLean, C. (2002) 'The changing man', *The Psychologist*, 15 (4), 182–6.

Huxley, R.R. and Jacobs, D.R. (2011) 'Size still matters ... but not in the way we thought', *The Lancet*, 377 (9771), 1051–2.

Iwawaki, S. and Lerner, R.M. (1974) 'Cross-cultural analyses of body-behavior relations. I. A comparison of body build stereotypes of Japanese and American males and females', *Psychologia*, 17 (2), 75–81.

LaFrance, M.N., Zivian, M.T. and Myers, A.M. (2000) 'Women, weight and appearance satisfaction: An ageless pursuit of thinness', in B. Miedema, J.M. Stoppard and V. Anderson (Eds) *Women's bodies, women's lives* (pp. 227–36), Toronto: Sumach Press.

Latner, J.D. (2012) 'Body weight and body image in adults', in T.F. Cash (Ed.) *Encyclopedia of body image and human appearance* (pp. 264–9), London: Elsevier.

Lee, C., Huxley, R, Wildman, R. et al. (2008) 'Indices of abdominal obesity are better discriminators of cardiovascular risk factors than BMI: A meta-analysis', *Journal of Clinical Endocrinology and Metabolism*, 61 (7), 646–53.

Luo, Y., Parish, W.L. and Laumann, E.O. (2005) 'A population-based study of body image concerns among urban Chinese adults', *Body Image*, 2 (4), 333–47.

Lupton, D. (2013) *Fat*, London: Routledge.

McCreary, D. (2012) 'Muscularity and body image', in T.F. Cash (Ed.) *Encyclopedia of body image and human appearance* (pp. 561–7), London: Elsevier.

McCreary, D.R., Karvinen, K. and Davis, C. (2006) 'The relationship of drive for muscularity and anthropometric measures of muscularity and adiposity', *Body Image*, 3 (2), 145–53.

Mazur, A. (1986) 'U.S. trends in feminine beauty and overadaption', *Journal of Sex Research*, 22, 281–303.

Meyer, R. (1991) 'Rock Hudson's body', in D. Fuss (Ed.) *Inside out: Lesbian theories, gay theories* (pp. 259–90), New York: Routledge.

Monaghan, L. (2005a) 'Discussion piece: A critical take on the obesity debate', *Social Theory and Health*, 3 (4), 302–14.

Monaghan, L. (2005b) 'Big handsome men, bears and others: Virtual constructions of "fat male embodiment"', *Body and Society*, 11 (2), 81–111.

Murray, S. (2016) *The 'fat' female body*, London: Palgrave.

Myers, B.S. and Copplestone, T. (1985) *Landmarks of Western art*, Feltham, UK: Newnes.

O'Kelly, L. (1994) 'Body talk', *The Guardian*, 23 October, 30–2.

Olivardia, R. (2002) 'Body image and muscularity', in T.F. Cash and T. Pruzinsky (Eds) *Body image: A handbook of theory, research, and clinical practice* (pp. 210–18), New York: Guilford Press.

Orbach, S. (1993) *Hunger strike: The anorectic's struggle as a metaphor for our age*, London: Penguin.

Pope, H.G., Phillips, K.A. and Olivardia, R. (2000) *The Adonis complex: The secret crisis of male body obsession*, New York: Free Press.

Public Health England (2015a) *Measurement of obesity*, available online at: www.noo.org. uk/NOO_about_obesity/measurement [accessed 20 December 2015].

Public Health England (2015b) *Health Survey for England: Factsheets*, available online at: www.noo.org.uk/NOO_pub/Key_data [accessed 20 December 2015].

Puhl, R.M. and Peterson, J.L. (2012) 'Physical appearance and stigma', in T.F. Cash (Ed.) *Encyclopedia of body image and human appearance* (pp. 588–94), London: Elsevier.

Pultz, J. (1995) *Photography and the body*, London: Orion.

Reid, S. (2000) 'Spot the lollipop ladies', *The Sunday Times Style Magazine*, 7 May, 10–11.

Rennels, J. (2012) 'Physical attractiveness stereotyping', in T.F. Cash (Ed.) *Encyclopedia of body image and human appearance* (pp. 636–43), London: Elsevier.

Rich, E. (2005) *Obesity, eating disorders, and the role of physical education*, paper presented at the British Sociological Association Sport Study Group Conference, Leicester University, 6 May 2005.

Rothblum, E.D. (1990) 'Women and weight: Fad and fiction', *Journal of Psychology*, 124, 5–24.

Sagoe, D., Andreassen, C.S. and Pallesen, S. (2014) 'The aetiology and trajectory of anabolic-androgenic steroid use initiation: A systematic review and synthesis of qualitative research', *Substance Abuse Treatment, Prevention, and Policy*, 9, 27.

Schoemer, K. (1996) 'Rockers, models, and the new allure of heroin', *Newsweek*, 26 August, 50–6.

Silverstein, B., Peterson, B. and Purdue, L. (1986) 'Some correlates of the thin standard of physical attractiveness of women', *International Journal of Eating Disorders*, 5 (5), 898–905.

Swami, V. (2015) 'Cultural influences on body size ideals: Unpacking the impact of Westernization and modernization', *European Psychologist*, 20 (1), 44–51.

Swami, V., Caprario, C., Tovee, M.J. and Furnham, A. (2006) 'Female physical attractiveness in Britain and Japan: A cross-cultural study', *European Journal of Personality*, 20 (1), 69–81.

Sweetman, P. (1999) 'Anchoring the (postmodern) self? Body modification, fashion and identity', *Body and Society*, 5 (2–3), 51–76.

Thompson, J.K. and Cafri, G. (Eds) (2007) *The muscular ideal*, Washington, DC: American Psychological Association.

Tiggemann, M. and Golder, F. (2006) 'Tattooing: An expression of uniqueness in the appearance domain', *Body Image*, 3 (4), 309–16.

Tiggemann, M. and Rothblum, E. (1988) 'Gender differences and social consequences of perceived overweight in the United States and Australia', *Sex Roles*, 18 (1), 75–86.

Tiggemann, M., Slater, A. and Smyth, V. (2014) 'Retouch free: The effect of labelling media images as not digitally altered on women's body dissatisfaction', *Body Image,* 11 (1), 85–88.

Tovee, M. (2012) 'Anthrometry', in T.F. Cash (Ed.) *Encylopedia of body image and human appearance* (pp. 23–29), London: Elsevier.

Uzoma, K. (2015) *Percentage of Americans who diet every year*, available online at: www. livestrong.com/article/308667-percentage-of-americans-who-diet-every-year/ [accessed 29 December 2015].

Webb, V.Z., Wadden, T.A. and Tsai, A.G. (2012) 'Weight-loss programs: Commerical and popular diets', in T.F. Cash (Ed.) *Encylopedia of body image and human appearance* (pp. 798–808), London: Elsevier.

Williams, L.K., Ricciardelli, L.A., McCabe, M.P., Waqa, G.G. and Bavadra, K. (2006) 'Body image attitudes and concerns among indigenous Fijian and European Australian adolescent girls', *Body Image*, 3 (3), 275–88.

Winter, K. (2014) *I wanted people to question the dangerous lengths people go to to attain beauty*, available online at: www.dailymail.co.uk/femail/article-2727727/-Former-anorexic-turned-plus-size-model-Crystal-Renn-wrote-memoirs-23.html#ixzz3u 17pehYS [accessed 14 August 2014].

World Health Organization (2015) *Mean body mass index*, available online at: www.who. int/gho/ncd/risk_factors/bmi_text/en/ [accessed 20 December 2015].

Yingling, T. (1991) 'AIDS in America: Postmodern governance, identity and experience', in D. Fuss (Ed.) *Inside out: Lesbian theories, gay theories* (pp. 291–310), New York: Routledge.

3

WOMEN AND BODY IMAGE

Slimness is seen as a desirable attribute for women in prosperous cultures, and is associated with self-control, elegance, social attractiveness and youth (Bordo, 2003; Murray, 2016). The ideal female shape is epitomized in the slim but full-breasted figures that Gail Marchessault (2000) describes as "the physically impossible, tall, thin and busty Barbie-doll stereotype" (p. 204). Women show a preference for an "hourglass" shaped figure (Grogan et al., 2013) with an underweight body mass index (BMI; e.g. Aghekyan et al., 2012) and large breasts, so long as they are not uncomfortably large (Reardon and Grogan, 2011; Swami et al., 2015). Muscle tone is also important, and the twenty-first century ideal is a firm-looking body for women as well as men (Lupton, 2013).

Chapter 2 showed how body shape ideals for women changed in the twentieth and twenty-first centuries. Despite changes in the feminine ideal, one thing remains constant through the decades: women have always been encouraged to change their shape and weight to conform to current trends. Through the ages, women have undergone pain to attempt to conform to the current ideal. This is clearest in relation to practices such as foot binding and the wearing of restrictive corsets, whereby women suffered discomfort and immobility in the name of particular fashions. In Western society today we have replaced these practices with strict diets (which weaken and debilitate) and cosmetic surgery (in which women undergo painful and potentially dangerous procedures) to try to attain culturally defined, attractive, slender body shapes.

This chapter evaluates evidence (mostly from the UK, the USA, Canada and Australia) to investigate women's body image. Body image is defined and measured in different ways depending on the specific backgrounds and aims of particular researchers. Some see body image in terms of perceptual factors (estimated size of the body), and others as attitudes to the body. Within attitudinal work, some authors have focused on satisfaction with, and evaluation of, the body (the affective-evaluative dimension) and others on rated importance of, and investment in, appearance (the cognitive-behavioural dimension). There has been a significant increase in measures in the last few decades (Thompson et al., 2012), and recently new measures focusing on body appreciation have also been developed (Tylka, 2012).

Researchers using a variety of different techniques have concluded that many women in Western cultures are dissatisfied with some aspect of their body weight and shape, and are taking behavioural steps to try to change the look of their bodies. A range of measures will be discussed in the first part of this chapter to illustrate how body image has been investigated, and how such work helps us to understand body dissatisfaction in women. The second part of the chapter will look at ways in which psychologists and sociologists have tried to make sense of women's dissatisfaction with body shape and weight.

Assessment of body image

Psychologists and sociologists have used various measures to assess body image. Many of these techniques were originally produced to assess body dissatisfaction in women who have problematic relations with food. This text aims to look at body image in women who have "normal" relations with food, rather than those who have been classified as *anorexic* or *bulimic*. Readers with a special interest in eating disorders are referred to the book chapter by Linda Smolak and Michael Levine (2015), or Linda Smolak and Kevin Thompson's (2008) edited text *Body image, eating disorders, and obesity in youth: Assessment, prevention, and treatment.*

The studies discussed below are ones that have looked at body image in women picked at random, or on an opportunity basis, rather than those referred to professionals as a result of problematic relations with food. As such, these women's experiences constitute majority views, rather than those of a more specific group. However, this does not imply that the women whose experiences are discussed in this chapter have unproblematic relationships with their bodies. Evidence shows that many women experience levels of dissatisfaction with weight and body shape and overestimate the size of key areas of their bodies, suggesting a problematic relationship.

Figure rating scales

Figure rating scales, or silhouette techniques, were developed in the 1950s and are still used to provide quantitative measures of degree and direction of body dissatisfaction. Using these techniques, silhouettes ranging from very thin to very fat are presented to the participant, who is usually asked to choose the silhouette closest to her own body size and the image representing her ideal size. The discrepancy between the two figures can be seen as an indication of (dis)satisfaction, and the figures chosen indicate whether her ideal is thinner or fatter than her current body type. Various versions of this kind of scale are now available, including photographic images of real women varying in BMI (Photographic Figure Rating Scale; Swami et al., 2012), and images varying one body part, such as breast size, alone (e.g. the Breast Size Rating Scale; Swami et al., 2015). However, many researchers continue to use the original Figure Rating

Scale developed by Albert "Mickey" Stunkard and colleagues (1983) which depicts a set of nine silhouette drawings of Caucasian-looking women of various sizes arranged from a very thin to a very heavy figure (see Grogan, 2008: 43).

Studies using figure rating scales have found that women show a reliable tendency to pick a thinner ideal than their current figure (Cororve-Fingeret et al., 2004; Vartanian, 2012). In one of the earliest published studies using figural rating scales, April Fallon and Paul Rozin (1985) asked 227 women studying psychology at the University of Pennsylvania to indicate their "ideal figure", their "current figure" and "the figure that most men would find attractive", using Stunkard et al.'s (1983) scale. In general, women picked a heavier figure for their "current figure" than for "the figure that most men would find attractive", and an even thinner figure for their "ideal figure". Fallon and Rozin (1985) concluded that the pursuit of thinness is motivated by self-imposed pressure to be thin rather than the desire to be attractive to men. This effect was replicated in Australian and British work in the 1990s (Huon et al., 1990; Tiggemann and Pennington, 1990; Wardle et al., 1993), showing that discrepancy in size between how women perceive themselves and how they would ideally like to look is not a specifically American phenomenon.

Guy Cafri and colleagues (2010) present a critical look at these techniques, noting that difference scores "suffer from numerous potential methodological problems, including reduced reliability, ambiguity, confounded effects, untested constraints, and dimensional reduction" (p. 361). Michelle Cororve-Fingeret and colleagues have also taken a critical look at figural rating scales, and in particular at potential demand characteristics inherent in the design of studies in which women are asked to choose their ideal and current sizes and the size that they think that men prefer. They reasoned that making all three choices in the same test session might encourage women to give socially appropriate responses. To investigate this, they designed a study where they varied the format to compare conditions where women either made all the choices in the same test session or picked only some of the target figures. They found that the ideal-current discrepancy was robust when measured in different formats, suggesting that this technique is a valid measure of ideal-current discrepancy, and they concluded that "the findings do provide evidence of robust and large effects for the current-ideal discrepancy as measured by figural rating scales" (Cororve-Fingeret et al., 2004: 207).

More recently, Lenny Vartanian (2012) has reviewed effects across a range of studies carried out in diverse cultures (including in Bahrain, Korea, Nigeria and China) and reports remarkable consistency in effects across cultures. He concludes that women show a preference for a thinner ideal body than their current bodies, and that there is now considerable evidence that self-ideal discrepancies are related to body dissatisfaction and to dieting, exercise and uptake of elective cosmetic surgery.

Questionnaire studies

Another way to assess body image is to ask women to complete self-report questionnaires. Body image questionnaires are designed to provide quantitative measures of aspects of body image, including body attitudes. The main focus here will be on measures designed to assess body satisfaction and positive body image, and the review below is necessarily selective. For a review of the full range of questionnaire measures designed to investigate all aspects of body image, please see the review chapter by Kevin Thompson and colleagues (2012).

Most body satisfaction measures ask respondents to indicate their degree of agreement or disagreement with statements relating to satisfaction with particular body parts or with the body as a whole. The Body Cathexis Scale is one of the earliest measures for assessing the degree of satisfaction with the body, and it is still widely used. This measure was developed in the 1950s by Secord and Jourard (1953). Participants indicate satisfaction with a wide variety of body parts, and the scale is scored so that each person ends up with a score indicating body satisfaction. Secord and Jourard argued that body satisfaction is highly associated with general self-esteem, so that a person who scores highly on the body satisfaction scale would also be likely to score highly on self-esteem scales. This link has been confirmed in many studies in women, men, and children (see Ben-Tovim and Walker, 1991, for a review). Researchers have tended to modify the scale, losing the items that relate to height, ankles, calves, and neck length which tend to produce unreliable results, and adding other body areas. For instance, Adrian Furnham and Nicola Greaves (1994) added lips, ears, biceps, chin, buttocks, arms, eyes, cheeks, legs, stomach, body hair and face. Fifty-five British women aged 18 to 35 were asked to rate, on a ten-point scale, how satisfied they felt with each body part (where 1 equals complete dissatisfaction and 10 equals complete satisfaction). Compared to a sample of 47 British men in the same age range, the women were significantly less satisfied with all body parts, and especially with thighs, buttocks and hips. Dissatisfaction with the lower part of the body, where flesh tends to accumulate in women, is widely documented in studies using various methods, as will be seen below.

The Multidimensional Body-Self Relations Questionnaire Appearance Scale (MBSRQ–AS) (Cash, 2000) measures appearance evaluation (seven items, e.g. "I like my looks just the way they are"), appearance orientation (12 items, e.g. "Before going out in public, I always notice how I look"), overweight preoccupation (four items, e.g. "I constantly worry about being or becoming fat"), and self-classified weight (two items, e.g. "I think I am very underweight/very overweight"), all scored on a five-point Likert scale. The Body Areas Satisfaction subscale asks about dissatisfaction with various parts of the body. This questionnaire is internally reliable (alphas for subscales range between 0.70 and 0.94), has been well validated on male and female samples in various Western populations, and has been used extensively in body image research (Cash, 2000). Women tend to score lower than men on appearance evaluation (satisfaction), and higher on overweight preoccupation and appearance orientation. According to Cash et al. (1986) and Garner (1997), the areas of the body that present most concern for women are mid-torso (stomach) and lower torso (hips and buttocks). This measure has been translated into several languages (including Spanish), and continues to show excellent reliability and validity in males and females of a range of ages (e.g. Roncero et al., 2015).

The Body Shape Questionnaire (Cooper et al., 1987) was designed specifically to study body image in women with "eating disorders". It includes thirty-four questions relating to antecedents and consequences of body shape concern, and asks the respondent how she has felt over the last four weeks in order to look at long-term dissatisfaction. Items include "Have you felt ashamed of your body?" and "Have you pinched areas of your body to see how much fat there is?" Evans and Dolan (1992) produced shortened versions of the scale with sixteen and eight items that retain the reliability and validity of the original version but have the advantage of greater ease of completion for participants. In a population of normal weight women with no history of "eating disorders", 17 per cent scored high levels of body shape concern on the original Cooper et al. (1987) questionnaire, showing – as might be expected – that body shape concern is not restricted to women with "eating disorders" but affects a significant proportion of women with no history of such problems. Elizabeth Welch and colleagues (2012) conducted a study of the psychometric properties of the eight-item version of the scale among 18- to 30-year-old Swedish women and found good reliability and validity, showing that it remains a valuable measure for the assessment of body shape dissatisfaction in young adult women.

The Body Attitudes Questionnaire (Ben-Tovim and Walker, 1991) covers six distinct aspects of body experience: fatness, self-disparagement, strength, salience of weight, attractiveness, and consciousness of lower-body fat. The scale is specifically designed for women, produces separate scores on each of the subscales, and covers a wider range of body-related attitudes than alternatives such as the Cooper et al. (1987) scale. Sample questions include "I worry that my thighs and bottom look dimply" and "I try to avoid clothes that make me especially aware of my shape". The authors found that concern about being fat was central to women's attitudes towards their bodies, and that this was particularly marked in relation to concern with the lower half of the body. They also found that "body disparagement" (where the woman agrees with statements such as "My life is being ruined because of the way I look" and "I prefer not to let other people see my body") was common in their sample of 504 Australian women respondents. This scale has been widely used and translated into several languages, including Japanese (Kagawa et al., 2007), and continues to show similar patterns of response in women in different cultures.

Questionnaire studies suggest that many women are dissatisfied with their bodies, particularly the lower half of the body (stomach, hips and thighs). These data support the results of silhouette studies, and also add detail about the specific body areas that present cause for concern. One of the problems with the way that figural rating scales work is that women are forced to choose a whole-body silhouette, which obscures perceptions of individual body parts. Questionnaires that ask specifically about different body parts allow a more detailed assessment of satisfaction with different parts of the body, and reveal that most women participants in the studies may be quite satisfied with the top half of the body while being dissatisfied with the lower torso and thighs.

Recently there has been a move to develop measures of positive body image. The Body Appreciation Scale (Avalos et al., 2005) focuses on key aspects of positive body image and has been found to be reliable and valid (Webb et al., 2015). The original scale uses thirteen items to measure body acceptance (e.g. "In spite of its imperfections I still like my body"), body respect ("I respect my body") and body protection (by resisting media influences, e.g. "I do not allow unrealistically thin images of women presented in the media to affect my attitudes towards my body"), and participants indicate degree of agreement on a five-point scale from 1 (never) to 5 (always). This measure has been validated in the US, Australia, the UK, Spain, Germany and Canada, and positive scores have been linked to healthy (intuitive) eating (Andrew et al., 2015) and enjoyment-based physical activity (Homan and Tylka, 2014). Since its development in 2005 the authors have reduced the original scale and have modified some items slightly to create the Body Appreciation Scale 2, which includes thirteen items and has been validated with US men and women (Tylka and Wood-Barcalow, 2015). Jennifer Webb and colleagues (2015) note that scores on the original scale tend to be inversely related to BMI, with heavier women showing lower levels of body appreciation across cultures.

Interview studies

Another way to find out how women feel about their body shape and size is to talk to them about experiences of body (dis)satisfaction in interviews. The advantage of doing this (rather than asking women to complete a questionnaire that asks specific questions) is that women are given the freedom to express how they feel, rather than just answering preplanned questions. This allows women interviewees to set the agenda to some extent, and to address issues that are important to them, giving this technique more flexibility than questionnaire work.

In one of the earliest published studies, Nickie Charles and Marion Kerr (1986) carried out an interesting investigation using the semi-structured interview technique. As part of a study on eating in the family they interviewed two hundred British women about their attitudes and experiences of dieting and their satisfaction with their current weight. Their results showed that most women were dissatisfied with their body image. Of the two hundred women they interviewed, only 23 had never dieted or worried about their weight. Of the 177 who had been concerned about their weight, 153 had been concerned enough to diet. When speaking about their ideal body, most were dissatisfied with the way they looked at the time of the interview. Charles and Kerr concluded:

What emerges from these comments is a strong dissatisfaction with their body image, a dissatisfaction which was not confined to women who were dieting or trying to diet but was shared by almost all the women we spoke to.

(Charles and Kerr, 1986: 541)

The women who were interviewed by Charles and Kerr seemed to have a mental yardstick for how they would like to look. For some of them, this was how they had looked when they were younger. For many, losing a "magic half-stone" (7 lb) was the goal. Most had not managed to accept their bodies as they were. The areas of the body that caused most dissatisfaction were breasts (too small or too large), legs (too fat or too thin), abdomen (not flat enough), and buttocks (too flabby or too skinny). Not all women felt too fat, but the majority did. Although being slimmer was linked with good health, women cited looks rather than health as the main reason for dieting. One woman needed to diet for medical reasons, but said that the main reason for losing weight was to look better.

In a series of interviews with women carried out at Manchester Metropolitan University in the 1990s, it was found that women of various ages reported body dissatisfaction. Fifty women aged 16 to 63 years were interviewed by Penny Cortvriend, Lisa Bradley, Helen Richards, Debbie Mee-Perone and myself between 1994 and 1996. The women were encouraged to talk about their experiences of body shape and weight, diet, and exercise. They reliably reported dissatisfaction with stomach, buttocks and thighs, irrespective of their ages. Pseudonyms and ages are noted here before the quotations:

Sheila (age 34): All the blub around my belly. I don't like that one bit.

Dawn (age 17): I'd like my thighs to be smaller. And my bottom's too big.

These findings supported those from quantitative questionnaire work, suggesting that stomach, thighs, buttocks and hips present most concern to women. Such comments were presented in almost all the interviews, irrespective of the objective sizes of the women being interviewed. Both slim and heavier women of all ages reported concern that their hips, buttocks and thighs were too big. In fact, there is some evidence from work on body size estimation that women also tend to overestimate the size of these body parts (see later in this chapter). These are areas of the body where women store fat, and also areas which are often the focus of media attention in advertisements for slimming products (Bordo, 2003; Murray, 2016).

The discourses used by women when asked to talk about their bodies are interesting. Most women objectified their bodies. Most were able to describe what was "wrong" with their bodies with no difficulty, but found it difficult to identify any part that was satisfactory. Most of the women interviewed, irrespective of their body size, reported that they would be delighted to lose half a stone (7 lb). For instance, one 26-year-old woman said "I'd kiss you!"; another, aged 25, said

"I'd be so delighted." The women reported that they would be more confident if they lost weight. Many women reported that they would change the way that they dressed if they lost weight, and that they would become like a different (better) person. For instance:

Susie (age 26): Yes. I'd be confident as hell. Oh, I'd wear stuff that was shorter and tighter.

Jodie (age 27): I'd completely change. My clothes, everything. I'd be a different person.

Women who had experienced weight loss reliably reported increased confidence. For instance:

Frankie (age 43): I remember once I did a diet from a magazine going back, er, fourteen years now when I was so slim. I felt so good, I felt like a different person. I felt so confident.

Feeling slender and feeling confident were intrinsically linked for most of the women interviewed. This was the case for both heavier and slimmer women. When asked to imagine putting on half a stone (7 lb) in weight, many women said that this would make them feel like hiding away and not going out.

Ruth (age 26): Oh God, no, I'd be gutted [really upset]. I wouldn't go out.

These feelings were expressed by women across the age range, who said that they would "feel fat" and avoid social activities if they put on 7 lb. The significant social effect of this relatively small increase in weight shows the importance of not increasing weight to most of the women we interviewed. This is particularly interesting, since researchers have shown that participants in psychology studies do not rate women's attractiveness higher when they lose (compared to when they gain) between 0.5 and 18 lb (Alley and Scully, 1994).

Many women reported that they felt happiest about their body first thing in the morning (before they had eaten), when they felt lightest and slimmest. For instance:

Caroline (age 32): When I first get up, my tummy looks flatter but then as soon as I have had a drink or a slice of toast or something, there it goes, there it is [laughs].

Women referred to media models as influences on body satisfaction. Many women said that models (in general) were too thin. For instance:

Jade (age 17): I used to think, oh models, perfect figure. And now sometimes I look at them and I think no. Too skinny. Definitely too skinny.

However, other women tended to be ambivalent about skinny models, saying that they were too thin but also that they would like to look like them. The discourse "they make me sick" was used repeatedly by respondents in these interviews. For instance:

> Beth (age 25): They make me sick. They are too thin. But I would kill for one of their bodies.

> Joanne (age 35): Some [models] I think, no, I wouldn't like to be like that. But I suppose the Naomis and the Claudia Schiffers, and things like that ... that seems reachable. You know, I mean, obviously, you couldn't get the youth and the flowing hair and that lot. But they make you sick, really, don't they [laughs]? Why her, not me?

The idea of "skinny but shapely" being the most attractive body shape was a recurring theme. For instance:

> Sally (age 17): I like a balance. A bit of curves but skinny curves.

> Nicki (age 43): I don't like thin thin at all. I mean, I would hate to be like that. But the shapely slim models, I might look at them and think it would be nice to look like that.

Women of all ages cited models and female actors as influential in determining body satisfaction. The ideal body for women aged from 16 to 60 was the tall, slim, cultural ideal. For instance:

> Sandi (age 26): I'd like firm breasts, thin legs, little tiny hips.

Many women cited pressure from the fashion industry to be slim, saying that fashionable clothes only come in small sizes (British size 14 or below), so that to dress fashionably you have to be slim. For instance:

> Suzanne (age 26): Fashion dictates really what size you are, because none of them go over a size 14 anyway, so you couldn't be fat and fashionable.

Many women said that the fact that their clothes became uncomfortable if they put on weight acted as a motivator to lose weight again. This was seen by many women as more important than how much they actually weighed. For instance:

> Betty (age 63): The fact that clothes get uncomfortable really. That's basically what it is, 'cos I don't look in the mirror to see how fat I am. And when I put on clothes that are tight around the waist. And the clothes

that I've got that are nice but that I can't get into. That's what motivates me to get my weight down. It's clothes.

Sharron (age 46): I don't feel comfortable at the moment in my jeans. That three pounds [recent weight gain] has made a tremendous difference on a skirt or a pair of jeans. That's the only thing. If you've got a pair of jeans, three pounds makes a difference on the waist. That's the only thing that I would diet for, if I went out of my clothes size. I would have to diet, because I could never afford to replace all my clothes. If I was growing out of my clothes I would definitely try and cut down.

Toni (age 27): I don't long to be under nine stone [126 lb] again, because I think that is an unrealistic weight for me, but I think just so that my clothes fit me nicely. Do you know what I mean? And I think that the emphasis has changed now in that I don't really weigh myself that often because it is not actually the weight that matters to me. It is how I feel myself and what I feel I look like.

Clothes fit is extremely important in determining women's body satisfaction. In 2013 we interviewed twenty UK women aged between 18 and 45 years in a study on body size and dress fit (Grogan et al., 2013). We recorded spontaneous speech as women selected a dress to wear from a number of dresses. Women were also body-scanned and photographed in their chosen dress, and discussed both the scan and the photograph in semi-structured interviews. All women reported some self-surveillance in relation to clothes fit, and tightness of clothes resulted in decreased body confidence even in women who were generally body-confident.

All women wanted to look slim in clothes, and showed a preference for an hourglass body shape. Clothes were used to try to produce this idealized hourglass shape, creating the appearance of being "in proportion" (a balanced body with equivalently sized breasts and hips) and hiding features that did not fit the ideal. Body image and clothes preferences were fluid, and on "fat" days (when they felt heavier) women reported that they would avoid wearing particular clothes that exposed more of their bodies and would opt not to shop for clothes. For instance:

Olivia (age 19): It's never a good idea to go and try on clothes when you're already feeling like a bit like rubbish.

Women were more critical and knowledgeable consumers of clothes than participants in previous studies, expecting clothes bought from different retailers to vary in size. However, being critical of clothes sizing did not seem to protect participants against feeling unhappy if they could not fit into clothes of their usual size. Although these women knew that size labelling was unreliable, they still used clothes size as a marker for weight gain, and were extremely unhappy if clothes were too tight and did not fit as expected. For instance, one young woman who was in other ways relatively satisfied with her body, reflecting on how she feels when she cannot fit into jeans her usual size, reported:

> Anna (age 29): Cause if I have to buy a bigger size, if I know that I have to buy a bigger size I feel a little bit rubbish [Interviewer: "Right, ok"] if I go into say, *Topshop*, and I try a pair of size 10 jeans and I can't get them past my thighs that does make me feel awful.

The physical changes associated with the aftereffects of pregnancy seem to present particular concerns for some women. Helen Skouteris and colleagues (2005) have suggested that women may feel less "fat" in late pregnancy than prior to, or in the earlier stages of, pregnancy (probably because this is a time when women are expected to put on weight to ensure the health of their baby). However, the post-natal period presents particular challenges for a lot of women.

In our interviews with women aged between 16 and 63 years carried out in the 1990s, women felt that their bodies had become less aesthetically pleasing after pregnancy, and that they had been relatively attractive in the "golden days" before pregnancy and childbirth. Pregnancy did not result in any positive effects that these women could identify. The main negative effects were stretched skin around the stomach and drooping breasts. For instance:

> Jude (age 25): I've got more stretch marks than I don't know what. I've got millions of them.

> Helen (age 35): All this breastfeeding has just ruined my boobs [breasts]. Yes, I'd change those if I could.

The post-partum period has been identified by many researchers as a time of augmented body dissatisfaction. However, results are not clear cut. Victoria Fern and colleagues (2012) found that UK women interviewed in the post-partum period did not seem to be particularly unhappy with their post-natal bodies, and felt sympathy for celebrities who were under pressure to look slender shortly after childbirth:

> Jayne (age 28 years; 3 months post-partum): I feel sorry for them. I feel sorry that they have got the pressure on them to look so good, yeah.

> Emma (age 26 years; 2 weeks post-partum): It's not fair that the media put pressure on them as well to lose weight too; they must feel really pressured to lose weight and to get toned.

In another study (Fern et al., 2014) we carried out email interviews with forty women aged 20 to 42 years who were up to three years post-partum. We found that women who had breastfed reported greater appreciation and acceptance towards their changed bodies. Although all participants had some degree of body dissatisfaction, women who had experience of breastfeeding were more accepting of the body changes that had occurred through pregnancy, seeing their bodies in more functional than aesthetic terms. This seemed to confer some protection from dissatisfaction with their changed bodies. For instance:

> Serena (age 42 years; 31 months post-partum): My body is more precious and important in its ability to carry and nurture a baby than how I look in terms of body image.

> Kadam B (age 31 years; 21 months post-partum): Seeing it go through the changes pregnancy brings has made me appreciate it more and the amazing things it can do.

Interviews with women across a wide age range, and over a twenty-year period, have shown that most women are dissatisfied with their body size, in particular the lower torso. Many report comparing themselves to models or actresses (though women may feel protected against this when post-partum), and most have a body ideal that is skinny but shapely. Very thin fashion models were seen as "too skinny" by some, and as an unrealistically slim target shape by others. Being slim (and shapely) was linked with self-confidence for most of the women we spoke to, and most have said that their life would change for the better if they lost weight (irrespective of current body size). One interesting aspect of the interviews that we conducted between 1990 and 2013 is that none of the women we interviewed reported wanting to put on weight (even those who were objectively very thin). In addition, all the women interviewed could identify one body site where they wanted to lose weight. Many women perceived their bodies to be heavier than they appeared to the outside observer. Some psychologists have suggested that women tend to overestimate the size of their body (particularly the lower torso). This phenomenon will be investigated next.

Body size estimation techniques

Interest in body size estimation originated in the 1960s when Bruch (1962) suggested that anorexic women showed a marked distortion in their size perception, perceiving themselves as fat even when very thin. We might expect that women with eating disorders would be exceptional and that the majority of women have a pretty good idea of their body size and shape. After all, women are accustomed to looking at themselves in mirrors, and to buying clothes that fit. In fact, research on body size estimation suggests that many women are poor at estimating the size of their body as a whole and the size of individual body parts, tending to think that they are larger than they really are.

Body size estimation techniques allow women to estimate the size of their bodies, and give a quantitative measure of the degree of distortion. In the 1970s the movable caliper technique (Slade and Russell, 1973) involved asking the participant to adjust two horizontally-mounted lights to match the width of a particular body part. This technique was modified in the 1980s by Thompson and Spana (1988) to include a simultaneous presentation of four light beams representing the cheeks, waist, hips and thighs. They called this instrument the "adjustable light beam apparatus". The participant was required to adjust the width of all four light beams to match her own estimate of the width of her cheeks, waist, hips and thighs. An assessment of the participant's actual width (measured with body calipers) was compared with her estimate; and a ratio of over- or underestimation was calculated. Kevin Thompson and colleagues found that women tended to overestimate the size of all four body parts by about 25 per cent, and that the waist was overestimated to the greatest degree (Thompson et al., 1990). Dolan and colleagues (1987) also found that women showed a tendency to overestimate the size of the waist region.

In the 1980s, the distorting photograph technique required participants to indicate their size by adjusting a photograph distorted from 20 per cent under to 20 per cent over actual size. Degree of distortion in body image (i.e. the extent to which a woman overestimates the size of her body) was measured by the discrepancy between actual size and perceived size. Women showed a reliable tendency to overestimate the size of their body, with slimmer women showing more of a distortion tendency than heavier women. Other researchers in Australia (Touyz et al., 1984) and the USA (Gardner and Moncrieff, 1988) used the distorting video technique, in which participants indicated their perceived size by adjusting a video image that was distorted by from 50 per cent under to 50 per cent over their actual size. Women tended to overestimate their size in this procedure, perceiving themselves as heavier than they actually were.

Whole-body estimation techniques were criticized in the 1990s. It was argued (e.g. by Thompson et al., 1990) that confrontation with a real-life image that increases in size may be very upsetting to an individual sensitive to appearance. Moreover, the techniques do not allow the participant to manipulate individual body sites separately. This is important because size estimation may be site-specific and not constant to the whole body (Thompson and Spana, 1988), so that a woman may overestimate the size of hips, stomach and thighs but not the rest of the body. An answer to this second problem may be found in computerized techniques that allow participants to alter specific areas of a visual image on the screen to match their body shape and size.

In the 1990s researchers (e.g. Emery et al., 1995) developed computerized measures that enabled them to "grab" a frame from a video of the participant in a leotard which could be re-sized and manipulated on the computer screen. The participant could observe the frame-grabbed image on the computer screen, and use the cursor to modify the shape of different parts of the image to produce what she felt was an accurate representation of her own body shape (when the image was initially shown as larger and smaller than actual size). The programme then calculated the degree of under- or overestimation of size for each body part. A study of twenty women aged between 19 and 32 years of age showed that the women tended to overestimate the size of legs, buttocks and abdomen, and underestimate the size of other body parts. The advantages of this method are that it allows study of the particular areas of the body that are over- or underestimated, and allows the participant to look at an image that realistically mimics weight loss or gain, rather than just widening or narrowing the image.

These techniques have become more and more sophisticated over the years with the development of more complex computer programs (Gardner, 2012). For instance, Marita McCabe and colleagues (2006) used a digital body image computer program that enables participants to manipulate a full frontal image of their entire body at five specific sites (chest, waist, hips, thighs and calves). The degree of over- and underestimation at each site is compared with the ability to manipulate the size of an on-screen, 10cm image of a vase (to check the accuracy of perception when perceiving non-body-related images). They found that their sample of 107 Australian women (with a mean age of 25 years) overestimated the size of their body. Although they also tended to overestimate the size of the vase, overestimates of body regions were significantly greater for all body regions. Actual size (BMI) did not predict degree of overestimation for women, consistent with the view that women of all shapes and sizes may be likely to overestimate their size. McCabe et al. conclude that estimation inaccuracies are not confined to women with eating disorders, but are also found in the normal population of women.

Recently, it has become possible to show women three-dimensional images of their bodies on the computer screen. Whole-body scanning enables accurate and detailed assessment of the body by measuring surface topography, and is used by people in the clothes industry who need to optimise garment fit (Istook, 2000). Whole-body scanners use image capture to produce an accurate three-dimensional image (Figure 3.1) that can be rotated in space so that women can see their bodies from all angles, presenting the possibility of a new kind of measure to study size distortion.

Although body scanning is a process that has been widely used to gather important body measurement data to inform the development of sizing systems for the clothing industry, there is very limited research where women have been asked to comment after viewing their body scans. In 2013 we carried out in-depth interviews with twenty women aged between 18 and 45 years with dress sizes between UK 10 and UK 14 who had been whole-body scanned (Grogan et al., 2013). Women reported that they looked slimmer and more "in proportion" than they had expected, suggesting that showing women realistic images of their bodies in a three-dimensional whole-body scan reduced body size overestimation, resulting in higher body satisfaction. For instance:

> Georgina (age 40): I'm surprised cause I'm, I thought I was a lot more weighty down here.

> Keira (age 31 years): I do feel a little bit better to know that my hips aren't as out of proportion as I expected.

To investigate these findings further, we asked ninety-one women with a wide range of age and BMI (aged between 18 and 81 years; BMI 19 to 42) to complete

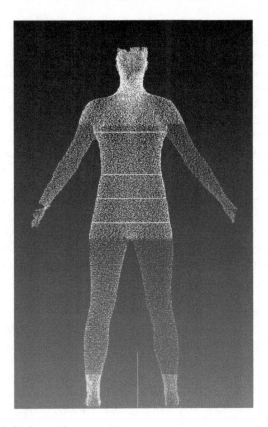

Figure 3.1 Whole-body scan image.

an online questionnaire after a whole-body scan and found somewhat different results (Grogan et al., 2016). Around a third (34 per cent) reported greater body dissatisfaction since the scan, and only six women (7 per cent) reported increased satisfaction. The effects were independent of BMI, and thematic analysis of responses to an open-ended question suggested that although women were comfortable being scanned, and wanted to see an accurate and objective view of their size and shape, they also felt threatened and vulnerable (one woman used the words "anxious" and "unhappy") when seeing their bodies on the printed output. These findings suggest that whole-body scanning should be used with caution, particularly with women with existing body concerns.

Studies using a variety of techniques show that the majority of women tend to perceive their bodies as heavier than they actually are. There is some disagreement over whether women who differ in weight/BMI differ in degree of overestimation. In an early review of relevant literature Kevin Thompson et al. (1990) argue that thinner women overestimate more than heavier women. However, more recent studies have failed to find a significant relationship between BMI and estimation accuracy (e.g. McCabe et al., 2006).

So, to conclude, evidence suggests that most women overestimate the size of (at least) parts of the body. It is important to bear in mind this tendency to overestimate body size when assessing data from studies of body satisfaction, because they need to be understood in the context that many women have unrealistic images of their body, particularly their waist, hips and thighs. These data also emphasize the importance of focusing on women's perceptions of body size, and discrepancy from the slim ideal, rather than on objective size. Perception of size is likely to be a much better predictor of body satisfaction than objectively measured body weight, a prediction borne out in studies that have found that perceived size is a better predictor of body satisfaction and self-esteem than BMI (e.g. Tiggemann, 2005).

Behavioural indicators of body dissatisfaction

One way to investigate body image is to monitor behaviours that would be expected to result from body dissatisfaction. Interview work has suggested that women engage in dieting and exercise as ways of trying to change body size and shape. This section will investigate body-relevant behaviours in women, including dieting, exercise and cosmetic surgery.

Dieting

One behavioural indicator of body dissatisfaction is the inclination to try to change body shape through diet. Most women have attempted to change weight and shape at some time in their lives by reducing the amount of food that they eat, and women's magazines promote dieting as an effective way to lose weight with front-page headlines such as "*7-Day Fat Loss Plan: Feel slimmer in just one week*" (*Women's Fitness*, February 2016). Estimates of the frequency of dieting in American and British women show that about 95 per cent of women have dieted at some stage in their lives, and approximately 45 million Americans diet each year (Uzoma, 2014: 1). Most of the women we have interviewed have used dieting as their primary way to try to lose weight. For instance:

> Sadie (age 34): The only way to get rid of it [weight], to feel more comfortable with yourself, is to diet.

Dieting was usually self-motivated, and women were keen not to be seen to have been duped into dieting by men:

> Betty (age 63): I don't diet for anyone else. Just me.

However, some women reported that their partners had encouraged them to lose weight and that they had been sufficiently upset when their partners commented negatively on their weight or shape, to lead them to change their eating habits:

Caroline (age 32): He said, "God, you aren't half getting fat." The cheeky pig. I cried and slept downstairs that night.

Continuous vigilance and awareness of body size were common features of women's discourse. Most reported dieting in cycles, losing weight by dieting for two to six weeks and then putting the weight on again when they started eating normally. For instance:

April (age 35): Well, I can't cut down. I have to go to extremes. I have to, once I manage it. I keep trying and trying, and once I start a diet, I can keep it going for six weeks as long as I don't cheat at all. If I have any cheats, that's it. I have to keep to a steady routine, so I'd have branflakes for breakfast, cottage cheese and soup for lunch, and a diet meal for tea [evening meal], and at weekends I'd probably allow myself to binge. But if I broke that pattern during the week, that's it. I'd start eating excessively then. From one extreme to another. When I do it, I go over the top really. So I can lose it quick, but that is probably why it goes on so quick.

Jackie (age 43): My whole life, I think, is going to be dieting and then nondieting, then dieting, and I know it's not good for your health.

Most of the women we interviewed distinguish between "normal" dieting (cutting down on fatty foods, generally eating less, and calorie counting) and what most of them referred to as "fad" (or "faddy") diets, which were usually liquid protein diets or all-fruit diets. As such, they presented themselves as experts on dieting who could distinguish between "real/normal" diets and "fad" diets. Liquid protein diets, which originated in the mid-1970s, involve replacing meals with low-calorie protein drinks (powder mixed with water), and are usually claimed to provide all the protein needed to be healthy while reducing calorie intake. There is some evidence that these diets, which were originally designed for obese people, may be dangerous for those who are within the normal range but "feel fat", although as Jane Ogden (1992) says, these diets are so boring that most people give them up before they can do any real harm. A similar argument can be made for all-fruit diets, whose authors recommend periods of starvation when only fruit is eaten. These could be dangerous for health. The authors often encourage dieters to engage in bulimic-type behaviour, bingeing (on off-diet days) and then purging (on diet days), and eating fruit, which acts as a diuretic, to encourage weight loss.

In interviews, most women said that they were against what they called "fad dieting" because such diets were seen to be ineffective in the long term (because they are boring and lead to cravings for other foods) and bad for health (because they do not contain necessary nutrients). For instance:

Paula (age 46): I think that fad diets are absolutely stupid. The only way to lose weight is to cut down generally and to exercise.

However, women commonly reported dieting to lose weight for special occasions, such as nights out with friends. For instance:

> Wendy (age 25): It's like when I go out on a Friday night, I can't eat so I can look slimmer that night when I go out. My belly is flatter if I don't eat.

This short-term change in behaviour was not usually seen as "dieting", which was characterized as a more long-term change in behaviour. Restriction of food, even when hungry, to look slimmer was reported by most of the women we spoke to.

Dieting is common among Western women. Many women deny themselves food, especially before a special occasion, to look slimmer. Women diet to look thinner, in the belief that thinness is associated with confidence. The slimming industry promotes this association, with images of self-confident-looking, thin models, and the rhetoric of a "new you" after the commercially available diet has helped the dieter to lose weight. Since commercial diets often fail the dieter (Chapter 2), this can lead large numbers of women to feel chronically guilty about not sticking to their diets, and dissatisfied with the way that they look (Lupton, 2013; Murray, 2016).

Exercise

Another behavioural indicator of dissatisfaction is exercising as a means to change body shape and size. Fewer women than men exercise in the USA, Canada and Britain, and the majority of women do not exercise sufficiently to achieve significant health benefits. The World Health Organization (2016) suggests that in order to protect heart function, adults aged between 18 and 64 years should do at least 150 minutes of moderate-intensity aerobic physical activity throughout the week. The Health Survey for England (Public Health England, 2015) reports that only 55 per cent of women (compared to 67 per cent of men) were achieving these recommended levels of physical activity in 2012, and that 29 per cent of women spend six hours or more being sedentary on week days, increasing to 35 per cent on weekend days. Physical exercise has well-documented effects on the incidence of coronary heart disease, blood pressure and diabetes in women (Centers of Disease Control, 2016), as well as the potential to improve body satisfaction (see Chapter 7).

Women's motivation for exercise may differ from that of men. In a study of exercise motivations among ninety-three British bar staff, we found that weight loss is a more important motivator for women who exercise than for men, and that women and gay men are more likely than heterosexual men to exercise to improve their appearance in general (Grogan et al., 2006a). This supports work by Adrian Furnham and Nicola Greaves in the 1990s showing that women are more likely than men to cite exercising for weight control, altering body shape and attractiveness (Furnham and Greaves, 1994). In interviews that we conducted with UK women, all either intended to use, or actually used, some form of exercise (usually walking, going to the gym or aerobics) as a way to lose weight and "tone" their bodies. The primary motivator to exercise for all the women interviewed was to improve muscle tone and lose weight, rather than for health (e.g. to improve cardiovascular fitness) or other (e.g. enjoyment) reasons. For instance:

> Caroline (age 32): [I exercise] entirely for weight. To try to firm up and try to use some calories, and I'm always thinking I'm not doing enough. Afterwards, like after I've been swimming, I feel great. I actually feel slimmer.

> Jade (age 17): I want to make my legs smaller. I do exercises for that.

The positive effects of exercise are not limited to changes in muscle tone and "feeling slimmer" (although this might be what motivates exercisers in the first place). Researchers have argued that women who exercise also experience positive changes in body image and self-concept due to an increase in physical mastery of the body through exercise. Precilla Choi (2000a, 2000b) suggested that exercise has the potential to develop physical mastery in women, leading to more positive body image and self-esteem. However, the construction of exercise as a beauty product may lead to unrealistic expectations (which may lead to women quitting exercise when these are not realized), and the competitive nature of sports environments may alienate women who do not conform to the slender, sporty ideal.

Jennifer Huberty and colleagues (2008) used a qualitative methodology to investigate why women may not adhere to exercise programmes, and found that in their 26- to 35-year-old participants, failed attempts to lose weight contributed to poor body image which adversely affected their motivation levels and self-worth. Other work by Kari Wasilenko and colleagues (2007) has also shown that exercise cultures that promote a focus on weight can lead to body dissatisfaction. Women exercising in a gym experienced significantly higher body dissatisfaction when exposed to a slender peer in comparison with participants exposed to the same peer wearing padding to appear heavier. Furthermore, when exposed to the slender peer they exercised on the machine for a shorter amount of time.

In the UK, Lisa Pridgeon interviewed women who had maintained their gym membership and women who had not (Pridgeon and Grogan, 2012). Unfavourable body comparisons with other women at the gym who were perceived to be more attractive were significant reasons why women had quit the gym. One woman contended that these feelings had a devastating effect on her self-esteem and could be so overwhelming as to make her leave immediately.

> Annie: They're all so much skinnier than me and then when all the skinny girls walk in it's like, "Oh my God I don't wanna be here", so I walk out.

Choi (2000a) argued that exercise cultures need to provide a welcoming environment for women of all shapes and sizes, to promote positive body image through successful engagement in exercise programmes:

> The potential for true physical and psychological health, as opposed to beauty, must be emphasised and the exercise culture must facilitate empowerment by emphasising mastery over outcomes, by celebrating the physical achievements of all participants, and by including all participants whatever their shape and size.
>
> (Choi, 2000a: 377)

The implications of these findings for promoting positive body image will be discussed in Chapter 7.

Bodybuilding

Bodybuilding is not always seen as appropriate for women, and pioneering women bodybuilders faced social censure as they entered the competitive bodybuilding world in the 1970s (St. Martin and Gavey, 1996). The first widely publicized women's bodybuilding event was held in 1979 in Los Angeles (previously the only choice for women bodybuilders was the "beauty pageant" added to the men's competitions). In the 1980s the Ms. Olympia competition started in the USA, and in Britain NABBA (National Amateur Body Building Association) renamed its "Miss Bikini International" competition "Ms. Universe".

In 1986 the Ms. Universe competition was divided into "Physique" and "Figure" classes. The "Physique" class caters for those aiming for a more muscular physique and less traditionally feminine presentation (minimal make-up and bare feet), and "Figure" for those who want traditionally feminine presentation (moderate degrees of muscularity, makeup and shoes with high heels). In the 1990s *"Fitness"* competitions were set up for women who engage in weight training as part of a general fitness regime. *"Fitness"* competitors engage in an aerobic performance as well as posing to reveal body shape and tone. In 2010 a new category of *"Bikini Fitness"* was officially recognized by the International Federation for Bodybuilding and Fitness. For this category women are expected to be lean, though with higher body fat than *"Figure"* competitors, and without visible muscle definition (framed as a "beach body"). In competition, *"Bikini Fitness"* bodybuilders are required to wear a two-piece posing suit, high heels, full make-up and styled hair as per *"Figure"* competitors, and the emphasis is on looking "healthy and fit" (International Federation for Bodybuilding and Fitness, 2016).

Women's bodybuilding has been conceptualized in many different ways. In the 1990s Sandra Lee Bartky (1990) saw it as a direct challenge to the cultural restrictions placed on women in terms of how their bodies should look, and argued that women bodybuilders represent a radical cutting edge of feminist resistance to cultural ideals. She represents an optimistic view of bodybuilding as a way to challenge dominant ideologies that represent women as physically weak, showing that muscularity (and, by inference, strength) is mostly a product of cultural practices. By showing that women's physical weakness is (mostly) culturally produced, she opens up the possibility that it is surpassable. This view sees bodybuilding as an empowering practice that challenges the cultural association of muscularity (and strength) with masculinity. An alternative view is presented by Susan Bordo (2003), who sees bodybuilding as women's response to cultural pressures to control their bodies into a culturally acceptable, firm, toned and solid form. She links bodybuilding with anorexia, seeing both as attempts to avoid "the soft, the loose, unsolid, excess flesh" (p. 191). She sees women bodybuilders as responding to cultural pressures to have a slim, firm body, but doing so in a different way from women who choose to try to attain the ideal through the usual means of restriction of food intake. For Bordo these women are not challenging cultural ideals, but merely responding to them in a different way.

In 2004 we interviewed an opportunity sample of women bodybuilders who all competed (or had competed in the past) in the "Physique" (highly muscled) bodybuilding class (Grogan et al., 2004), to investigate their motivations for bodybuilding. These women were engaging in behaviours that placed them outside the mainstream norms of how it is appropriate for women to look, and were resisting the social pressures to be more slender that other women report. We were interested in what motivated them to start bodybuilding and what maintained their bodybuilding. Given that mainstream Western cultures expect women's bodies not to take up space (e.g. Murray, 2016), we were also interested in these women's experience of other people's reactions to their increased size. We wondered how they experienced the reactions of those outside and also inside the bodybuilding world, and what sources of social support these women used.

The women who took part in our interviews presented accounts in which they represented themselves as feeling better about their bodies, and about themselves generally, than in their pre-bodybuilding days, stressing control of the body. This is a traditional feminine discourse, drawing on notions of bodily restraint (Bordo, 2003), although in this case the women were talking about increasing rather than reducing the size of their bodies. These women had shifted their body ideal (with support from within the bodybuilding community) to a more muscular figure:

> I mean their bodies are beautiful. Their shape. Like the Figure and the Fitness, and your Americans – Universe and Miss Galaxy. They're beautiful, and this is what people are looking for now. That athletic shape of the female. The waist, and the toned, and umm you know that. But healthy.

> We are used to it. We get *Muscle and Fitness* [magazine]. We get *Flex* [magazine]. We read them monthly. We get them every day and we have become conditioned to see the female body like that. It doesn't look any different to us. So, when you are in that environment, unless you are huge you're not going to be, if you like, a freak to them.

58

The only people whose reactions concerned them were other bodybuilders and competition judges. This effectively negated the importance of reactions from those who may not find a hard and muscular body appealing, enabling these women to feel physically and mentally strong and raising their self-esteem and self-confidence. However, they also reported that they were under constraint from the bodybuilding community in terms of what size was acceptable, and this restricted how muscular they could get and still be able to succeed in competition:

> I think I look feminine on stage. I'll never be the biggest girl on stage, but, do you know what I mean? I think I've got a nice shape and still look feminine and that's what I base it on.

This raises the crucial question of whether these women should be seen as complying with mainstream social pressures to be "feminine" – as Jane Ussher (1997) puts it, to "do girl" – or whether, as Sandra Bartky (1990) and Leena St. Martin and Nicola Gavey (1996) argue, they are resisting these pressures. I suggest that they are doing both. In actively changing their bodies to be "unacceptably" muscular, and by explicitly rejecting the judgements of mainstream views of their bodies, these women are resisting mainstream cultural norms. They are also complying with a narrow set of ideals, determined by the largely male bodybuilding community. If we had interviewed women who had not competed we may have identified more evidence of resistance and individuality, since they would be likely to be under less pressure from the bodybuilding community. These women bodybuilders were engaged in a complex balancing act in which they want to be muscular, toned and athletic looking, but do not want to get unacceptably muscular. Their experiences provide a model of how women can resist mainstream cultural pressures to be slender, providing they have support from a salient subcultural group. They show that contesting the dominant slender ideal can lead to feelings of empowerment and the forging of alternative body ideals. The fact that these women are subject to alternative pressures from within the bodybuilding community to present as "feminine" should not detract from the fact that they have found a way to resist mainstream pressure to be slim, and to feel good about the look and feel of their bodies.

Anabolic steroid use

The use of anabolic steroids as an aid to bodybuilding is becoming more and more prevalent (Smith et al., in press). Steroids help to maximize the effects of weight training in increasing muscle mass, but carry with them risks of serious side effects such as kidney and liver damage and hypertension, as well as risks of HIV infection and hepatitis for those who use injectable steroids (National Health Service, 2016). Most work on anabolic steroid use has focused on men, as most bodybuilders are men and most steroid users are male (Lennehan, 2003; Smith et al., in press). However, women's use of anabolic steroid drugs for bodybuilding has increased in the twenty-first century, with recent studies showing that around 4 per cent of adolescent girls report using steroids in the previous twelve months (Eisenberg et al., 2012). Jenny O'Dea and Renata Cinelli (in press) suggest that there has been an increase in usage of anabolic steroids in young women in the last decade.

In order to try to understand why women engage in anabolic steroid use, risking their health to become highly muscled, we have investigated experiences of steroid use in interviews with women who use anabolic steroids as part of their bodybuilding regime (Grogan et al., 2006a). Social support, especially from within the bodybuilding community, was an important motivator for use, and these women believed that it would be impossible to compete in bodybuilding without steroids. The masculinizing effects of steroids (male pattern baldness and deepening of the voice) and the threat to reproductive health were cited as the biggest disincentives for women, and more of a disincentive than more serious long-term risks such as kidney and liver damage or the risk of blood-borne diseases caused by sharing needles. For instance, one respondent was concerned about her fertility:

> [reproductive health] is a bit of a worry but I've had kids before and to be quite honest I haven't been on the pill [oral contraceptive] for three years. But when you've been dieting and taking gear [steroids], it's not a good time. So we need to have a full term to be clean, and, you know what I mean. You know, we'll go to the doctors and get everything checked out anyway.

In relation to the masculinizing effects of some steroids, such as lowering of the voice, male pattern baldness and increased hair growth on the body and face, one of the women reported:

> I could sing before and I can't now. Umm, I find if I try and sing, it breaks, which is not particularly great. Also I've found I have been quite lucky on the hair side, as on my body my hair hasn't grown, but I have found on my face, umm, I had what you would call downy hair, which was like fair downy hair. When I competed, it was noticeable and it was the steroid use and it was my own fault for shaving it off a couple of years back, which caused my hair to grow back even worse. You could argue whether it was or it wasn't steroid use, that. But I do have hair problems now so I do have to shave in certain areas, which is a disadvantage, I feel. Skin – my skin has never been particularly good either on steroid use.

No women reported concerns about liver or kidney damage. Nor did they express concerns about contracting HIV/AIDS through infected needles. The only side-effects that were experienced as significant deterrents were those that had a direct effect on body image and fertility. However, these (and fertility problems) were outweighed by the importance of wanting to gain muscle for competition. An unexpected finding in this study was that the women's primary concern about maintaining a "feminine" look was to increase their chances of winning in competition through being able to present on stage as looking "feminine" (defined as having a hair-free body and clear skin). Interventions designed to reduce or prevent steroid use in women need to take into account the fact that the desire to maintain a traditionally feminine look and reproductive health may act as a disincentive for their use.

Cosmetic surgery

The twenty-first century has seen a significant increase in the number of women having cosmetic surgery. The International Society of Aesthetic Surgeons (2015) notes that over 20 million cosmetic procedures were performed in 2014. Botulinum toxin (botox) was the most prevalent cosmetic procedure for women and men and breast augmentation the most prevalent surgical procedure for women, closely followed by liposuction. Twenty per cent (4,064,571) of procedures performed internationally were carried out in the US, followed by Brazil (10 per cent; 2,058,505) and Japan (6 per cent; 1,260,351). Women had more than 17 million cosmetic procedures (87 per cent of the total), an increase on previous years. Clearly, more and more women are turning to cosmetic surgery as a way to change the shape of their bodies. Susan Bordo (2003) notes that the increased availability of cosmetic surgery has changed expectations about how women's bodies should look as they age, and has reduced the range of body and facial types that are considered acceptable. Cosmetic surgical procedures are now "normal" and accessible:

> These homogenized images normalize – that is, they function as models against which the self continually measures, judges, "disciplines" and "corrects" itself. Cosmetic surgery is now a $1.75-billion-a-year industry in the United States, with almost 1.5 million people a year undergoing surgery of some kind from face lifts to calf implants.
>
> (Bordo, 2003: 25)

Cosmetic surgery is not a recent phenomenon. It is possible to trace its history from 1000 BC; the first plastic surgery was reported in India, when rhinoplasty (nose reconstruction) was carried out on individuals whose noses had been cut off as a form of punishment (Haiken, 1997). However, it was not until the mid-twentieth century that cosmetic surgery (surgery performed for the aesthetic improvement of healthy bodies) emerged. Naomi Wolf (1991) traces the beginnings of what she calls the "Surgical Age" in which cosmetic surgery became a mass phenomenon, showing how it became more and more accessible to women who were dissatisfied with the way that they looked, partly fed by the promotion of cosmetic surgery techniques aimed at women. Fabienne Darling-Wolf (2000) notes that cosmetic surgeons and popular media promote the idea of the female body as inherently flawed and in need of technological reconstruction in order to create a demand for their services, and that there has been a disturbing shift in the 1990s from an emphasis on ornamentation of the body to actual reshaping of the "flawed" female body:

> Such a construction contributes to an ideology – clearly present in the language used by plastic surgeons – of the female body as inherently flawed and pathological. In the United States the American Society of Plastic Surgeons managed to convince the Federal Food and Drink Administration to let silicone breast implants stay on the market by arguing that the condition of having small breasts was actually a disfiguring disease called "micromastia". Cosmetic surgery journals similarly abound with references to "abnormalities" and "deformities" needing to be corrected.
>
> (Darling-Wolf, 2000: 285–6)

This trend has progressed in the twenty-first century with the genesis of reality television shows in which women receive "extreme makeovers" including cosmetic surgery to correct perceived flaws. *Ten Years Younger,* which originally aired in the UK in 2004 and has since been released in Australia, New Zealand, Brazil and the US, and *Extreme Makeover* in the US (2002–2007) and Australia (2007–) give viewers access to before, during and after footage of cosmetic procedures. These have the effect of normalizing these procedures and also raise women's awareness of cosmetic procedures that would be available to them if they could afford them.

The question of why women are willing to undergo unnecessary surgery to make their bodies conform more closely to accepted norms may help us to understand the nature of body dissatisfaction in women. Kathy Davis (1995) in *Reshaping the Female Body: The Dilemma of Cosmetic Surgery* looks at cosmetic surgery from a broadly feminist viewpoint. She argues that understanding why women engage in a practice which is painful and dangerous must take women's explanations as a starting point. She attempts to explore cosmetic surgery as one of the most negative aspects of Western beauty culture without seeing the women who opt for the "surgical fix" as what she calls "cultural dopes" (i.e. by taking seriously their reasons for having cosmetic surgery). She carried out her work in the Netherlands, where there had been a general increase in cosmetic surgery in the preceding years (to more than twenty thousand cosmetic operations in 1994 – more per capita than in the USA). Since cosmetic surgery is freely available to all women in the Netherlands provided their appearance is classified as falling "outside the realm of the normal", it was possible to investigate women's decisions without financial considerations being an issue.

She spoke with women who had had a variety of different kinds of cosmetic surgery. She found that women gave accounts that dispelled the notion that they were simply the duped victims of the beauty system. They had long histories of suffering with bodies that they experienced as unacceptable, different or abnormal.

She argues that cosmetic surgery is about wanting to be normal rather than wanting to be beautiful. Women she interviewed reported that they experienced the decision to have cosmetic surgery as a way of taking control of their lives, and that cosmetic surgery was something that they had decided upon for themselves, rather than under pressure from partners or knife-happy surgeons. They were clear that they had made informed choices, based on weighing up the risks and possible benefits of surgery.

Davis takes the position that cosmetic surgery may be an informed choice, but it is always made in the context of culturally limited options. She argues fiercely against the idea expressed by many authors, including Kathryn Morgan (1991), that women who opt for cosmetic surgery are victims of male lovers, husbands or surgeons. She also disagrees that women who opt for cosmetic surgery are duped by ideologies that confuse and mystify with the rhetoric of individual choice.

Davis (1995) sees women as active and knowledgeable agents who make decisions based on a limited range of available options. She argues that women see through the conditions of oppression even as they comply with them. The women she interviewed reported that they had made free choices, although these "choices" were limited by cultural definitions of beauty and by the availability of particular surgical techniques. She cautions against closing the debate by accepting the politically correct line, and suggests that:

> As concerned critics of the explosion in surgical technologies for reshaping the female body and of women's continued willingness to partake in them, we simply cannot afford the comfort of the correct line.
>
> (Davis, 1995: 185)

In 2006 Jo Ann Campbell at Staffordshire University used the internet to recruit fifty-nine women who were due to undergo cosmetic surgery (Campbell, 2006). The women answered a series of open-ended questions about expectations and experiences of cosmetic surgery before and one month after having cosmetic surgery. She found that most of these women argued that they had been motivated to undertake cosmetic surgery by the feeling that the targeted body part was socially unacceptable and abnormal. For instance:

> I want to feel normal. All my life (since childhood), I was called names and pointed out for being ugly and flat-chested. I know I can never be pretty. But normal would be heaven for me.

Accounts supported suggestions from other authors that women referred for cosmetic surgery are not necessarily dissatisfied with the whole of their bodies but tend to believe that one rogue body part was out of line with the rest of their body (e.g. Cepanec and Payne, 2000). Although women referred for breast reduction surgery tended to cite health problems as the primary motivator for surgery (pain, rashes), aesthetic reasons were the main motivator for all other kinds of cosmetic surgery. Most women reported a significant improvement in quality of life and self-esteem post-operatively. Many women had spent considerable time researching the surgeon and surgery involved. Consistent with suggestions by Kathy Davis (1995, 2002), women argued that cosmetic surgery was a personal choice and a way to become "normal" and to take control over their bodies. For instance:

> Cosmetic surgery has given me a sense of power and control over my life for the first time. It gives me hope that I can be the real me.

It may be difficult for women to express wanting to be attractive and not open themselves to socially unacceptable charges of vanity. It may also be challenging to report anything other than agency over the decision to have surgery and still ensure that one is not seen as a "cultural dope". Diane Cepanec and Barbara Payne (2000) argue that the claim that women are taking their lives into their own hands deflects attention from the sociocultural contact in which women's agency operates. They are also critical of Davis's position that cosmetic surgery can be both disempowering and a road to empowerment, as this position can be used to endorse cosmetic surgery. Susan Bordo (2003) believes that to have plastic surgery is to support a system that is oppressive to women:

> Unlike Davis I do not view cosmetic surgery as being first and foremost "about" self-determination or self-deception. Rather my focus is on the complexly and densely institutionalized system of values and practices within which girls and women – and increasingly boys and men as well – come to believe that they are nothing (and are frequently treated as nothing) unless they are trim, tight, lineless, bulgeless, and sagless.
>
> (Bordo, 2003: 32)

In the twenty-first century it is not difficult to find examples of media promoting women's "choice" to "resculpt" their bodies. A random selection of advertisements in women's magazines in Britain from 2007 showed how the advertisers stress improvements in confidence (BUPA: "The real secret to looking good is feeling good"; Transform: "Years of development in plastic surgery enables women to have beautiful breasts and the confidence to enjoy life to the full") and in rationality (the Hospital Group: "If you're not happy with the way you look ... change it!"; the Pountney Clinic: "[Liposuction] is the logical way to complete a 'trim' figure"), and avoid any mention of pain, stressing instead the virtues of care and reassurance (Transform: "With 30 years' experience and highly qualified and experienced surgeons, we've transformed the lives of over 150,000 patients so you can be confident you're in safe hands"). Pictures of conventionally attractive models appear in the advertisements, along with statements such as "For making me comfortable in sleeveless tops, for letting me relax in photographs, for showing me my best asset is me. Thank you" (BUPA); and "Cosmetic surgery changed my life" (Belvedere Private Clinic).

In 2012 the UK Advertising Standards Authority noted a move to ban advertising of cosmetic surgery in the UK:

> Following recent headlines and public health concerns about faulty breast implants, the British Association of Aesthetic Plastic Surgeons (BAAPS) and its members are calling for a ban on the advertising of cosmetic surgery. While any ban would have to be passed by Government through legislation; the ASA is committed to ensuring that all ads for cosmetic procedures stick to the strict Advertising Codes which require ads to be prepared responsibly and avoid being misleading, harmful or offensive.
>
> (Advertising Standards Authority, 2012: 1)

However, private cosmetic surgery clinics in the UK and elsewhere continue to publish advertisements for cosmetic surgery, including "luxury perks" as inducements for surgery, with incentives that are time-sensitive, to pressure people into booking quickly (Wiseman, 2014).

Social construction of the feminine body

Since the 1980s authors have debated reasons why so many women are dissatisfied with their bodies. Feminist authors have suggested that a system of unrealistic beauty norms promoted through media and internalized by women has set up impossible body ideals for women. These unrealistic ideals have been seen as a way to keep women in a subordinate position, by ensuring that they put their energies into vigilance over their bodies and these energies are channeled into the "fight" for a perfect body.

Susan Brownmiller (1984), in *Femininity*, presented a seemingly light-hearted but intelligent and hard-hitting analysis of women's relationships with their bodies. Brownmiller traced the history of the prevailing vogue for extreme slimness, showing how slenderness became identified with refinement, willpower and chic, and success at dieting became an important form of competition among women within a context where women were encouraged to compete in terms of their physical appearance. She argued that striving for physical perfection was a distraction for women, causing chronic self-monitoring:

> [We are] never quite satisfied, and never secure, for desperate unending absorption in the drive for a perfect appearance – call it feminine vanity – is the ultimate restriction on freedom of mind.
>
> (Brownmiller, 1984: 33)

Developing some of these ideas in the 1990s, Susie Orbach (1993) argued that women are taught from an early age to view their bodies as commodities. She showed how women's bodies are used to humanize and sell products in Western consumer culture, and how the fact that women's bodies themselves are objectified creates body image problems for women:

> The receptivity that women show (across class, ethnicity, and through the generations) to the idea that their bodies are like gardens – arenas for constant improvement and resculpting – is rooted in the recognition of their bodies as commodities. A consumer society in which women's bodies perform the crucial function of humanising other products while being presented as the ultimate commodity creates all sorts of body image problems for women, both at the level of distortion about their own and others' bodies, and in creating a disjuncture from their bodies.
>
> (Orbach, 1993: 17)

Also in the 1990s, Sandra Bartky saw women as engaging actively with the representation of the female body. She argued that what she called the "fashion-beauty complex" seeks (on the surface) to provide opportunities for women to indulge themselves, but covertly depreciates women's bodies by constantly presenting messages that women fail to measure up to the current ideals:

> We are presented everywhere with images of perfect female beauty – at the drugstore cosmetics display, the supermarket magazine counter, on television. These images remind us constantly that we fail to measure up. Whose nose is the right shape, after all, whose hips are not too wide – or too narrow? The female body is revealed as a task, an object in need of transformation. ... The fashion–beauty complex produces in women an estrangement from her bodily being: on the one hand, she is it and is scarcely allowed to be anything else; on the other hand, she must exist perpetually at a distance from her physical self, fixed at this distance in a permanent posture of disapproval.
>
> (Bartky, 1990: 40)

Bartky noted that every aspect of women's bodies is objectified, so that women feel estranged from their bodies. She suggested that the pleasures that women report in body-maintenance procedures result from the creation of "false needs" by the fashion–beauty complex, which produces the needs themselves (through indoctrination, psychological manipulation and the denial of autonomy), and also controls the conditions through which these needs can be satisfied. She argued that the repressive narcissistic satisfactions promoted by the fashion–beauty complex stand in the way of authentic delight in the body. She suggested a revolutionary aesthetic of the body, which allows an expansion of ideas of beauty and allows body display and play in self-ornamentation. She promoted the release of our capacity to apprehend the beautiful from the narrow limits within which it is currently confined, to produce an aesthetic for the female body controlled by women. She proposed that women should produce a model of feminine beauty that celebrates diversity. This could be an ideal that actually makes women feel better about themselves, rather than one that breeds body insecurity among those who do not conform to the slender, well-toned ideal.

Towards the end of the 1990s Barbara Frederickson and Tomi-Ann Roberts developed Objectification Theory (Frederickson and Roberts, 1997). According to this theory, women's bodies are socially constructed as objects to be watched and evaluated. In order to gain social approval girls learn to practice self-surveillance, watching and judging themselves against prevailing societal standards as though they were an outside observer. This habitual self-monitoring leads to body shame and dissatisfaction. In one study, Frederickson et al. (1998) randomly assigned US student women to conditions in which they were asked to try on either a swimsuit or a sweater (the swimsuit condition was intended to increase self-objectification). When the groups were compared the swimsuit group had higher levels of body shame on average, ate less when food was available, and performed worse on a mathematics test. These data suggest that body surveillance can cause body shame and reduced performance in cognitive spheres, probably due to distraction and deflection of cognitive resources.

In the twenty-first century, feminist scholars have continued to focus on the social construction of the female body. Susan Bordo (2003) argued that preoccupation with fat, diet and slenderness in women was still normative. She suggests that Western culture surrounds women with clear messages that overweight (described as "bulges" and "bumps") must be "destroyed", "eliminated" or "burned". The ideal is a body completely under control, toned and contained, an ideal that can be achieved through dieting or extreme exercise and bodybuilding. She argued that the seemingly disparate areas of bodybuilding and compulsive dieting are linked in their rejection of loose, soft flesh:

> The two ideals, though superficially very different, are united in a battle against a common enemy: the soft, the loose, unsolid, excess flesh. It is perfectly permissible in our culture (even for women) to have substantial weight and bulk – so long as it is tightly managed.
>
> (Bordo, 2003: 191)

Bordo's analysis places women's preoccupation with slimness into a cultural context in order to explain why women are especially susceptible to pressures from the beauty system. She is pessimistic about women's ability to really resist these pressures. She argues that women cannot help but collude in the system because they are submerged in the culture in which slimness in women is associated with a specific (positive) set of cultural meanings. She says that feminists should be sceptical about the possibility of developing free, feminine identities that are independent of the mainstream beauty culture, and she shows how women's attempts to escape the system may be reabsorbed into negative discourses of femininity. Citing the Foucauldian position that individual self-surveillance and self-correction to prevailing social norms may be just as effective at controlling behaviour as physical violence and material constraints, she relates this to appearance-related behaviours:

> When it comes to the politics of appearance such ideas are apt and illuminating. In my work they have been extremely helpful both to my analysis of the contemporary disciplines of diet and exercise and to my understanding of eating disorders as arising out of and reproducing normative feminine practices in our culture, practices which train the female body in docility and obedience to cultural demands while at the same time being experienced in terms of power and control.
>
> (Bordo, 2003: 27)

Feminist writers have continued to critique cultural pressures on women in relation to their bodies. In 2014, in the second edition of her book *Beauty and Misogyny*, Sheila Jeffreys argues that beauty practices such as cosmetic surgery (and other arguably more innocuous beauty practices such as wearing high heels that make walking difficult and can lead to injury) are harmful to women and undertaken primarily for the benefit of men. She also argues that cultural discourses around 'choice' act to normalize dangerous health-related behaviours such as cosmetic surgery for women. She also argues that there has been minimal improvement in the position of women in 2014 compared to 2005 (when she published the first edition of her book), and that new developments, including the normalization of botox and other cosmetic procedures, new and dangerous clothing trends, and expectations that women will depilate their bodies as a matter of course, have added to the sociocultural body-related pressures that were present when she wrote the previous edition of her book.

Feminist accounts of women's experience of the body are important in helping to make sense of why women in particular may show normative body concern. There can be no doubt that Western culture in the twenty-first century promotes unrealistic body ideals to women, and that non-conformity to these ideals leads to social disapproval. The question of women's active involvement in restrictive beauty practices (such as dieting and cosmetic surgery) is more complex, and discourses of "choice" are promoted by cosmetic surgery companies and others invested in women's continued uptake of beauty products.

Women's bodies are subject to critical evaluation to the extent that they differ from an established norm based on a youthful, slender ideal. Women who have social support for an alternative body type (such as the "Physique" level bodybuilders whose interviews are described above) report relative satisfaction with their bodies, but only to the extent that their bodies comply with an alternative norm (too muscled or too much body hair and they will no longer be satisfactory), and women who are pregnant or have recently given birth and are still breastfeeding also report more positive body image through focusing on the functional rather than the aesthetic aspects of their bodies. Chapter 6 investigates factors that may predict higher satisfaction in some groups of women. Chapter 7 investigates ways of using what we know about body dissatisfaction to promote a more positive body image in women.

Summary

- Many women in Western societies are dissatisfied with their bodies, particularly their stomach, hips and thighs.
- Most women would choose to be thinner, and women tend to overestimate the size of key body sites, irrespective of actual size.
- Questionnaires and interviews have found a similar pattern of dissatisfaction in British, Canadian, US and Australian women.
- Work focusing on the social construction of femininity assists our understanding of women's body dissatisfaction. This work suggests that social pressure to strive for the slender, toned body shape that is associated with youth, control and success encourages the objectification of the body and the disproportionate allocation of energies to body maintenance.
- A positive way forward is indicated by feminist scholars who promote the development of a new aesthetic that would push back the limits of acceptable body shape and size.

Bibliography

Advertising Standards Authority (2012) *Cosmetic surgery advertising*, available online at: www.asa.org.uk/News-resources/Media-Centre/2012/Cosmetic-surgery-advertising. aspx#.VqooZxErGUk [accessed 25 January 2012].

Aghekyan, M., Ulrich, P. and Connell, L. (2012) 'Using body scans in assessing perceptions of body attractiveness and size: Cross-cultural study', *International Journal of Fashion Design, Technology and Education*, 5 (2), 81–89.

Alley, T. and Scully, K. (1994) 'The impact of actual and perceived changes in body weight on women's physical attractiveness', *Basic and Applied Social Psychology*, 15 (4), 535–42.

Andrew, R., Tiggemann, M. and Clark, L. (2015) 'Predictors of intuitive eating in adolescent girls', *Journal of Adolescent Health*, 56 (2), 209–14.

Avalos, L., Tylka, T.L. and Wood-Barcalow, N. (2005) 'The Body Appreciation Scale: Development and psychometric evaluation', *Body Image*, 2 (3), 285–97.

Bartky, S.L. (1990) *Femininity and domination: Studies in the phenomenology of oppression*, New York: Routledge.

Ben-Tovim, D. and Walker, K. (1991) 'Women's body attitudes: A review of measurement techniques', *International Journal of Eating Disorders*, 10 (2), 155–67.

Blashill, A., Williams, A., Grogan, S. and Clark-Carter, D. (2015) 'Negative appearance evaluation is associated with skin cancer risk behaviors among American men and women', *Health Psychology*, 34 (1), 93–6.

Bordo, S. (2003) *Unbearable weight: Feminism, Western culture, and the body*, 10th anniversary edition, Berkeley, CA: University of California Press.

Brownmiller, S. (1984) *Femininity*, New York: Linden Press.

Bruch, H. (1962) 'Perceptual and conceptual disturbances in anorexia nervosa', *Psychological Medicine*, 24 (2), 187–94.

Cafri, G., van den Berg, P. and Brannick, M.T. (2010) 'What have the difference scores not been telling us? A critique of the use of self-ideal discrepancy in the assessment of body image and evaluation of an alternative data-analytic framework', *Assessment*, 17 (3), 361–76.

Campbell, J. (2006) 'Cosmetic surgery: Women's experiences', unpublished MSc Health Psychology dissertation, Staffordshire University.

Cash, T. (2000) *User manuals for the Multidimensional Body-Self Relations Questionnaire*, available from the author online at: www.body-images.com

Cash, T., Winstead, B. and Janda, L. (1986) 'The great American shape-up: Body image survey report', *Psychology Today*, 20 (4), 30–7.

Centers of Disease Control and Prevention (2016) *Physical activity and health*, available online at: www.cdc.gov/physicalactivity/basics/pa-health/index.htm [accessed 4 January 2016].

Cepanec, D. and Payne, B. (2000) '"Old bags" under the knife: Facial cosmetic surgery among women', in B. Miedema, J.M. Stoppard and V. Anderson (Eds) *Women's bodies, women's lives* (pp. 121–41), Toronto: Sumach Press.

Charles, N. and Kerr, M. (1986) 'Food for feminist thought', *Sociological Review*, 34, 537–72.

Choi, P.Y.L. (2000a) 'Looking good and feeling good: Why do fewer women than men exercise?' in J. Ussher (Ed.) *Women's health* (pp. 372–9), Leicester: BPS Books.

Choi, P.Y.L. (2000b) *Femininity and the physically active woman*, London: Routledge.

Cooper, P., Taylor, M., Cooper, Z. and Fairburn, C. (1987) 'The development and validation of the Body Shape Questionnaire', *International Journal of Eating Disorders*, 6 (4), 485–94.

Cororve-Fingeret, M., Gleaves, D.H. and Pearson, C.A. (2004) 'On the methodology of body image assessment: The use of figural scales to evaluate body dissatisfaction and the ideal body standards of women', *Body Image*, 1 (2), 207–12.

Darling-Wolf, F. (2000) 'From air-brushing to liposuction: The technological reconstruction of the female body', in B. Miedema, J.M. Stoppard and V. Anderson (Eds) *Women's bodies, women's lives* (pp. 277–93), Toronto: Sumach Press.

Davis, K. (1995) *Reshaping the female body: The dilemma of cosmetic surgery*, London: Routledge.

Davis, K. (2002) 'A dubious equality: Men and women in cosmetic surgery', *Body and Society*, 8 (1), 49–65.

Dolan, B.M., Birchnell, S.A. and Lacey, J.H. (1987) 'Body image distortion in non-eating disordered men and women', *Journal of Psychosomatic Research*, 31 (4), 513–20.

Eisenberg, M.E., Wall, M. and Neumark-Sztainer, D. (2012) 'Muscle-enhancing behaviors among adolescent girls and boys', *Pediatrics*, 130 (6), 1019–26.

Emery, J., Benson, P., Cohen-Tovee, E. and Tovee, M. (1995) 'A computerised measure of body image and body shape', personal communication.

Evans, C. and Dolan, B. (1992) 'Body Shape Questionnaire: Derivation of shortened "alternate forms"', *International Journal of Eating Disorders*, 13 (3), 315–32.

Fallon, A. and Rozin, P. (1985) 'Sex differences in perceptions of desirable body shape', *Journal of Abnormal Psychology*, 94 (1), 102–5.

Fern, V.A., Buckley, E. and Grogan, S. (2012) 'Women's experiences of body image and weight loss after childbirth', *British Journal of Midwifery*, 20 (12), 860–5.

Fern, V., Buckley, E. and Grogan, S. (2014) 'Postpartum body image and feeding choices: Dealing with the pressure to be slender', *British Journal of Midwifery*, 22 (11), 788–94.

Frederickson, B.L. and Roberts, T. (1997) 'Objectification theory: Towards understanding women's lived experience and mental health risks', *Psychology of Women Quarterly*, 21 (2), 173–206.

Frederickson, B.L., Roberts, T., Noll, S.M., Quinn, D.M. and Twenge, J.M. (1998) 'That swimsuit becomes you: Sex differences in self-objectification, restrained eating and math performance', *Journal of Personality and Social Psychology*, 75 (1), 269–84.

Furnham, A. and Greaves, N. (1994) 'Gender and locus of control correlates of body image dissatisfaction,', *European Journal of Personality*, 8 (3), 183–200.

Gardner, R. (2012) 'Measurement of perceptual body image', in T.F. Cash (Ed.) *Encyclopedia of body image and human appearance* (pp. 526–32), London: Elsevier.

Gardner, R.M. and Moncrieff, C. (1988) 'Body image distortion in anorexics as a non-sensory phenomenon: A signal detection approach', *Journal of Clinical Psychology*, 44 (2), 101–7.

Garner, D.M. (1997) 'The 1997 body image survey results', *Psychology Today*, 30 (1), 30–48.

Grippo, K.P. and Hill, M. (2008) 'Self-objectification, habitual body monitoring, and body dissatisfaction in older European American women: Exploring age and feminism as moderators', *Body Image*, 5 (2), 173–182.

Grogan, S. (2008) *Body image: Understanding body dissatisfaction in men, women, and children* (2nd edition), London: Routledge.

Grogan, S., Conner, M. and Smithson, H. (2006a) 'Sexuality and exercise motivations: Are gay men and heterosexual women most likely to be motivated by concern about weight and appearance?' *Sex Roles*, 55 (7–8), 567–72.

Grogan, S., Evans, R., Wright, S. and Hunter, G. (2004) 'Femininity and muscularity: Accounts of seven women bodybuilders', *Journal of Gender Studies*, 13 (1), 49–63.

Grogan, S., Gill, S., Brownbridge, K., Kilgariff, S. and Whalley, A. (2013) 'Dress fit and body image: A thematic analysis of women's accounts during and after trying on dresses', *Body Image*, 10 (3), 380–388.

Grogan, S., Gill, S., Brownbridge, K., Warnock, D. and Armitage, C. (2016) 'Women's long-term reactions to whole-body scanning: A mixed methods approach', *Clothing and Textiles Research Journal*, 34 (1), 75–83.

Grogan, S., Shepherd, S., Evans, R., Wright, S. and Hunter, G. (2006b) 'Experiences of anabolic steroid use: Interviews with men and women steroid users', *Journal of Health Psychology*, 11(6), 849–60.

Haiken, E. (1997) *Venus envy: A history of cosmetic surgery*, Baltimore and London: Johns Hopkins University Press.

Homan, K.J. and Tylka, T.L. (2014) 'Appearance-based exercise motivation moderates the relationship between exercise frequency and positive body image', *Body Image*, 11 (2), 101–8.

Huberty, J.L, Ransdell, L.B., Sidman, C. et al. (2008) 'Explaining long-term exercise adherence in women who complete a structured exercise programme', *Research Quarterly for Exercise and Sport*, 79 (3), 374–84.

Huon, G. (1988) 'Towards the prevention of eating disorders', in D. Hardoff and E. Chigier (Eds) *Eating disorders in adolescents and young adults* (pp. 447–54), London: Freund.

Huon, G., Morris, S. and Brown, L. (1990) 'Differences between male and female preferences for female body size', *Australian Psychologist*, 25, 314–17.

International Federation of Bodybuilding and Fitness (2016) *Rules*, available online at: www.ifbb.com/rules/ [accessed 20 January 2016].

International Society of Aesthetic Plastic Surgery (2015) *Global statistics on cosmetic procedures*, available online at: www.isaps.org [accessed 5 December 2015].

International Society of Aesthetic Surgeons (2016) *ISAPS Global Statistics*, available online at: www.isaps.org/news/isaps-global-statistics [accessed 5 January 2016].

Istook, C.L. (2000) 'Rapid prototyping in the textile and apparel industry: A pilot project', *Journal of Textile and Apparel Technology and Management,* 1 (1), 1–14.

Jeffreys, S. (2014) *Beauty and misogyny: Harmful cultural practices in the West*, London: Routledge.

Kagawa, M., Uchida, H., Uenishi, K., Binns, C.W. and Hills, A.P. (2007) 'Applicability of the Ben-Tovim Walker Body Attitudes Questionnaire (BAQ) and the Attention to Body Shape scale (ABS) in Japanese males and females', *Eating Behavior,* 8 (3), 277–84.

Lennehan, P. (2003) *Anabolic steroids*, London: Taylor and Francis.

Lupton, D. (2013) *Fat*, New York: Routledge.

Marchessault, G. (2000) 'One mother and daughter approach to resisting weight preoccupation', in B. Miedema, J.M. Stoppard and V. Anderson (Eds) *Women's bodies, women's lives* (pp. 203–26), Toronto: Sumach Press.

McCabe, M.P., Ricciardelli, L.A., Sitaram, G. and Mikhail, K. (2006) 'Accuracy of body size estimation: Role of biopsychosocial variables', *Body Image,* 3 (2), 163–73.

Morgan, K. (1991) 'Women and the knife: Cosmetic surgery and the colonization of women's bodies', *Hypatia,* 6 (3), 25–53.

Murray, S. (2016) *The 'fat' female body*, London: Palgrave.

National Health Service (2014) *Start losing weight*, available online at: www.nhs.uk/ Livewell/loseweight/Pages/start-losing-weight.aspx [accessed 26 June 2014].

National Health Service (2016) *Anabolic steroid misuse*, available online at: www.nhs.uk/ conditions/anabolic-steroid-abuse/Pages/Introduction.aspx [accessed 6 January 2016].

O'Dea, J. and Cinelli, R.L. (in press) 'Use of drugs to change appearance in girls and female adolescents', in M. Hall, S. Grogan, and B. Gough (Eds) *Chemically modified bodies: The use of diverse substances for appearance enhancement,* London: Palgrave Macmillan.

Ogden, J. (1992) *Fat chance: The myth of dieting explained*, London: Routledge.

Orbach, S. (1993) *Hunger strike: The anorectic's struggle as a metaphor for our age*, London: Penguin.

Pridgeon, L. and Grogan, S. (2012) 'Understanding exercise adherence and dropout: An interpretative phenomenological analysis of men's and women's accounts of gym attendance and non-attendance', *Qualitative Research in Sport, Exercise and Health,* 4 (3), 382–99.

Public Health England (2015) Health Survey for England: Factsheets, available online at: www.noo.org.uk/NOO_pub/Key_data [accessed 16 December 2015].

Reardon, R. and Grogan. S. (2011) 'Women's reasons for seeking breast reduction: A qualitative investigation', *Journal of Health Psychology,* 16 (1), 31–41.

Ricciardelli, L.A. and Yager, Z. (2015) *Adolescence and body image: From development to preventing dissatisfaction,* London: Routledge.

Roncero, M., Perpina, C., Marco, J.H. and Sanchez-Reales, S. (2015) 'Confirmatory factor analysis and psychometric properties of the Spanish version of the Multidimensional Body-Self Relations Questionnaire – Appearance Scales', *Body Image,* 14, 47–53.

Secord, P.F. and Jourard, S.M. (1953) 'The appraisal of body cathexis: Body cathexis and the self', *Journal of Consulting Psychology*, 17 (5), 343–7.

Skouteris, H., Carr, R., Wertheim, E.H., Paxton, S.J. and Duncombe, D. (2005) 'A prospective study of factors that led to body dissatisfaction during pregnancy', *Body Image*, 2 (4), 347–61.

Slade, P. and Russell, G. (1973) 'Awareness of body dimensions in anorexia nervosa: Cross-sectional and longitudinal studies', *Psychological Medicine*, 3 (2), 188–99.

Smith, D., Rutty, M.C. and Olrich, T. (in press) 'Muscle dysmorphia and anabolic-androgenic steroid use', in M. Hall, S. Grogan and B. Gough (Eds) *Chemically modified bodies: The use of diverse substances for appearance enhancement*, London: Palgrave Macmillan.

Smolak, L. and Levine, M.P. (2015) 'Body image, disordered eating, and eating disorders', in L. Smolak and M.P. Levine (Eds) *The Wiley handbook of eating disorders*, Chichester, UK: John Wiley and Sons Ltd.

Smolak, L. and Thompson, J.K. (Eds) (2008) *Body image, eating disorders, and obesity in youth: Assessment, prevention, and treatment*, Washington, DC: American Psychological Association.

St. Martin, L. and Gavey, N. (1996) 'Women's bodybuilding: Feminist resistance and/or femininity's recuperation', *Body and Society*, 2 (4), 45–57.

Stunkard, A.J., Sorensen, T. and Schulsinger, F. (1983) 'Use of the Danish adoption register for the study of obesity and thinness', in S. Kety (Ed.) *The genetics of neurological and psychiatric disorders*, New York: Raven Press.

Swami, V., Cavelti, S., Taylor, D. and Tovee, M.J. (2015) 'The Breast Size Rating Scale: Development and psychometric evaluation', *Body Image*, 14, 29–38.

Swami, V., Stieger, S., Harris, A.S. and Tovee, M.J. (2012) 'Further investigation of the validity and reliability of the Photographic Figure Rating Scale for body image assessment', *Journal of Personality Assessment*, 94 (4), 404–9.

Thompson, J.K., Burke, N.L. and Krawczyk, R. (2012) 'Measurement of body image in adolescence and adulthood', in T.F. Cash (Ed.) *Encyclopedia of body image and human appearance* (pp. 512–20), London: Elsevier.

Thompson, J.K. and Spana, R.E. (1988) 'The adjustable light beam method for the assessment of size estimation accuracy: Description, psychometrics and normative data', *International Journal of Eating Disorders*, 7 (4), 521–6.

Thompson, J.K., Ata, R., Roehrig, M. and Chait, S. (2012) 'Tanning: Natural and artificial', in T.F. Cash (Ed.) *Encyclopedia of body image and human appearance* (pp. 783–9), London: Elsevier.

Thompson, J.K., Penner, L. and Altabe, M. (1990) 'Procedures, problems, and progress in the assessment of body images', in T. Cash and T. Pruzinsky (Eds) *Body images: Development, deviance and change* (pp. 21–46), New York: Guilford Press.

Tiggemann, M. (2005) 'Body dissatisfaction and adolescent self-esteem: Prospective findings', *Body Image*, 2 (2), 129–36.

Tiggemann, M. and Pennington, B. (1990) 'The development of gender differences in body-size dissatisfaction', *Australian Psychologist*, 25 (3), 306–13.

Touyz, S.W., Beaumont, P.J.V. and Collins, J.K. (1984) 'Body shape perception and its disturbance in anorexia nervosa', *British Journal of Psychiatry*, 144, 167–71.

Tylka, T. (2012) 'Positive psychology perspectives on body image', in T.F. Cash (Ed.) *Encylopedia of body image and human appearance* (pp. 657–63), London: Elsevier.

Tylka, T. and Wood-Barcalow, N. (2015) 'A positive complement', *Body Image*, 14, 115–17.

Ussher, J. (Ed.) (1993) *The psychology of the female body*, London: Routledge.

Uzoma, K. (2014) *Percentage of Americans who diet every year*, available online at: www.livestrong.com/article/308667-percentage-of-americans-who-diet-every-year/ [accessed 20 December 2014].

Vartanian, L.R. (2012) 'Self-discrepancy theory and body image', in T.F. Cash (Ed.) *Encylopedia of body image and human appearance* (pp. 711–17), London: Elsevier.

Wardle, J., Bindra, R., Fairclough, B. and Westcombe, A. (1993) 'Culture and body image: Body perception and weight concern in young Asian and Caucasian British women', *Journal of Community and Applied Social Psychology*, 3 (3), 173–81.

Wasilenko, K.A., Kulik, J.A. and Wanic, R.A. (2007) 'Effects of social comparisons with peers on women's body satisfaction and exercise behaviour', *International Journal of Eating Disorders*, 40 (8), 740–5.

Webb, J.B., Wood-Barcalow, N.L. and Tylka, T.L. (2015) 'Assessing positive body image: Contemporary approaches and future directions', *Body Image*, 14, 130–45.

Webb, V.Z., Wadden, T.A. and Tsai, A.G. (2012) 'Weight-loss programs: Commerical and popular diets', in T.F. Cash (Ed.) *Encylopedia of body image and human appearance* (pp. 798–808), London: Elsevier.

Welch, E., Lagerström, M. and Ghaderi, A. (2012) 'Body shape questionnaire: Psychometric properties of the short version (BSQ-8C) and norms from the general Swedish population', *Body Image*, 9 (4), 547–50.

Wiseman, E. (2014) *Is cosmetic surgery now a normal part of modern life?* Available online at: www.theguardian.com/lifeandstyle/2014/feb/09/is-cosmetic-surgery-normal-modern-life [accessed 11 December 2014].

Wolf, N. (1991) *The beauty myth: How images of beauty are used against women*, New York: William Morrow.

World Health Organization (2016) *Physical activity and adults*, available online at: www.who.int/dietphysicalactivity/factsheet_adults/en/ [accessed 14 January 2016].

4

MEN AND BODY IMAGE

The study of the psychology and sociology of male body image is a relatively recent phenomenon. Until the 1980s research on body image and embodiment was largely restricted to women, particularly within psychology. Women's bodies have historically been represented more frequently in the media than men's, and descriptions of women have tended to be more embodied than those of men (Bordo, 2003).

In the last decade psychologists (e.g. Gough and Robertson, 2009; McCreary, 2012; Ricciardelli et al., 2007; Thompson and Cafri, 2007) and sociologists (e.g. Holliday and Cairnie, 2007; Monaghan, 2008) have become increasingly interested in men's body image and male embodiment. This is largely due to the fact that the male body has become more visible in popular culture, producing interest in the effects of this increased visibility on men's images of their bodies. This chapter summarizes current research and assesses what we know about men's body image in the twenty-first century.

There is a general consensus that most men aspire to a muscular mesomorphic shape characterized by average build with well-developed muscles on chest, arms, and shoulders, and slim waist and hips, rather than an ectomorphic (thin) or endomorphic (fat) build (e.g. Franko et al., 2015). Harrison Pope and colleagues in *The Adonis Complex* (2000) have argued that men idealize the slender, muscled physique presented in popular Western media. Low body fat levels are a crucial part of this ideal physique, as they allow muscles to be more visible (Thompson and Cafri, 2007). Having a flat and toned stomach is seen by some as a status symbol in its own right. For instance, in an interview with *The Observer Magazine* in Britain, David Zinczenko (author of *The Abs Diet*) says:

> In some ways being thin is more of a status symbol than it's ever been because of how overweight some people are. If you have a flat stomach, you're probably in control under very trying circumstances. These days, everybody has an iPod. Everyone can afford a plasma TV. A flat stomach is a much more difficult thing to come by. It's a way to stand out.
>
> (Leith, 2006: 33)

The slender, muscular shape is the masculine ideal because it is intimately tied to Western cultural notions of maleness as representing power and strength. Mansfield and McGinn (1993: 49) argue that "muscularity and masculinity can be, and often are, conflated". However, although moderate muscularity is rated highly, extreme muscularity (such as seen in male bodybuilders) is not universally acceptable, and may be perceived as unnatural and as reflecting narcissism (Aoki, 1996). The Western cultural ideal is generally slender and moderately muscular rather than being heavily muscled (Franko et al., 2015).

Assessment of body image

A similar array of techniques has been used to assess body image in men as that used for women (see Chapter 3) – indeed, most measures were developed for women and have been adapted for men. However, some were originally developed to be gender-free (e.g. Cash, 2000), and measures of drive for muscularity have been designed specifically for use with men (e.g. McCreary and Sasse, 2000). Results from studies using a range of measures will be considered below to evaluate the degree and direction of body dissatisfaction in men.

As in the previous chapter on women's body image, this chapter will focus on body image in men without clinical diagnoses of body image problems such as muscle dysmorphia. Muscle dysmorphia (characterized by feeling insufficiently muscular, and focusing on weight training and diet to the exclusion of other areas of life) was first discussed by Harrison Pope and colleagues who initially used the term "reverse anorexia" (Pope et al., 1993). In 1997 they revised the term to "muscle dysmorphia" (Pope et al., 1997), and this is now recognized as a subtype of body dysmorphic disorder (American Psychiatric Association, 2013). For further discussion see work by Guy Cafri and colleagues (2008) in the US, and by Dave Smith and colleagues (in press) in the UK.

Figure rating scales

Studies using male silhouette figures have produced interesting findings. In one of the earliest studies, April Fallon and Paul Rozin (1985) showed nine male silhouettes of varying size to 248 US undergraduate students and asked them to indicate the figures that approximated their own current figure, the figure they would like to look like, and the figure that they thought women would prefer. There was no significant discrepancy between these men's ideal, the figure they would expect women to prefer, and their perceived current shape. Fallon and Rozin concluded that men's perceptions served to keep them satisfied with their figures, and related the findings to the lower incidences of dieting, anorexia and bulimia in US men than in US women. In line with most other researchers using figure rating scales with women at this time, Fallon and Rozin based their conclusions on scores averaged across their samples. However, although body dissatisfaction in women usually relates to feeling overweight, body dissatisfaction in men may relate to feeling either overweight or underweight. Averaging has the effect of combining together men who believe they are either overweight or underweight compared to their ideal, so that on average they may appear to have no discrepancy between their ideal and current body (Drewnowski and Yee, 1987).

Marc Mishkind and colleagues (1986) took this methodological problem into account when designing their study. They found that when shown a similar set of silhouette drawings of male body types ranging from very thin to very fat, 75 per cent of men reported that their ideal was discrepant from their current body size. Roughly half wanted to be bigger, and half wanted to be thinner than they were. In this respect, there is an important difference between men and women on these silhouette tasks. Women reliably pick a slimmer ideal than their current shape. Men are equally likely to pick a thinner or a larger ideal. Wanting to be larger and wanting to be thinner both represent body dissatisfaction. These differences between men are lost when researchers average across groups. Mishkind et al.'s data suggested that a significant proportion of men were dissatisfied with their body shape.

Another problem with the figure rating scale methodology when applied to men is that men may be primarily concerned with the degree of muscularity of the target figures rather than size per se. Shawn Lynch and Debra Zellner (1999) investigated the effects of increased levels of muscularity by producing a set of male figures with the same body fat levels but increased muscularity, and they found that their sample of US male college students chose ideals that were significantly more muscular than their current shape, and that these men assumed that women preferred a significantly more muscular body than the men's current size. Lynch and Zellner's (1999) finding is interesting in showing that young men, on average, desire to be more muscular, but their methodology did not enable men to indicate any interaction in preference between fat levels and desired muscularity.

Amanda Gruber, Harrison Pope and colleagues developed the Somatomorphic Matrix at the end of the twentieth century (Pope et al., 2000). This is a computerized body image test that enables men to choose between male figures that vary along the two crucial dimensions of muscularity and fatness. Images are displayed on a computer screen, and men can adjust the images by clicking on the screen to make them more or less muscular and more or less fat. This method has enabled Pope and colleagues to produce data on preferred degree of muscularity and body fat in samples of US, Austrian and French men, finding that college-aged men in all three countries showed a preference for an ideal that was significantly more muscular than the men's current body shape, and believed that women preferred a significantly more muscular body for men than their own current body. This result has been replicated in several more recent studies (e.g. Frederick et al., 2005), though Don McCreary (2012) notes that the Somatomorphic Matrix can produce unreliable results. He also argues that we need to know more about how men other than those from college student populations score on these kinds of measures.

Questionnaire studies

Most of the early body satisfaction questionnaires were designed to look at body dissatisfaction in women, and contain items that are not relevant to men. Questionnaires aimed at women tend to be designed to assess desire to be thinner and concern about lower-body fatness, whereas male body concerns tend to centre on wanting to gain muscle from the waist upward which may mean that questionnaire instruments are not ideal for use with men (Cafri and Thompson, 2004; Dakanalis and Riva, 2013). However, some of the early measures have been shown to be appropriate for use with men, and others have been developed recently that are specifically for use with men.

One of the earliest scales that could be used with male samples was the Body Esteem Scale (Franzoi and Shields, 1984), which assesses satisfaction with a number of body parts and can be applied to men as well as to women. According to Franzoi and Shields, the crucial determinants of men's body satisfaction are physical attractiveness (face and facial features), upper body strength (biceps, shoulder width, arms and chest) and physical conditioning (stamina, weight and energy level), and when the scale is used with a male sample a thirteen-item physical condition subscale score and a nine-item upper body strength subscale score can be calculated in addition to the thirteen-item physical attractiveness subscale score. These subscales have good internal reliability and validity (Franzoi and Shields, 1984), and the questionnaire has been used effectively in a number of studies with US and British male samples. For instance, Adrian Furnham and Nicola Greaves (1994) administered the measure to forty-seven British men aged 18 to 35 (mostly university undergraduates). Participants were asked to rate, on a ten-point scale ranging from 1 (complete dissatisfaction) to 10 (complete satisfaction), how satisfied they were with their nose, lips, waist, thighs, ears, biceps, chin, buttocks, width of shoulders, arms, chest, eyes, cheeks, hips, legs, feet, stomach, body hair, face and weight. They were also asked to rate how likely they were to "attempt to change" each body part on a similar ten-point scale. Men were least satisfied with biceps, width of shoulders and chest measurement, and were most likely to try to change these aspects of the body. This finding coincides with current ideals of male body shape, where the emphasis is on broad shoulders and well-muscled chests and arms.

Don McCreary and colleagues in Canada have developed a questionnaire that is specifically designed to assess attitudes and behaviours relating to drive for muscularity, so it is particularly appropriate for use with men (McCreary and Sasse, 2002; McCreary et al., 2004). The Drive for Muscularity Scale is a fifteen-item questionnaire that measures the extent to which people desire to have a more muscular body. The items are a mix of questions relating to attitudes and behaviours scored on a six-point Likert scale from "always" to "never". Sample questions include "I wish I were more muscular" and "I feel guilty if I miss a weight-training session". The questionnaire gives three scores: a total drive for muscularity score, and subscale scores for muscularity-related attitudes and behaviours. McCreary and colleagues report good levels of internal reliability (alphas between 0.87 and 0.92) and validity (McCreary et al., 2006). Scores on this questionnaire have indicated that drive for muscularity in men is unrelated to actual muscularity (McCreary et al., 2006), although it is related to psychological variables such as self-esteem and depression (McCreary and Sasse, 2002). The measure has now been translated into various languages including Spanish, and has been shown to have excellent internal consistency and validity (e.g. Compte et al., 2015).

Tracy Tylka and colleagues (2005) have also developed a body attitudes scale specifically designed for use with men. The Male Body Attitudes Scale assesses three dimensions of body attitudes (muscularity, low body fat and height), and has good internal reliability, test-retest reliability and validity. Items include "I think I have too little muscle on my body" (muscularity subscale), "I think my body should be leaner" (low body fat subscale), and "I wish I were taller" (height subscale). Scores on all subscales and total score were correlated significantly with men's self-esteem, suggesting that low self-esteem is linked to body dissatisfaction in men as well as in women and supporting suggestions by other authors (McCabe and Ricciardelli, 2003). This scale is useful for assessing male body image since it covers height, which has been largely ignored in body image research but which has emerged in interviews as a key determinant of men's satisfaction (Grogan and Richards, 2002). It has also been translated into several languages and has been shown to have good reliability and validity. For instance, Emilio Compte and colleagues (2015) administered a translated form of the measure to 423 male students in Argentina and concluded that the Spanish version was an acceptable and valid instrument to assess body dissatisfaction in Argentinian men.

Thomas Cash's Multidimensional Body-Self Relations Questionnaire (MBSRQ) (Cash, 2000) is validated for both men and women and has a series of body area satisfaction items that enable the identification of relative satisfaction with different areas of the body. Thomas Cash and colleagues (1986) found that 34 per cent of men who responded to a survey in *Psychology Today* magazine were generally dissatisfied with their looks, 41 per cent with their weight, 32 per cent with muscle tone, 28 per cent with upper torso, 50 per cent with mid-torso, and 21 per cent with lower torso. In 1997 David Garner replicated the study with another set of readers of *Psychology Today* and found that 43 per cent of men were generally dissatisfied with their looks, 52 per cent with their weight, 45 per cent with muscle tone, 38 per cent with upper torso, 63 per cent with mid-torso, and 29 per cent with lower torso (Garner, 1997). In a parallel UK study Clare Donaldson (1996) administered the MBSRQ body area satisfaction subscales and some additional body image items to one hundred 18- to 43-year-old male students in Manchester. She found that 27 per cent of men in the sample were dissatisfied with their weight, showing that men in this sample were, on average, more satisfied than Cash et al.'s (1986) US men. However, 38 per cent were dissatisfied with their muscle tone, 25 per cent with lower torso, 28 per cent with mid-torso, and 37 per cent with upper torso. When asked about general body satisfaction, only 10 per cent of the men reported that they were generally dissatisfied with their bodies. In 2004 Helen Fawkner administered the MBSRQ (and other measures) to a sample of 369 Australian men aged 17 to 89 years accessed through community groups. She found that 29 per cent were dissatisfied with their weight – lower than Cash's 1980s American sample and similar to Donaldson's British men. Twenty-four per cent were dissatisfied with their muscle tone, 21 per cent with upper torso, 41 per cent with mid-torso, and 18 per cent with lower torso. Only 10 per cent were dissatisfied with their overall appearance. More recently David Frederick and colleagues (2007) administered the MBSRQ to 2,206 US undergraduate men and women, and found that 15 per cent of men were dissatisfied with their bodies.

Results of studies using the MBSRQ suggest an increase in men's body dissatisfaction since the 1980s. However, comparisons need to be made with caution since different studies have accessed different samples of men of varying ages, and the MBSRQ subscales may produce variable results with people of different ages (Rusticus and Hubley, 2006). Also, samples of men accessed by Thomas Cash and colleagues, and by David Garner, were readers of *Psychology Today* who may differ in important ways from the university students sampled by Clare Donaldson and by David Frederick and colleagues, and from the community sample accessed by Helen Fawkner. Samples have also varied in geographical location as well as in instructions given to respondents and scoring systems used (Frederick et al., 2011). However, across studies, data suggest that a small but significant proportion of men in Western cultures are dissatisfied with their bodies, which is perhaps the key finding here.

Interview studies

One of the limitations of questionnaires measuring aspects of body evaluation is that they do not tell us why men are dissatisfied, and how this dissatisfaction affects the rest of their lives. Interviews enable men to explain more about their experiences of embodiment, and help to develop further our understanding of men's experiences of body dissatisfaction.

In a study that we conducted in 2002, men aged 16 to 25 years talked about body image and body dissatisfaction in focus groups (Grogan and Richards, 2002). Older men in the sample (aged 18 to 25 years) were in agreement that the ideal male body is toned and muscular. Being muscular was linked with being healthy and fit. These ideals correspond exactly with the cultural ideal of the well-toned mesomorph. These men believed that the ideal body was within their reach (through exercise), but were not motivated to exercise to change their body shape, since it was not sufficiently important to them. They believed that women were more likely to be motivated to exercise to change body image, but that body shape mattered less to men. They agreed that feeling they were looking good affected their self-esteem, linking looking good (having a well-toned, muscular body) with feelings of confidence and power in social situations.

Similar findings emerged from focus groups with younger men aged 16 to 17 years (Grogan and Richards, 2002). These younger men's ideal build was muscular and relatively slender. Several of them said that they wished that they were bigger and had more muscle. The desire to be big and muscular was clearly distinguished from a fear of being big and fat. Being fat rather than muscular was related to weakness of will and lack of control. Two of the young men felt fat (although they were within the normal weight range), and explained how they laughed about excess weight as a way of covering up their embarrassment about feeling fat. All these young men were concerned with the way that they looked, believing either that they were too thin and needed to put on muscle, or that they were too fat and needed to lose weight. When asked whether they felt external pressure to look a certain way, all felt pressure from others. Pressure came mainly from male peers. Competing with peers and fitting in with their social group in terms of size were given as an explicit reason by some of the interviewees, who wanted to be as big as their friends. We have rarely encountered such explicit competition with peers when talking to women. For instance:

I need to be a bit bigger because my brothers are like six foot, and I'm a couple of inches shorter than all my friends as well, and I feel pressure.

If you've got friends who are, like, quite big in build, you want to be the same as them. Although you might not be able to do anything about it, it's on your conscience all the time. You want to be that sort of size.

However, these young men were clear that they were only willing to put limited resources into trying to attain their ideal body shape. For instance:

It would be nice to look rather large, but I'm not really bothered if I don't look that big, and I wouldn't mind looking like that [the *Chippendales* dance troupe]. But I wouldn't put myself out to look like it, you know.

Reporting that they were not sufficiently concerned about the look of their bodies to exercise or diet reflects traditional male discourses on self-reliance and detachment, and may underestimate these men's investment in their bodies. Dieting in particular has been seen as a feminine activity and inappropriate for men, who are expected to eat heartily and not be concerned with either dieting or healthy eating (Gough, 2007). Muscle tone and muscle mass were important to these young men, supporting suggestions that muscle tone is central to male physical attractiveness. Men compared themselves with their male friends, and wanted to "fit in" with them in terms of body size. To be smaller or fatter than the ideal was seen to be problematic, suggesting that men want to look "average".

Self-confidence and self-esteem were related to how good they felt about their bodies, supporting questionnaire work cited earlier and conflicting with Jane Ogden's (1992) suggestion that men's body image is independent of their self-esteem. It is possible that the cultural shift in the importance attached to the appearance of the body for men in the 1990s and 2000s (Pope et al., 2000; Thompson and Cafri, 2007) has led to an increased association between self-esteem and body satisfaction in men. This would explain the difference between Ogden's results from the early 1990s and other, more recent work that has found an association between self-esteem and body satisfaction in men (Grogan and Richards, 2002; McCabe and Ricciardelli, 2003; Tylka et al., 2005).

Brendan Gough and colleagues (2016) ran interviews with thirty obese UK men aged 30 to 69 years, twenty-seven of whom were enrolled in a weight management programme. They were asked about consciousness of body shape and weight, and about issues around weight and weight loss. The authors found that although men minimized the importance of body weight and associated problems, body image was clearly a key concern for them, and there were many examples of body consciousness and body dissatisfaction evident in accounts. This study is important in showing that body image concerns are salient for older men as well as for younger men. Post-programme weight loss was associated with a significant increase in body confidence, self-esteem and psychological well-being.

Helen Fawkner (2004) ran focus groups with thirty-four Australian men in which they discussed body image and media imagery of the body. The results showed that many men reported that appearance was important to them and had considerable influence on their day-to-day interactions. The men reported that comments from partners or potential partners were influential in evaluating their own attractiveness and influencing their body image. Their ideal images were tall, slim and V-shaped. All men reported some degree of comparison with media imagery. However, few men reported negative impacts of these comparisons, and few would modify their behaviour to try to emulate these ideals. Exercisers and gay men were most likely to report negative affect as a result of comparisons with idealized media imagery, and were most likely to engage in unhealthy behaviours to try to change their body shapes. Fawkner (2004) suggests that exercise may increase narcissistic investment in one's body in vulnerable men, particularly in gay men. This will be investigated further in Chapter 6.

In a UK interview study conducted by Gillian Adams and colleagues, men aged 18 to 32 took part in semi-structured interviews in which they discussed experiences of body dissatisfaction (Adams et al., 2005). The men interviewed described body dissatisfaction in cognitive, behavioural and affective terms, and dissatisfaction was reflected in perceived discrepancy between their current and ideal bodies. Triggers for feeling dissatisfied were usually interpersonal. Negative feedback from others, especially sexual partners, was particularly salient, and comparison with other men's bodies also caused distress. In the absence of social contact, body dissatisfaction was not sufficient to promote behaviour change, and most men did not engage in appearance-fixing behaviours such as exercise and diet simply because they were aware of a discrepancy between ideal and current body, supporting the findings of the Grogan and Richards (2002) and Fawkner (2004) studies described above.

Body size estimation techniques

There have been fewer studies of size estimation with men than with women, probably because early work focused on size overestimation in young women with eating problems. However, recent work has suggested that men tend to overestimate their body size to a similar extent to women.

In a sophisticated study on body size estimation, Marita McCabe and colleagues (2006) used their digital body image computer program to enable men to manipulate a full frontal image of their body at five points: chest, waist, hips, thighs and calves. Their eighty-two male participants were aged between 18 and 36 years, with BMI ranging from 18 to 36. Relative to a control condition in which the men estimated the size of a vase, they overestimated the size of all five body regions on average. The degree of overestimation was comparable to a female sample tested by the same procedure. The authors concluded that size overestimation may bring men's bodies more in line with the muscular male ideal, and so may have quite a different effect from size overestimation in women. Men with higher BMI were more likely to overestimate the size of their bodies, contrary to suggestions that heavier men underestimate the size of their bodies (e.g. Smeets et al., 1998). Future work needs to go further in terms of differentiating between perceptions of adiposity (fatness) and degree of muscularity, which may be particularly relevant to a male sample (McCreary, 2012). This work is informative in relation to gender and size estimation in showing that both men and women tend to overestimate the size of key body areas.

Behavioural indicators of body dissatisfaction

There are a number of appearance-fixing (Walker and Murray, 2012) behaviours in which men might engage to try to change the look of their bodies and reduce body dissatisfaction. The focus here will be on four kinds of body-relevant behaviours: dieting and taking diet pills, exercise and bodybuilding, steroid use, and cosmetic procedures.

Dieting and diet pills

Dieting is significantly less frequent among men than among women, and is generally seen as not gender appropriate for men (Gough, 2007). Most UK surveys tend to find that more women than men diet at any one time (e.g. 42 per cent of women, 25 per cent of men; Leith, 2006), although significantly more men in England are overweight than women (57 per cent of women, 67 per cent of men; Health and Social Care Information Centre, 2015). Dieting is generally perceived as a feminine-appropriate behaviour (Gough et al., 2014), and men tend to exercise rather than diet if they want to lose weight (e.g. Grogan and Richards, 2002; Grogan et al., 2006a). However, a relatively small proportion of men within the normal weight range do diet to try to lose weight, and the number of men who refer for eating disorders is on the increase, particularly among gay men (Morgan and Arcelus, 2009; Strong et al., 2000).

Dieting may be more frequent in men who are sensitive to health issues than in the more general male population. For instance, in a survey commissioned by *Men's Health* magazine in the 1990s, six out of ten men who responded had dieted to lose weight, and all reported that they were successful in losing weight in the long term (Chaudhary, 1996). Men's style magazines such as *Men's Health* and *Men's Fitness* tend to promote low-fat diets rather than calorie counting, and emphasize looking and feeling good rather than slimness. In an interview with *The Observer Magazine* in Britain, Morgan Rees, editor of *Men's Health*, is clear that the aim of the magazine is to encourage men to adopt more healthy eating patterns, rather than to diet:

> Pictures of six-packs, far from making you feel bad about how you are, exist to make you feel good about how you might become. Morgan Rees says, "We want the image to look achievable." And Men's Health, he adds, does not encourage men to diet. "We don't really favour diets," he says, "we favour healthy eating".
>
> (Leith, 2006: 32)

The Atkins diet, which focuses on high-protein, low-carbohydrate food, has had a relatively high uptake by men, and it has been suggested that this is because Robert Atkins focuses on health as well as weight loss, and because his diet is male-appropriate in that men can continue to eat meat:

> It was a lean, mean, hunter's diet. In a way it was like eating muscles.
>
> (Leith, 2006: 32)

Eating less to lose weight has generally been seen as a feminine activity (Bordo, 2003; Gough et al., 2014), and would not be expected to lead directly to the muscular physique that is the cultural ideal for men, so it is perhaps not surprising that men are less likely to diet than women. Men are more likely to try to bulk up by eating a high-protein diet, such as the Atkins diet, or to reduce the fat in their diets, than to reduce calorie intake in order to try to attain a slender physique (Leith, 2006; McCreary and Sasse, 2002).

Dieting practices and associated pressures may differ for heterosexual and gay men (Conner et al., 2004). John Morgan and Jon Arcelus (2009), in interviews with gay and heterosexual men, found that all participants reported some dissatisfaction and all had considered dieting, although only four of the fifteen men (all gay) had actually dieted, with one man losing extreme amounts of weight on a diet of mostly coffee and cigarettes. These kinds of "crash diets" are obviously not healthy for either men or women. Differences in health-related behaviours between gay and heterosexual men will be addressed in Chapter 6.

Diet pills such as ephedrine are being used more frequently in the twenty-first century than previously to reduce body fat levels. Ephedrine is used in decongestants and cold medicines as ephedrine hydrochloride. Since the 1990s ephedrine has been promoted as a way to lose weight, particularly on bodybuilding websites, as it tends to reduce appetite and increase metabolic rate. As it tends to target fat while saving lean muscle, it is very popular among bodybuilders who use it in 'cutting' phases ahead of competition when they reduce fat as a way of making muscles more visible (Kanayama et al., 2001; Steroidal.com, 2014).

Matthew Hall and colleagues (2015a) focused on how men talk to each other about ephedrine use on the *Men's Health* website. They found that risk was downplayed, and that men positioned themselves as rational, knowledgeable and in control. Weight loss for men in the context of ephedrine use was linked to sport and muscularity. There are key similarities between men's accounts in relation to ephedrine use and reports from other studies that have focused on anabolic steroid use, in that men presented use as safe and beneficial so long as it was carried out by well-informed users (e.g. Grogan et al., 2006b; Hale and Smith, 2012).

Compounds of ephedrine are widely available over the internet, and include caffeine and aspirin (known as an ephedrine–caffeine–aspirin or ECA stack; ephedrineweb.com, 2014). Incidence of ephedrine use for weight loss is difficult to determine as many men buy ephedrine from bodybuilding websites, but Lina Ricciardelli (2012) estimates lifetime prevalence of ephedrine use in men at 4.5 per cent. This is a serious health concern that is directly related to men's body image concerns, and further work is needed to investigate men's motivations for use more fully.

Cosmetic procedures

Men are increasingly likely to have cosmetic surgery to change the way they look. In 2014, men underwent more than 2.5 million cosmetic procedures worldwide. The most common operations were eyelid surgery, rhinoplasty, liposuction, gynecomastia (removal of breast tissue) and fat grafting (International Society of Aesthetic Plastic Surgeons, 2015). Clearly a significant proportion of men are opting for the surgical fix to modify the look of their bodies, and seem to accept the associated health problems and other risks. For many men body image is sufficiently important to make the risks worth taking and the costs worth paying. Ruth Holliday and Allie Cairnie (2007) report a study where they interviewed post-operative men and suggest that multiple factors are at work in men's decisions to have cosmetic surgery; these include social identity, work-related pressures and key life events. They argue that men's surgery can best be understood as investment in "body capital":

> Drawing on the work of Bourdieu, we argue that men's consumption of aesthetic surgery (and perhaps women's as well) often constitutes an investment in 'body capital' that can be deployed in a variety of different

fields. We tentatively predict that the reconstitution of the aesthetic surgery recipient from 'patient' to 'consumer' will facilitate the development of a burgeoning market for men's aesthetic surgery.

(Holliday and Cairnie, 2007: 57)

In addition to medically-administered cosmetic procedures, there has also been a rise in do-it-yourself muscle-enhancement procedures in the twenty-first century. Site enhancement oils were developed at the start of the twentieth century for use in cosmetic procedures such as wrinkle reduction (Di Benedetto et al., 2002). More recently they have been used by bodybuilders to enhance muscle size (Ghandourah et al., 2012). Oils used in the UK and USA include paraffin, sesame and walnut oil. When injected directly into muscle, site enhancement oils cause swelling, so they tend to be used to inflate the size of muscles that are not so fully developed as others. They may also be used in large quantities to produce the appearance of a generally muscular body, although effects may be "freakish" and "bizarre" (Childs, 2007).

Synthol has become one of the most popular site enhancement oils in recent years, and it is widely available through internet bodybuilding sites (Arnold, 2014). Synthol is a mix of 85 per cent oil (usually sesame), 7.5 per cent lidocaine (a local anaesthetic) and 7.5 per cent alcohol (a sterilizer), and may be attractive to some bodybuilders who believe that it does not cause some of the more severe side effects linked with anabolic steroid use (Ghandourah et al., 2012). Reasons for continued use are poorly understood, though Matthew Hall and colleagues (2015b) have investigated ways that users talk about their synthol use in online posts and have shown that men avoided recognizing potential health dangers, focusing instead on cosmetic issues (how to get a "natural" look and reduce unsightly bumps).

Medical reports cite various health complications in patients following injections of paraffin, sesame and walnut oil, with links to stroke and pulmonary embolism, localized skin problems such as nerve damage and oil filled cysts, and muscle damage (Banke et al., 2012; Darsow et al., 2000), so although site enhancement oils may give bodybuilders a way to rectify perceived shortcomings in particular muscles or muscle groups, use destroys the injected muscle and may produce severe long-term health consequences (Ghandourah et al., 2012). This development is therefore a significant health concern, and men's motivations for the use of site enhancement oils requires further research.

Exercise and bodybuilding

Although men are significantly less likely than women to be motivated to exercise for appearance reasons (Grogan et al., 2006a), a significant proportion of men use exercise to try to change the way that they look. In Clare Donaldson's (1996) study, 65 per cent of her respondents reported engaging in sport specifically to improve their body image. Kyrejto et al. (2008) found that drive for muscularity scores were linked with a number of health-related behaviours for men including exercise participation (resistance training, aerobic training and participation in sport). They asked men to complete the statement "To manage my desire to become more muscular I..." and found that 74.6 per cent of men reported that they exercised to try to change the look of their bodies, presenting statements such as "I work out" or "I pump iron". The authors suggest that drive for muscularity (wanting to be more muscular and toned) has the potential to impact positively on health through encouraging engagement in exercise among men.

The activities most obviously linked to improvement in body image for men are weight training and bodybuilding, activities that would be expected to lead to development of muscle mass, to bring the male body more into line with the slender and muscular ideal. Peter Baker (1994) reported that half a million British men regularly used weights to get into shape, and an increasing number used steroids to accelerate the effects of exercise. Harrison Pope et al. (2000) also noted a significant increase in weight training among US men, linked with concerns about being insufficiently muscular (see also Thompson and Cafri, 2007).

Bodybuilding is becoming more and more popular worldwide as a way for men to attain the culturally valued slender, muscular body (Pope et al., 2000; Thompson and Cafri, 2007). In 1996 Paul Husband and I carried out a study of body image in bodybuilders specifically for the first edition of this book (Grogan, 1999). We administered in-depth questionnaires and interviews to ten male bodybuilders in their twenties and thirties in Manchester gyms. The men were between 5 feet 7 inches and 6 feet 3 inches tall (mean height 5 feet 10 inches), and ranged in weight from 9 stone (126 lb) to 17 stone (238 lb), with a mean of 12.7 stone (178 lb). They all trained with weights regularly (most days), although one had only recently joined the gym. When asked about activities engaged in specifically to improve body image, four out of ten had dieted, one had cut out meals, five had cut out alcohol, three had played more sport, three had stopped eating takeaway food, three had been running, four had used sunbeds, and one had used fake tan. The percentage of men in this small group who had dieted (40 per cent) is significantly higher than most estimates of dieting in men; for instance, Clare Donaldson (1996) found that 20 per cent of her sample of undergraduate students (in the same age range as these bodybuilders) had dieted. This is not surprising, since diet (and nutrition in general) is as important as weight training in the manipulation of fat-to-muscle ratios. Prior to competition (for instance), professional bodybuilders reduce body fat to an absolute minimum to reveal muscle definition and detail (Francis, 1989). These men were significantly more satisfied with their lower torso than with any other part of their bodies, in line with other work on men's body satisfaction (Donaldson, 1996; Fawkner, 2004; Garner, 1997). On average they were "somewhat satisfied" with their weight, height, upper, mid- and lower torso, and overall appearance.

When asked whether they would like to look more like magazine models, these men, on average, said that they sometimes wished they could look more like the models (with a range from never to always), but when asked how satisfaction with their own appearance was affected by such images, these men, on average, said they were unaffected, and that such images did not make them feel like improving their physical appearance. It may be important here that we asked about images of male models in general (to which these bodybuilders may not aspire, since such models may be perceived to be insufficiently muscular). Interview work with these young adult male bodybuilders has suggested that they may compare themselves unfavourably to other highly muscled men, and this may motivate them to train harder. For instance:

> Before I started being interested in lifting weights, when I saw a competitive bodybuilder, when I saw the Gladiators on television, you know, it made you think, you know, it made you want to be like them.

These results suggest that other highly muscled men became a standard for comparison, against which these men compared themselves unfavourably, prompting the decision to weight train. All our interviewees described how they made unfavourable comparisons with other bodybuilders seen at the gym, and how these motivated them to try to gain more muscle. For instance:

> I remember one time when I was about 17 stone [238 1b], I thought I was getting really good. And a really, really big bodybuilder came to work out at the gym, and he was absolutely enormous, and he had a big effect on me, you know, and I really kind of felt rubbish after that. I looked rubbish, felt crap. That kind of spurred me on to get bigger and bigger. In fact, it had that much influence on me, when I actually left the gym kind of looking at him, it was on my mind, and I got knocked off my bike on the way home. I was actually on the wrong side of the road. But, you know, I saw, not him, but, you know, the muscles, and that's how I wanted to be. It just completely dominated my thoughts.

Reports of other people's reactions when these men started to put on large amounts of muscle were interesting. Other bodybuilders were generally positive. For instance:

> Other bodybuilders and bouncers and people like that, they kind of painted a picture of me and, you know, put me on a pedestal, and there was this big guy and he was strong, nothing could bother you, and I started to believe I had nine lives.

> My friends and family ... my friends in bodybuilding, you know, in that you meet a lot of, that's the good thing about going to a gym, you meet a lot of friends, so a lot of my friends do also train, you know, and some of the friends who don't train have respect in, you know, the way that I've done what I've done, you know, in the short period of time I've achieved it. The family are one hundred per cent behind me.

88

Some bodybuilders reported generally favourable comments from strangers:

I have noticed it on holiday in that people kind of look and nudge each other. I've not really had nasty comments. I've just had good comments. … You get the odd comment like "Do you weight train?" or "Do you do weights?"

However, men and women outside the bodybuilding culture tended to react negatively:

When I was about 18 and a half, around Christmas time or whatever, people were quite different with me then. I was in a pub and one person pushed me, one person tripped me up as, you know, I was going past.

I found men found me threatening on the whole, even though I wasn't. I didn't get eye contact. I didn't talk to them. But if I was out socializing, I got quite a lot of ignorant remarks. I got people saying, "What are you taking?", you know, um. I got people who actually spat at me. I was pushed downstairs in a club. I felt that men were really offended and threatened by how I looked. Women reacted the same, really. They felt threatened. They avoided me and just generally assumed that because I was big, I was nasty. I was using steroids, so therefore I was nasty and aggressive.

These negative reactions relate to a general social prejudice against bodybuilding men. Doug Aoki (1996) notes that even academics tend to present negative views of bodybuilders and bodybuilding in general:

Usually circumspect about not denigrating minorities of any type, they nonetheless too often sneer at body-builders for the appearance of their bodies and for their presumed narcissism.

(Aoki, 1996: 59)

It is interesting that bodybuilders attract negative reactions from others. It might be expected that an extreme form of the V-shaped body would be culturally favoured. Perhaps there is a ceiling on acceptable levels of muscularity (Aoki, 1996), or perhaps it is the implied narcissism and body objectification (both seen as culturally inappropriate for men; Gough et al., 2014) that result in negative reactions. The perceived unnaturalness of the highly muscled body may be an additional factor, and this could be expected to be particularly marked if the muscles are seen to be the results of artificial means such as anabolic steroid intake.

Anabolic steroids

The use of anabolic steroids to improve athletic performance is well documented (see Hildebrandt and Alfano, 2012; Lennehan, 2003). Anabolic steroids have long been used by professional bodybuilders to increase muscle bulk. The earliest documented use was by members of a Soviet weightlifting team in the 1950s (Strauss and Yesalis, 1991). More recent data suggest that they are now being used by a number of young men who want to build up their bodies to a more pleasing muscular shape (Grogan et al., 2006b; Hildebrandt and Alfano, 2012; Smith et al., in press). Steroids enable the user to build muscle bulk much more quickly than is possible through weight training alone, so they are an attractive option for some young men who wish to become more muscular for cosmetic reasons.

It is not possible to know the extent of non-medical steroid use. However, it is well known that steroids are widely available in public gyms and health clubs used by bodybuilders across a range of countries (Hildebrandt and Alfano, 2012; Sagoe et al., 2014). Data from needle exchanges in Britain show that steroid users constitute a significant proportion of the group which makes use of the service, and these statistics probably underestimate use, since users often share needles in the gyms to avoid having to access appropriate needles themselves (Lennehan, 2003). US figures suggest that usage there may be more widespread, with recent studies suggesting that most professional bodybuilders, weightlifters and powerlifters use anabolic steroids (Hildebrandt and Alfano, 2012) and steroid use has been found to be prevalent even in high school boys (Laure et al., 2004).

Steroid use is not restricted to athletes and sportsmen, but is also found in other men who want to increase their muscularity (Hildebrandt and Alfano, 2012). In a recent literature review, Sagoe et al. (2014) note a range of reasons for anabolic steroid use, but a key one was to overcome negative body image. This has been supported in other work showing that body image is an important initial motivator for initial uptake of steroids.

In 2000 we asked bodybuilders to complete questionnaires on their motivation for steroid use. We found that 59 out of 135 (44 per cent) bodybuilders who completed questionnaires that we placed in two bodybuilding magazines had used steroids. We applied content analysis to the responses and found that motivations to use steroids were complex and person specific (Wright et al., 2000, 2001). However, there were some commonalities in the results. Wanting to get bigger/ more muscular was the most frequent incentive for starting to use steroids (31 per cent of steroid users), demonstrating the importance of the "look" produced by the drugs (as opposed to strength and endurance). Non-users of steroids were more likely to be concerned about the negative physical side effects of steroid use (95 per cent of non-users versus 64 per cent of users), and steroid users were significantly more likely to agree that steroids are necessary for effective bodybuilding, are necessary for competition, and maximize hard training. Steroid users were also significantly more likely to agree that only "ignorant people" criticized steroids, that steroids are not harmful in moderation, and that they are harmful only if used in excess.

In other work we interviewed men about motivations for steroid use (Grogan et al., 2006a). Men told consistent stories about their reasons for starting to use steroids. Most had tried steroids after becoming frustrated at lack of muscle gain through intensive weight training and a high-protein diet:

> I was training let's say 12 months, and, you know, I'd seen people looking bigger than me, and we got talking, and then I decided, you know, after a long time to take steroids. Really I needed, I felt I needed, to be bigger, and basically I thought steroids would do it. Literally I decided to take them because other people were kind of getting bigger than me, and they were taking them, so it was just like a knock-on effect. They do it, so, like, you do it.

All the men we interviewed cited pressures from images in bodybuilding magazines, and images from movies and television, as being influential in their decision to take steroids:

> The more I trained, the more magazines I looked at, the bigger I wanted to be ... and there was a TV programme, and when I watched these people, it made me feel really depressed, I didn't look as good as them, and it had a massive effect on my decision to take steroids. In fact, it was probably one of the biggest reasons why I did take them, seeing other people bigger than me.

Several respondents cited the bodybuilding gym culture as being influential in their decision to take steroids, because steroids were available and because people talked about them at the gym. For instance:

> In a hard-core bodybuilding gym you are going to see steroids readily available, you know, you are going to hear them talked about. You might see them, you know. So, yeah, people will talk to you about steroids, you know, different things you can take. So, yeah, if someone starts off at the gym intending just to train, they could be influenced by taking steroids because they can see, you know, they are in an atmosphere where people are taking steroids.

In terms of the effects of steroids on muscularity, reports were generally favourable (as might be expected). These men enjoyed the increased strength and muscularity that resulted from intensive training coupled with steroid intake, linking it with increased self-confidence:

It made me look how I wanted to look, which was a lot more muscular ... it made me feel a lot more confident and gave me more reassurance.

I became more muscular, and, um, stronger, you know, a bigger look. It made me feel more confident in two ways. In the way with me being only quite short, it gave me a lot more confidence, you know, in general public, it made me feel better in myself.

However, the attention that large muscles attract was not always welcome. One bodybuilder described how he would hide his muscles when outside the gym:

I used to wear clothes in the street to make me look smaller, you know, like a black baggy jumper just to make me look smaller. It started to bother me after a bit, everybody staring at me. When I was 20 stone [280 lb], people in the street were staring back at me. It started to bother me after a bit.

The men we interviewed were keen to explode the myth that steroids alone would make someone muscular, and stressed the amount of work that goes into creating a well-muscled body, even when steroids are used as a catalyst:

There's no drug makes a bodybuilder. People who talk about things like this are often people who have never trained a day in their life. They don't understand the first thing to do with bodybuilding. They just see a bodybuilder, and all they can see in their minds is the drugs that made that bodybuilder. They don't see how much hard dieting, how much hard training, how much real dedication has gone into it.

Interviewees were keen to show us how much work went into their physiques, representing themselves as creating "natural" muscle and only using the steroids as a catalyst. As such, they were emphasizing the fact that the muscles gained were not synthetic, not produced by the steroids, but produced through their own hard work. They wanted to take responsibility, to retain ownership of their bodies, resenting the impression of people outside bodybuilding who (they believed) thought of steroids as being a lazy way to achieve a muscular body. This links to Gaines and Butler's (1980) suggestion of a cultural belief that steroid users' muscles are somehow "sinful" and "useless" since they are not the result of hard physical labour (which would not, presumably, be sinful or useless), but the result of pharmacological intervention. It is no surprise, then, that bodybuilders who used steroids felt it necessary to explain at length how hard they had to work to attain their body shape and size.

Steroid use presents particular tensions between the appearance of the body (the muscularity of the body implying strength and fitness) and the felt body (fitness/health as experienced by bodybuilders themselves who may feel weak and ill). One of the most important questions to be answered is how men who choose to use steroids make sense of the paradoxical relationship between the apparently healthy (muscled) external appearance and the (often) unhealthy internal state of their bodies.

In our interviews (Grogan et al., 2006b), men reported that they had experienced serious health side effects (liver and kidney damage and hypertension), but saw these only as minor irritations and not significant disincentives for use. Side effects were linked with "abuse" (uninformed use involving overdose), and all users believed that steroids used in moderation presented no significant health risks. Participants argued that (taken in moderation) steroids served a useful function and are safe. For instance, one respondent argued that all drugs (including steroids) are potentially dangerous if taken in huge quantities, likening anabolic steroids to over-the-counter analgesics and alcohol, which (he argued) would be equally dangerous if taken in large quantities. Information from healthcare professionals tended to be mistrusted because it was not based on firsthand experience of use. Trusted sources of information on safe use were books written by those within the bodybuilding community ("steroid bibles"), websites run by steroid users, and word-of-mouth information from other users. Social support, especially from within the bodybuilding community, was an important motivator, and men believed that it would be impossible to compete in bodybuilding competitions without steroids.

Dave Smith and colleagues (in press) argue that health-related messages are unlikely to be effective on their own in reducing use because of the generally positive impacts on users, including muscle mass, strength, and self-confidence. They suggest assisting those who are attempting to quit by reducing their reliance on their bodies as their key source of self-esteem, encouraging transfer to a training environment where steroids are less widely used and where they will meet a wider range of clientele, and assisting with nutritional advice to optimize lean muscle mass. Clearly, any attempts to encourage steroid avoidance need to be developed with the support of the bodybuilding community to be maximally effective.

Social construction of the masculine body

Various social commentators have noted that there has been a radical change in social pressure on men to look slender and muscular that started in the late 1980s and that has continued to the present day with the rise of the "metrosexual" (defined as "a heterosexual urban man who enjoys shopping, fashion, and similar interests traditionally associated with women or homosexual men"; Oxford Dictionaries, 2016). These factors have been linked with body dissatisfaction and body-fixing behaviours because of the positive social capital attached to having a slender and muscular body.

In the 1980s Frank Mort argued that there had been a significant change in Western societies that meant an increased interest in the way that men look. He argued that men in the 1980s were being targeted by the advertising industry, and were becoming more aware than ever before of how they looked:

Young men are being sold images which rupture traditional icons of masculinity. They are stimulated to look at themselves – and other men – as objects of consumer desire.

(Mort, 1988: 194)

Mort argued that this change was significant, and required a rethinking of the meaning of "masculinity". Focusing on a 1980s advertisement for Levi's jeans, he showed how it used the standard technique for the sexual display of women, but pointed out that the target is now a man. Interestingly, one British newspaper also felt sufficiently uncomfortable about the follow-up Levi's TV commercial showing James Mardle in the bath in his Levi's to run a story stressing Mardle's heterosexuality. The move of male models from the gay press to the mainstream market obviously presented conflicts for some newspaper editors. Mort argued that changes in the acceptability of the visual display of the male body prompted men to look differently at themselves and other men, and to be generally more aware of the ways that their bodies looked and of the ways that they dressed. However, he noted that this new awareness was not necessarily positive for women, arguing that although the "new man" may be more aware of his looks, this did not necessarily change the traditional codes of masculinity. Analyzing Levi's jeans advertisements, he shows how the hero is played off against stereotyped images of women (the sweetheart, the fat lady, the harassed mum and the giggling girls). The "new man" image may just be another version of the old, macho image of the man going it alone, without/above women.

This theme was also taken up in the 1980s by Rowena Chapman (1988), who argued that the "new man" (nurturant and narcissistic) was largely the result of the British style culture of the early 1980s, promoted by the "style press" (music and fashion magazines aimed at a young and fashionable audience such as *i-D*, *The Face* and *Arena*). The culture legitimized men's concern with their bodies and the consumerism necessary to adopt the role. The "new man", she argued, was not a major departure from the traditional, John Wayne-style macho man, but was simply an adaptation of the role better suited to survive in a culture that rejected obvious machismo, largely due to the power of feminism.

This leads me to the conclusion that the new man represents not so much a rebellion but an adaptation in masculinity. Men change, but only to hold on to power, not to relinquish it. The combination of feminism and social change may have produced a fragmentation in male identity by questioning its assumptions, but the effect of the emergence of the new man has been to reinforce the existing power structure, by producing a hybrid masculinity which is better able and more suited to retain control.

(Chapman, 1988: 235)

Chapman noted the historic reticence in Western culture about male nudity, and the shift in the 1980s in the visibility of the male body. She argued that the dawning recognition of the marketability of the male body to women led to an increase in the representation of the male body on the cards, calendars and posters produced by companies such as Athena, whose poster *L'Enfant*, featuring a muscular man holding a baby, was its biggest seller in the late 1980s. However, she argued that women were still the objects of gaze more frequently and more completely than men, and that the objectification of the male body did nothing significant to reduce the power of men in society.

This trend continued in the 1990s. Harrison Pope and colleagues (2000) noted the increase in visibility of the male body, and that images of the male body had become increasingly muscular over the years. They commented on the increased visibility of the "supermale" (muscular) body in mainstream Western media:

> Look at television over the last several decades. The hard-bodied lifeguards in Baywatch are viewed by over 1 billion viewers in 142 countries – figures unmatched by any previous television series. Or look at the movies. Hollywood's most masculine men of the 1930s, 1940s and 1950s – John Wayne, Clark Gable, Gregory Peck – look like wimps in comparison to modern cinema's muscular action heroes – Arnold Schwarzenegger, Sylvester Stallone, or Jean-Claude van Damme. Today while growing up a young man is subjected to thousands of these supermale images.
>
> (Pope et al., 2000: 12–13)

In the twenty-first century, the male body continues to be seen as a commodity used to increase sales. Lee Monaghan (2008) argues that we have seen the development in recent years of a "cult of male beauty" where slender, toned and muscular male bodies have become eroticized and objectified. Darren Langdridge and colleagues (2013) have also noted the recent commodification of the penis, arguing that new possibilities in penile enhancement, linked to market forces which capitalize on men's concerns about aesthetic as well as functional shortcomings, may create additional body image pressures for men:

> In the past medical discourse has focused primarily upon the 'traditional' functionality of the penis, more recently it has focussed upon pharmaceutical innovations such as *Viagra*. However, we suggest that now there appears to be the emergence of a new penile discourse, a penile aesthetic that focuses upon penile appearance as much as function. This shift has been facilitated by the Internet, the deregulation of pornography and changes in sexual mores.
>
> (Langdridge et al., 2013: 121)

Recently, various authors have focused on the impact of endorsement of traditional hegemonic (dominant) masculinity on men's drive for muscularity and leanness. It has been suggested that men's conformity to masculine norms is important in determining their drive for muscularity, and that those who endorse more masculine norms have a higher drive for muscularity and leanness. Kristina Holmqvist-Gattario and colleagues (2015) accessed a large sample of men from the US, UK, Australia and Sweden and found that conformity to masculine norms was a significant predictor of men's drive for muscularity, leanness and fitness in all four countries. Conformity to the masculine norm of winning predicted body image across cultures, but there were also interesting cultural differences, with risk-taking predicting body image in the Australian group and conformity to the norm of violence predicting body image in the UK sample. Debra Franko and colleagues (2015) have suggested that internalization of body ideals mediates this relationship. They suggest that endorsing social constructions of masculinity leads to greater pursuit of societal body ideals for men as a central aspect of masculinity. Internalization of athletic ideals was a particularly powerful mediator in US and Australian men in their study, and the authors suggest that young men idealize and internalize the body types of sports figures:

> Our data would suggest that one of the mechanisms accounting for the association between conformity to masculinity and body image concerns is through the extent to which these athletic figures have been internalized by young men. This would indicate, perhaps, that the men in this study viewed athletes as an excellent representation (prototype) of masculinity and the male body.
>
> (Franko et al., 2015: 59)

Mathew Hall (2015) also notes that men are becoming increasingly interested in their body image and are spending more of their income on "beautification products and services" than ever before, citing these practices as necessary for employment and social progression. He notes that the promotion of "metrosexuality" in the twenty-first century has meant that body-related practices that might historically have been linked with femininity (such as the use of grooming products) have entered the mainstream and have made the use of male make-up and other grooming products more palatable to a heterosexual male audience through explicit links to socially acceptable (and overtly heterosexual) "metrosexual" global football superstars such as David Beckham and Cristiano Ronaldo (Hall, 2015).

Kathy Davis (2002) suggests that the commodification of the male body has created a "dubious equality" between the sexes in which young men's bodies are now objectified in a similar way to women's. This will be discussed further in Chapter 5 in relation to media influences on men's body image, and Chapter 6 in terms of impact of sexuality, age, social class and ethnicity on body image.

Summary

- The ideal male body shape in Western societies is slender and moderately muscular.
- Work on men's body satisfaction has suggested that a significant proportion of men are dissatisfied with some aspect of their body shape and weight.
- Men who are dissatisfied with their body shape are equally likely to want to be thinner or heavier (a different pattern from women, who mostly want to be slimmer).
- The main areas that produce dissatisfaction are the mid-torso, biceps, shoulders, chest and general muscle tone. Muscle tone and muscle mass are important to men.
- Men tend to use exercise (rather than diet) to try to change body shape.
- Interviews and questionnaires with bodybuilders demonstrate a strong social comparison effect, whereby bodybuilders compare their bodies to those of other men in the gym, encouraging them to train harder to try to develop more muscle.
- Some bodybuilders choose to take anabolic steroids to speed up the process of muscle development, despite unwanted side effects and the negative reactions of people outside the bodybuilding community.
- The incidence of cosmetic surgery and non-surgical procedures such as site enhancement oils has increased in the twenty-first century.
- Since the late 1980s there has been a significant increase in the visibility and marketability of the male body, and this is continuing into the twenty-first century, along with the promotion of "metrosexuality". All of these factors may operate to increase body image pressures for men.

Bibliography

Adams, G., Turner, H. and Bucks, R. (2005) 'The experience of body dissatisfaction in men', *Body Image*, 2 (3), 271–84.

American Psychiatric Association (2013) *American Psychiatric Association diagnostic and statistical manual of mental disorders* (5th edition), Washington, DC: APA.

Aoki, D. (1996) 'Sex and muscle: The female bodybuilder meets Lacan', *Body and Society*, 2 (4), 45–57.

Arnold, M. (2014) 'Anabolic steroid site injections', *IronMag*, February 10. Available online at: www.ironmagazine.com/2014/anabolic-steroid-site-injections/ [accessed 30 August 2014].

Baker, P. (1994) 'Under pressure: What the media is doing to men', *Cosmopolitan*, November, 129–32.

Banke, I.J., Prodinger, P.M., Waldt, S., Weirich, G., Holzaofel, B.M., Gradinger, R. and Rechl, H. (2012) 'Irreversible muscle damage in bodybuilding due to long-term intramuscular oil injection', *International Journal of Sports Medicine*, 33 (10), 829–34.

Bordo, S. (2003) *Unbearable weight: Feminism, Western culture, and the body* (10th anniversary edn), Berkeley, CA: University of California Press.

Cafri, G. and Thompson, J.K. (2004) 'Measuring male body image: A review of the current methodology', *Psychology of Men and Masculinity*, 5 (1), 18–29.

Cafri, G., Olivardia, R. and Thompson, J.K. (2008) 'Symptom characteristics and psychiatric comorbidity among males with muscle dysmorphia', *Comprehensive Psychiatry*, 49 (4), 374–9.

Cafri, G., Thompson, J.K., Ricciardelli, L., McCabe, M., Smolak, L. and Yesalis, C. (2005) 'Pursuit of the muscular ideal: Physical and psychological consequences and putative risk factors', *Clinical Psychology Review*, 25 (2), 215–39.

Cash, T., Winstead, B. and Janda, L. (1986) 'The great American shape-up: Body image survey report', *Psychology Today*, 20 (4), 30–7.

Cash, T.F. (2000) *User's manual for the Multidimensional Body-Self Relations Questionnaire*, available from the author at http://www.body-images.com.

Chapman, R. (1988) 'The great pretender: Variations on the new man theme', in R. Chapman and J. Rutherford (Eds) *Male order: Unwrapping masculinity* (pp. 225–48), London: Lawrence and Wishart.

Chaudhary, V. (1996) 'The state we're in', *The Guardian*, 11 June, 14.

Childs, D. (2007) *Like implants for the arms: Synthol lures bodybuilders*, available online at: http://abcnews.go.com/Health/Fitness/story?id=3179969 [accessed 14 June 2014].

Conner, M., Johnson, C. and Grogan, S. (2004) 'Gender, sexuality, body image and eating behaviours', *Journal of Health Psychology*, 9 (4), 505–15.

Compte, E.J., Sepulveda, A.R., de Pellegrin, Y. and Blanca, M. (2015) 'Confirmatory factor analysis of the Drive for Muscularity Scale-S (DMS-S) and Male Body Attitudes Scale-S (MBAS-S) among male university students in Buenos Aires', *Body Image*, 14, 13–19.

Dakanalis, A. and Riva, G. (2013) 'Current considerations for eating and body-related disorders among men', in L.B. Sams and J.A. Keels (Eds) *Handbook on body image: Gender differences, sociocultural influences and health implications* (pp. 195–216), New York, NY: Nova Publishers.

Darsow, U., Bruckbauer, H., Worret, W.-I., Hofmann, H. and Ring, J. (2000) 'Subcutaneous oleomas induced by self-injection of sesame seed oil for muscle augmentation', *Journal of the American Academy of Dermatology*, 42 (2), 292–4.

Davis, K. (2002) 'A dubious equality: Men and women in cosmetic surgery', *Body and Society*, 8 (1), 49–65.

Di Benedetto, G., Pierangeli, M., Scalise, A. and Bertani, A. (2002) 'Paraffin oil injection in the body: An obsolete and destructive procedure', *Annals of Plastic Surgery*, 49 (4), 391–6.

Donaldson, C. (1996) *A study of male body image and the effects of the media*, unpublished BSc dissertation, Manchester Metropolitan University.

Drewnowski, A. and Yee, D.K. (1987) 'Men and body image: Are males satisfied with their body weight?' *Psychosomatic Medicine*, 49 (6), 626–34.

Ephedrineweb.com (2014) *ECA stack*, available online at: http://dietpill-rx.com/eca-stack-ephedrine-caffeine-aspirin/ [accessed December 2014].

Fallon, A. and Rozin, P. (1985) 'Sex differences in perceptions of desirable body shape', *Journal of Abnormal Psychology*, 94 (1), 102–5.

Fawkner, H. (2004) *Body image attitudes in men: An examination of the antecedents and consequent adjustive strategies and behaviors*, unpublished PhD thesis, University of Melbourne.

Fawkner, H.J. (2012) 'Body image development: Adult men', in T. Cash (Ed.) *Encyclopedia of body image and human appearance* (pp. 194–201), London: Elsevier.

Francis, B. (1989) *Bev Francis' power bodybuilding*, New York: Stirling.

Franko, D.L., Fuller-Tyszkiewicz, M., Rodgers, R., Holmqvist Gattario, K., Frisen, A., Diedrichs, P.C., Ricciardelli, L.A., Yager, Z., Smolak, L., Thompson-Brenner, H. and Shingleton, R. (2015) 'Internalization as a mediator of the relationship between conformity to masculine norms and body image attitudes and behaviors among young men in Sweden, US, UK, and Australia', *Body Image*, 15, 54–60.

Franzoi, S. and Shields, S. (1984) 'The body esteem scale: Multidimensional structure and sex differences in a college population', *Journal of Personality Assessment*, 48 (2), 173–8.

Frederick, D.A., Fessler, D.M.T. and Haselton, M.G. (2005) 'Do representations of male muscularity differ in men's and women's magazines?' *Body Image*, 2 (1), 81–6.

Frederick, D.A., Forbes, G.B., Grigorian, K. and Jarcho, J.M. (2007) 'The UCLA Body Project I: Gender and ethnic differences in self-objectification and body satisfaction among 2,206 undergraduates', *Sex Roles*, 57 (5–6), 317–27.

Frederick, D.A., Jafary, A., Daniels, E.A. and Gruys, K. (2011) 'Surveys and the epidemiology of body image', in T. Cash (Ed.) *The encyclopedia of body image and human appearance* (pp. 766–73), San Diego: Academic Press.

Furnham, A. and Greaves, N. (1994) 'Gender and locus of control correlates of body image dissatisfaction', *European Journal of Personality*, 8 (3), 183–200.

Gaines, C. and Butler, G. (1980) *Pumping iron: The art and sport of bodybuilding*, London: Sphere.

Garner, D.M. (1997) 'The 1997 body image survey results', *Psychology Today*, 30 (1), 30–48.

Ghandourah, S., Hofer, M.J., Kiebling, A., El-Zayat, B. and Dietmar Schofar, M. (2012) 'Painful muscle fibrosis following synthol injections in a bodybuilder: A case report', *Journal of Medical Case Reports*, 6, 248.

Gough, B. (2007) '"Real men don't diet": An analysis of contemporary newspaper representations of men, food and health', *Social Science and Medicine*, 64 (2), 326–37.

Gough, B. and Robertson, D.S. (2009) *Men, masculinities and health: Critical perspectives*, London: Palgrave MacMillan.

Gough, B., Hall, M. and Seymour-Smith, S. (2014) 'Straight guys do wear make-up: Contemporary masculinities and investment in appearance', in S. Robertson (Ed.) *Debating modern masculinities: Change, continuity, crisis?* (pp. 106–24), Basingstoke: Palgrave Macmillan.

Gough, B., Seymour-Smith, S. and Matthews, C.R. (2016) 'Body dissatisfaction, appearance investment and wellbeing: How older obese men orient to "aesthetic health"', *Psychology of Men and Masculinity*, 17 (1), 84–91.

Grogan, S. (1999) *Body image: Understanding body dissatisfaction in men, women, and children*, 1st edition, London: Routledge.

Grogan, S. and Richards, H. (2002) 'Body image: Focus groups with boys and men', *Men and Masculinities*, 4 (3), 219–32.

Grogan, S., Conner, M. and Smithson, H. (2006a) 'Sexuality and exercise motivations: Are gay men and heterosexual women most likely to be motivated by concern about weight and appearance?' *Sex Roles*, 55 (7–8), 567–72.

Grogan, S., Shepherd, S., Evans, R., Wright, S. and Hunter, G. (2006b) 'Experiences of anabolic steroid use: Interviews with men and women steroid users', *Journal of Health Psychology*, 11 (6), 849–60.

Hale, B.D. and Smith, D. (2012) 'Bodybuilding', in T. Cash (Ed.) *Encyclopedia of body image and human appearance* (pp. 66–74), London: Elsevier.

Hall, M. (2015) *Metrosexual masculinities*, London: Palgrave Macmillan.

Hall, M., Grogan, S. and Gough, B. (2015a) '"It is safe to use if you are healthy": A discursive analysis of men's online accounts of ephedrine use', *Psychology and Health,* 30 (7), 770–82.

Hall, M., Grogan, S. and Gough, B. (2015b) 'Bodybuilders' accounts of synthol use: The construction of lay expertise', *Journal of Health Psychology* [E-pub ahead of print DOI: 10.1177/1359105314568579].

Health and Social Care Information Centre (2014) *Statistics on obesity, physical activity and diet: England 2014*, available online at: www.hscic.gov.uk/catalogue/PUB13648 [accessed 30 January 2016].

Hildebrandt, T. and Alfano, L. (2012) 'Drug use, appearance- and performance-enhancing', in T. Cash (Ed.) *Encyclopedia of body image and human appearance* (pp. 392–8), London: Elsevier.

Holliday, R. and Cairnie, A. (2007) 'Man made plastic: Investigating men's consumption of aesthetic surgery', *Journal of Consumer Culture*, 7 (1), 57–78.

Holmqvist-Gattario, K., Frisen, A., Fuller-Tyszkiewicz, M., Ricciardelli, L, Diedrichs, P., Yager, Z., Franko, D.L. and Smolak, L. (2015) 'How is men's conformity to masculine norms related to their body image? Masculinity and muscularity across Western countries', *Psychology of Men and Masculinity*, 16 (3), 337–47.

International Society of Aesthetic Plastic Surgery (2015) *Global statistics on cosmetic procedures*, available online at: www.isaps.org [accessed 14 December 2015].

International Society of Aesthetic Surgeons (2016) *ISAPS Global Statistics*, available online at: www.isaps.org/news/isaps-global-statistics [accessed 5 January 2016].

Kanayama, G., Gruber, A.J., Pope, H.G. Jr., Borowiecki, J.J. and Hudson, J.I. (2001) 'Over-the-counter drug use in gymnasiums: An underrecognized substance abuse problem?' *Psychotherapy and Psychosomatics*, 70 (3), 137–40.

Kyrejto, J.W., Mosewich, A.D., Kowalski, K.C., Mack, D.E. and Crocker, P.R.E. (2008) 'Men's and women's drive for muscularity: Gender differences and cognitive and behavioral correlates', *International Journal of Sport and Exercise Psychology*, 6 (1), 69–84.

Langdridge, D., Flowers, P., Gough, B. and Holliday, R. (2013) 'On the biomedicalisation of the penis: The commodification of function and aesthetics', *International Journal of Men's Health*, 12 (2), 121–37.

Laure, P., Lecerf, T., Friser, A. and Binsinger, C. (2004) 'Drugs, recreational drug use and attitudes towards doping of high school athletes', *International Journal of Sports Medicine*, 25 (2), 133–8.

Leith, W. (2006) 'We used to settle for one like this; now we all want one like this', *Observer Woman*, February, 30–5.

Lennehan, P. (2003) *Anabolic steroids*, London: Taylor and Francis.

Lynch, S.M. and Zellner, D.A. (1999) 'Figure preferences in two generations of men: The use of figure drawings illustrating differences in muscle mass', *Sex Roles*, 40 (9), 833–43.

Mansfield, A. and McGinn, B. (1993) 'Pumping irony: The muscular and the feminine', in S. Scott and D. Morgan (Eds) *Body matters* (pp. 49–68), London: Falmer.

McCabe, M.P. and Ricciardelli, L.A (2003) 'Sociocultural influences on body image and body changes among adolescent boys and girls', *Journal of Social Psychology*, 143 (1), 5–26.

McCabe, M.P., Ricciardelli, L.A., Sitaram, G. and Mikhail, K. (2006) 'Accuracy of body size estimation: Role of biopsychosocial variables', *Body Image*, 3 (2), 163–73.

McCreary, D.R. (2012) 'Muscularity and body image', in T. Cash (Ed.) *Encyclopedia of body image and human appearance* (pp. 561–7), London: Elsevier.

McCreary, D.R. and Sasse, D.K. (2000) 'An exploration of the drive for muscularity in adolescent boys and girls', *Journal of American College Health*, 48 (6), 297–304.

McCreary, D.R. and Sasse, D.K. (2002) 'Gender differences in high school students' dieting behaviour and their correlates', *International Journal of Men's Health*, 1 (2), 195–213.

McCreary, D.R., Karvinen, K. and Davis, C. (2006) 'The relationship of drive for muscularity and anthropometric measures of muscularity and adiposity', *Body Image*, 3, 145–53.

McCreary, D.R., Sasse, D.K., Saucier, D.M. and Dorsch, K.D. (2004) 'Measuring the drive for muscularity: Factorial validity of the Drive for Muscularity Scale in men and women', *Psychology of Men and Masculinity*, 5 (1), 49–58.

Medicinenet.com (2014). *Ephedrine-oral*, available online at: http://www.medicinenet.com/ephedrine-oral/article.htm

Mishkind, M., Rodin, J., Silberstein, L. and Striegel-Moore, R. (1986) 'The embodiment of masculinity: Cultural, psychological, and behavioral dimensions', *American Behavioral Scientist*, 29 (5), 545–62.

Monaghan, L.F. (2008) *Men and the war on obesity: A sociological study*, London: Routledge.

Morgan, J.F. and Arcelus, J. (2009) 'Body Image and sexual orientation in men', *European Eating Disorders Review,* 17 (6), 435–44.

Mort, F. (1988) 'Boys' own? Masculinity, style and popular culture', in R. Chapman and J. Rutherford (Eds) *Male order: Unwrapping masculinity*, London: Lawrence and Wishart.

National Health Service (2016) *Anabolic steroid misuse*, available online at: www.nhs.uk/conditions/anabolic-steroid-abuse/Pages/Introduction.aspx [accessed 20 January 2016].

Ogden, J. (1992) *Fat chance: The myth of dieting explained*, London: Routledge.

Oxford Dictionaries (2016) *Definition of metrosexual*, available online at: www.oxforddictionaries.com/definition/english/metrosexual [accessed 20 January 2016].

Pope, H., Katz, D. and Hudson, J. (1993) 'Anorexia nervosa and "reverse anorexia" among 108 male bodybuilders', *Comprehensive Psychiatry*, 34 (6), 406–9.

Pope, H.G., Gruber A.J., Choi, P., Olivardia, R. and Phillips, K.A. (1997) 'Muscle dysmorphia: An underrecognized form of body dysmorphic disorder', *Psychosomatics: Journal of Consultation and Liaison Psychiatry*, 38 (6), 548–57.

Pope, H.G., Phillips, K.A. and Olivardia, R. (2000) *The Adonis complex: The secret crisis of male body obsession*, New York: Free Press.

Public Health England (2015) *Health Survey for England: Factsheets*, available online at: www.noo.org.uk/NOO_pub/Key_data [accessed 20 December 2015].

Ricciardelli, L.A. (2012) 'Body image development: Adolescent boys', in T. Cash (Ed.) *Encyclopedia of body image and human appearance* (pp. 180–7), London: Elsevier.

Ricciardelli, L.A., McCabe, M.P., Mussap, A.J. and Holt, K.E. (2009) 'Body image in preadolescent boys', in L. Smolak and J.K. Thompson (Eds) *Body image, eating disorders and obesity in youth* (2nd edition), Washington, DC: APA.

Ricciardelli, L.A., McCabe, M.P., Williams, R.J. and Thompson, J.K. (2007) 'The role of ethnicity and culture in body image and disordered eating among males', *Clinical Psychology Review,* 27 (5), 582–606.

Rusticus, S. and Hubley, A.M. (2006) 'Measurement invariance of the Multidimensional Body-Self Relations Questionnaire: Can we compare across age and gender?' *Sex Roles,* 55 (11), 827–842.

Sagoe, D., Andreassen, C.S. and Pallesen, S. (2014) 'The aetiology and trajectory of anabolic-androgenic steroid use initiation: A systematic review and synthesis of qualitative research', *Substance Abuse Treatment, Prevention, and Policy,* 9, 27.

Smeets, M.A.M., Smit, F., Panhuysen, G.E.M. and Ingleby, J.D. (1998) 'Body perception index: Benefits, pitfalls, ideas', *Journal of Psychosomatic Research,* 44 (3–4), 457–64.

Smith D., Rutty, M.C. and Olrich, T. (in press) 'Muscle dysmorphia and anabolic-androgenic steroid use', in M. Hall, S. Grogan and B. Gough (Eds) *Chemically modified bodies: The use of diverse substances for appearance enhancement,* London: Palgrave Macmillan.

Steroidal.com (2014) *Ephedrine cycle,* available online at: www.steroidal.com/fat-loss-agents/ephedrine/ephedrine-cycle/ [accessed 25 March 2014].

Strauss, R.H. and Yesalis, C.E. (1991) 'Anabolic steroids in the athlete', *Annual Review of Medicine,* 42, 449–57.

Strong, S.M., Williamson, D.A., Netemeyer, R.G. and Geer, J.H. (2000) 'Eating disorder symptoms and concerns about body differ as a function of gender and sexual orientation', *Journal of Social and Clinical Psychology,* 19 (2), 240–55.

Thompson, J.K. and Cafri, G. (Eds) (2007) *The muscular ideal,* Washington, DC: American Psychological Association.

Tylka, T.L., Bergeron, D. and Schwartz, J.P. (2005) 'Development and psychometric evaluation of the Male Body Attitudes Scale (MBAS)', *Body Image,* 2 (2), 161–75.

Walker, D.C. and Murray, A.D. (2012) 'Body image behaviors: Checking, fixing and avoiding', in T.F. Cash (Ed.) *Encyclopedia of body image and human appearance* (pp. 166–72), London: Elsevier.

Wright, S., Grogan, S. and Hunter, G. (2000) 'Motivations for anabolic steroid use among bodybuilders', *Journal of Health Psychology,* 5 (4), 566–72.

Wright, S., Grogan, S. and Hunter, G. (2001) 'Body-builders' attitudes towards steroid use', *Drugs: Education, Prevention and Policy,* 8 (1), 91–5.

5

MEDIA EFFECTS

There is general agreement that media pressures on women to be a particular shape and size are more pronounced than similar pressures on men. Studies that have investigated media portrayal of men's and women's bodies have found that men and women are portrayed in markedly different ways in relation to body weight.

Media portrayal of women's bodies

Content analysis (where the frequency of portrayal of particular images is coded) has revealed that women are portrayed as abnormally slim in the media. Linda Smolak (2004) notes that fashion models in the 2000s are thinner than 98 per cent of US women, and Erin Strahan and colleagues (2006) argue that:

> Images of thin women are ubiquitous in the media, and women's magazines contain more messages about physical attractiveness than do men's magazines.
>
> (Strahan et al., 2006: 211)

Magazines aimed at girls and young women tend to present traditional slim images of attractiveness. The US National Eating Disorders Association (2013) note that size 0 (UK size 4) is now standard within the modelling industry, putting pressure on models to maintain an unrealistically low body weight in order to gain work, as well as putting viewers under pressure to emulate those ideals. Digital manipulations of pictures of models' bodies mean that women in the twenty-first century are faced with even more idealized and more slender bodies than previously (Bordo, 2003; Tiggemann, 2014); and playing with Barbie dolls, with their thin, unrealistic proportions, has been shown to reduce body esteem in 5- to 8-year-old British girls (Dittmar et al., 2006) as well as reduce career aspirations in 4- to 7-year-old girls in the US (Sherman and Zurbriggen, 2014).

Various authors have concluded that print media, particularly magazines aimed at young women, have powerful effects on their readers, serving to foster and maintain a "cult of femininity" and supplying definitions of what it means to be an attractive woman. Women's magazines are read by a large proportion of women (about half the adult female population of the UK). In the 1980s Marjorie Ferguson (1985) argued that there are interesting parallels between the practices promoted by women's magazines and the characteristic elements of the religious cult:

> I have argued that women's magazines collectively comprise a social institution which serves to foster and maintain a cult of femininity. In promoting a cult of femininity these journals are not merely reflecting the female role in society; they are also supplying one source of definitions of, and socialisation into, that role.
>
> (Ferguson, 1985: 184)

Ferguson saw the media as doing much more than simply reflecting current values, arguing that women's magazines may actually change a woman's view of herself by teaching her socially acceptable ways in which to behave.

Maggie Wykes and Barrie Gunter (2005) have argued that popular print media have continued to promote a narrow body ideal for women (as young, white and slender), but that they do this in different and more subtle ways in the twenty-first century to appeal to a more knowing audience than in previous years. While critiquing the dieting industry, magazines and newspapers present very slender images and subtly derogate women who do not conform to a very slender ideal. Wykes and Gunter argue that women are expected to work on their bodies (through diet, exercise and cosmetic surgery) to attain a socially acceptable body shape, and the underlying message is that if they do not achieve this look they will not be attractive to men:

> The modern print media are perhaps more covert operators on the body than explicitly overt as they were suggested to be in these earlier content analyses. At the outset of the twenty-first century, there are of course publications like *Shape* which are explicitly engaged in reconstructing women's bodies, but the print media analysed here are not, and are even critical of the diet and slimming industries. Despite this, the stories that they do tell about femininity are insidiously, repetitively and systematically engaged in a very particular construction of femininity that is deeply body-conscious and embedded within a particular gendered narrative.
>
> (Wykes and Gunter, 2005: 95)

Recently, researchers have become interested in the ways that men's and women's bodies are portrayed in video games, and possible impacts on body image. Almost half of "gamers" are now thought to be women (Entertainment Software Association, 2015). When playing video games women often use avatars to represent themselves in the game, and also interact with avatars of other women, making it important to understand how women's bodies are portrayed in games. Women characters in video games tend to be thin and youthful with large breasts (Martins et al., 2009), and Anastasia Salter and Bridget Blodgett (2012) link women's portrayal in video games with sexism within the gaming community. Portrayal has been argued to be unrealistic and over-sexualized, and to mimic and even exaggerate the thin and curvy body types seen in other mass media (Williams et al., 2009).

Another recent development is the proliferation of thin-ideal imagery on social media, referred to as "thinspiration". Thinspiration ("thin" + "inspiration") is usually defined as media content (words and/or images) that promotes weight loss, often in ways that glorifies eating disordered behaviour (National Eating Disorders Association, 2013). Visual images tend to portray extremely thin women (normally young and white) alongside messages promoting dieting and other strategies to promote weight loss. Jannath Ghaznavi and Laramie Taylor (2015) carried out a systematic content analysis of three hundred thinspiration images on Twitter and Pinterest and report:

> Images tended to be sexually suggestive and objectifying with a focus on ultra-thin, bony, scantily clad women.
>
> (Ghaznavi and Taylor, 2015: 54)

The authors conclude that the exposure to these kinds of images, in a context where they are socially endorsed, presents serious risks to women engaged in online communities.

Michael Levine (2012) reviews available literature and confirms that thin bodies are normative for women portrayed on the television, in magazines, in video games and on the internet, and that unhealthy messages about gender, attractiveness, body objectification and weight management abound. He is concerned about the fact that these kinds of images are a major part of the lives of adults and children around the world:

> As American girls and women have become heavier over the last 30–40 years, the ideal female featured in the mass media is now prototypically young, tall, thin, and White, with at least moderately large breasts.
>
> (Levine, 2012: 540)

Media portrayal of men's bodies

Cultural norms for men's bodies are more flexible than women's, and although there is a cultural preference for a slender but muscular body type (see Chapter 2), there is a greater range of media representations of attractive male bodies (e.g. Strahan et al., 2006). However, there has been a change in frequency of the portrayal of idealized images of men's bodies in the media that started in the late twentieth century.

In the 1980s and 1990s the male body became more "visible" in the popular media in both Britain and the USA. Frank Mort (1988) and Rowena Chapman (1988) noted the increasing prevalence of the well-muscled male body in British advertising. Marc Mishkind and colleagues (1986) argued that examination of US magazines and other media demonstrated that body image concern was strong for men. They suggested that media images of the young, lean, muscular male body represent changes in society's attitudes to the male body, as a result of which men are under increased pressure to look slender and muscular:

> Advertisements celebrate the young, lean, muscular male body, and men's fashions have undergone significant changes in style both to accommodate and to accentuate changes in men's physiques toward a more muscular and trim body.
>
> (Mishkind et al., 1986: 545)

They went on to suggest that the pressures of society to conform to the slender, muscular male body ideal may be producing an increase in body dissatisfaction and low self-esteem in men. Stuart Elliot (1994) also documented this trend, describing how *Sports Illustrated* magazine opted to use male models to advertise swimwear for the first time in 1994, and Peter Baker (1994) noted the increased use of attractive men (young, handsome, and muscular) in advertisements and movies and argued that this had led to an increase in men's self-consciousness about their bodies:

> Men's self-consciousness about their appearance is probably greater now than ever before. How could it be otherwise, given the massive exposure of men's bodies in the media?
>
> (Baker, 1994: 130)

More recently, other researchers have been concerned that images of men's bodies in video games tends to be hyper-muscular (e.g. Sylvia et al., 2014), and that even boys' toys have become more muscular in the twenty-first century (e.g. Smith et al., in press).

Philippa Diedrichs (2012) reviews data on the representation of men's bodies in magazines, television and children's media. She notes that images of men's bodies in popular media have become increasingly muscled and leaner, as well as being portrayed more frequently in objectifying poses and idealized through airbrushing (digital alteration to "perfect" the images), and that it is not surprising that when male consumers are exposed to these kinds of images they report greater body dissatisfaction. She concludes that:

> Collectively, this research demonstrates that media aimed at children and adults has increasingly depicted and promoted a cultural ideal for male beauty that emphasizes leanness, muscularity and youth. Furthermore, the idealized and objectified presentation of body types that fit with this ideal suggests to male consumers that this is what they should and can achieve, if they want to be attractive and successful.
>
> (Diedrichs, 2012: 548)

Surveys relating media exposure to body image

Psychology researchers have conducted surveys to investigate the link between media exposure and body dissatisfaction by asking participants to complete questionnaires in which they report exposure to magazine and television and in which body image is also measured (usually through questionnaires assessing body dissatisfaction). Botta (2000) found that magazine exposure (mediated by social comparison processes) was linked to body dissatisfaction in boys as well as girls, and in 2003 argued that:

> Magazine reading, social comparisons, and critical body image processing are important predictors of body image and eating disturbances in adolescent boys and girls.
>
> (Botta, 2003: 389)

Exposure to images of men's and women's bodies on the internet may also be important, and Marika Tiggemann and Jessica Miller (2010) included internet appearance exposure in their list of media-related appearance measures. In this study, 156 Australian female high school students (mean age 15 years) completed questionnaires where they indicated their media consumption and also answered questions relating to body image. Exposure to appearance-related materials on the internet and magazine reading were associated with internalization of thin ideals and weight dissatisfaction, suggesting that both kinds of media were important in presenting standards of attractiveness to young women. Marika Tiggemann and Amy Slater (2013, 2014) have also shown that girls aged 10 to 12 and 13 to 15 who used social networking sites scored significantly higher on body concern than non-users, suggesting that internalization of thin ideals mediates the relationship between social media exposure and body concerns.

Meta-analytic reviews (where authors analyse data across a range of studies) have shown consistently that girls and women who have higher levels of exposure to appearance-focused media imagery tend to be less satisfied with the way that they look, and are more likely to internalize the thin ideal than those with lower levels of exposure (e.g. Grabe et al., 2008).

Michael Levine (2012), in a review of available evidence, suggests that negative body image is more closely associated with fashion magazines than television in general, and that exposure to magazines aimed at adults and adolescents has been linked to awareness and endorsement of dieting in girls as young as 6 years. Studies with men have also produced similar findings and reviews have suggested that UK, New Zealand, US and Australian men who have greater self-reported appearance-related media exposure (such as viewing and purchasing fitness magazines) tend to show higher levels of body dissatisfaction (e.g. Diedrichs, 2012).

One of the problems with survey work that provides evidence of a correlation between exposure and body dissatisfaction is that it is impossible to tell whether the media exposure produced changes in satisfaction, or whether people who are less satisfied with their bodies gravitate toward particular kinds of media. In order to disentangle these effects, studies need either to investigate the direction of the relationship through prospective work in which media exposure and body image are both tested and then participants are followed up to look at changes in satisfaction, or to investigate experimentally the direct effects of media imagery on satisfaction.

Prospective studies are rare in the body image literature. However, Eric Stice and colleagues (2001) ran an interesting study where they randomly assigned 219 US adolescent girls to fifteen-month fashion magazine subscription or no-subscription conditions and followed them up over time. They found that there were no main effects of long-term exposure to thin images on thin-ideal internalization, body dissatisfaction, dieting, negative affect or bulimic symptoms. However, vulnerable adolescents, who scored highly on perceived pressure to be thin and body dissatisfaction at pre-test and who had poor social support, *were* adversely affected. The authors conclude that exposure to thin-ideal images may have lasting negative effects for vulnerable youth.

Marika Tiggemann (2006) also ran a prospective study of body image and media exposure with 214 Australian girls (mean age 14 years). At time 1 they completed questionnaire measures of media exposure (including both magazines and television), internalization of appearance ideals, appearance schemas, body dissatisfaction and drive for thinness. One year later, at time 2, they completed the same measures. Tiggemann found that none of the media exposure measures at time 1 predicted body image at time 2. She also found that body image at time 1 did not predict change in media exposure. She reports:

> It was concluded that for this age group, media exposure and body image seem to co-occur but that neither one is temporally antecedent to the other. Thus the study demonstrated no causal role for media exposure in the body image of adolescent girls.
>
> (Tiggemann, 2006: 523)

Clearly, mere exposure to media imagery may not be sufficient to modify body image. Vulnerability to these kinds of images may vary between young women, with those with high initial body dissatisfaction, high perceived pressure to be thin and poor social support at particular risk. The meanings attached to the images (and the importance attached to the thin ideal), the extent to which the person compares his or her own body to the images, and the size and direction of any perceived gap between the idealized image and the self may all be crucial in determining the effect of exposure.

Studies investigating direct effects of media images on body image

Rather than looking at associations between media exposure and body dissatisfaction, some authors have run experimental studies to investigate the effects of media imagery on body dissatisfaction in controlled laboratory situations. Most researchers have measured body satisfaction in women after (and sometimes before and after) observing slender/muscular models in various media. Most have found a decrease in body esteem after viewing, although some have found no change, and one study even found an increase in satisfaction.

In an early study, Thomas Cash et al. (1983) showed female students pictures of female models taken from magazines. One group saw pictures of women previously rated as physically attractive, one group saw pictures of physically attractive women whom they were told were professional models, and the third group saw pictures previously rated as not attractive. Women in the groups exposed to attractive models rated their own attractiveness less highly after viewing these images than those who had viewed the less attractive models. This was particularly the case in the condition where the attractive women were not labeled as models, suggesting that perceived similarity to viewed images is important, as suggested by social comparison theory (Major et al., 1991; see below).

Leslie Heinberg and Kevin Thompson (1995) investigated the effects of televised images on body satisfaction. A ten-minute tape of either appearance-related or non-appearance-related commercials was viewed by 139 women. Pre-test and post-test measures of body dissatisfaction revealed that participants who were high on "body image disturbance" (rated by Schulman et al.'s (1986) Bulimia Cognitive Distortions Scale – physical appearance subscale) and/or high on awareness or acceptance of societal attitudes to thinness and attractiveness (as measured by Heinberg and Thompson's Societal Attitudes Toward Appearance Questionnaire) were significantly less satisfied after viewing the appearance-related images. Participants below the median on body image disturbance showed no change or showed improved satisfaction. The authors suggested that media images of thinness are particularly salient for certain susceptible individuals, and that this group may use media models as social comparison targets when assessing their own physical attractiveness. Their data suggest that only a specific subsection of the population – those who agree with statements such as "being physically fit is a priority in today's society" (awareness of societal attitudes), "photographs of thin women make me wish that I were thin" (acceptance of societal attitudes), or "my value as a person is related to my weight" (cognitive distortions related to physical appearance) – are "at risk" from such images.

Philip Myers and Frank Biocca (1992) ran a fascinating study in which seventy-six female university students aged 18 to 24 viewed either body-image-oriented or neutral programming. The participants then completed questionnaires measuring mood, and estimated body size by the light-adjustment technique described in Chapter 3. They found that most of the young women overestimated their body size (in agreement with the research cited in Chapter 3). Watching a thirty-minute tape of body-image-oriented advertisements and programming had a significant effect on body size estimation and mood levels. Surprisingly, the body-image-oriented material reduced body size overestimation and also reduced depression levels.

Myers and Biocca explain these counter-intuitive results by suggesting that the young women may have imagined themselves in the ideal body presented in the tape. They may have felt more in control, and may have seen the ideal as more attainable and within reach. They use these findings to suggest a two-stage process of building a distorted body image. In the first stage, young women "bond" with the models, visualizing themselves in the socially represented ideal body. At this stage the "elastic" present body image moves toward the internalized ideal body, making the woman feel good about her body. The self-criticism that comes from a realization of the gap between the objective body and the internalized ideal body comes later. So the short-term effect is to make the woman feel that she is closer to her ideal (through identification with the models and consequent change in her current body image). However, once the identification has "worn off" she will make unfavourable comparisons between her objective body and her internalized ideal, leading to dissatisfaction. Unfortunately, Myers and Biocca did not look at the longer-term effects of the images. Their argument about long-term effects would be more convincing if it were accompanied by evidence that this long-term shift does in fact take place. It would also have been useful to have measured body dissatisfaction directly, rather than inferring it through body size estimation and depression levels.

Jill Cattarin and colleagues (2000) showed television advertisements to female students. These either depicted slim, attractive models or were not appearance-focused. Participants were told to compare themselves with the models in the advertisements, to focus on the product, or were given non-specific instructions. They found that the group viewing the appearance-related advertisements who had been told to compare themselves with the models had the lowest body satisfaction after viewing the images. This explicit social comparison manipulation showed that women who are prompted to focus on the bodies of models are likely to become significantly less satisfied with their own looks after viewing. Other work has also shown that self-discrepancy moderates the influence of these social comparison processes. Gayle Bessenoff's (2006) study found that women with high levels of body image self-discrepancy were most likely to engage in social comparison with media images, as well as being more likely to experience negative consequences as a result of such comparisons.

Exposure to social media use has also been linked with disordered eating and body concerns in adult women and adolescent girls. Annelise Mabe et al. (2014) argue that the use of social media sites such as Facebook merges two possible kinds of influences, media and peer pressure, so it may be particularly problematic. They assigned eighty-four women randomly to either a Facebook or a control (alternative internet activity) condition for twenty minutes, and found that Facebook exposure was associated with higher weight and shape concerns compared to the control condition. They conclude that use of social media sites such as Facebook may promote negative body image, and should be targeted directly in intervention and prevention programmes.

In a meta-analysis of twenty-five studies conducted up until 2001, Lisa Groetz and colleagues (2002) concluded that young women feel worse after exposure to thin images than to other types of images, with those with a history of body dissatisfaction being more negatively affected by the images than other women. In 2008 Shelley Grabe and colleagues conducted a meta-analysis that examined seventy-seven experimental and correlational studies investigating associations between media exposure, women's body dissatisfaction and internalization of the thin ideal, and concluded that although methodological factors impacted on the effects found, findings in general supported the link between exposure to media images depicting thin-ideal body types and body-related concerns in groups of women.

There is some evidence that initial positive body image may be protective against negative effects of media images in experimental studies. Emma Halliwell (2013) examined whether positive body image can protect women from negative media exposure effects. One hundred and twelve female UK university students were allocated at random to conditions where they viewed advertisements featuring ultra-thin models or control images. Women who reported high levels of body appreciation did not report negative effects of seeing the thin images. Halliwell suggests that positive body image protects women from negative media appearance messages, and that promoting positive body image may be an effective intervention strategy to reduce the effects of media images.

In a similar study, Rachel Andrew and colleagues (2015) asked sixty-eight Australian female university students to complete measures of body appreciation and media protective strategies before viewing thin-ideal advertisements. Results showed that participants with low body appreciation reported increased body dissatisfaction after exposure, whereas participants with high body appreciation did not show an increase. The authors conclude that body appreciation may protect young women against the impacts of media imagery on body dissatisfaction, and support Halliwell in suggesting that interventions to facilitate body appreciation may be effective in protecting women from the negative effects of media imagery on body image.

Work in this area has tended to focus on women. Some recent studies have considered effects on men. The issue of men's body esteem is of particular interest at present because of recent suggestions that Western cultural attitudes to the male body are in a state of change, and that men are becoming more and more concerned with body image (see Chapter 4). In a study conducted in 1995 we looked at the effects on both men and women of viewing same-gender, slim, conventionally attractive models. The study was designed to investigate these effects on body esteem. Body esteem scales were completed by forty-nine men and forty-five women (aged 17 to 32) before and after viewing pictures of same-gender photographic models (experimental group) or landscapes (control group). Women scored significantly lower than men on the body esteem scale irrespective of whether they were in the experimental or control group, showing that these women were generally less satisfied with their bodies than were the men. There were interesting differences between the experimental and control groups after seeing the photographs. Body esteem scores decreased significantly (and to a similar degree) in men and women after viewing the same-gender photographic models, whereas men and women in the control group (who viewed landscapes) showed no change (Grogan et al., 1996).

This suggests that these men and women felt significantly less satisfied with their bodies after viewing attractive same-gender models. At least in the short term, these participants felt less good about the way that their bodies looked after comparison with those of well-toned, slender models. The data are particularly interesting since they show an equivalent shift in satisfaction for both men and women. The effect does not seem to be mediated by problematic relationships with food. Scores on the Eating Attitude Test (a measure of such relationships) did not correlate significantly with body esteem changes in the experimental groups, suggesting that the effect is independent of attitudes to eating. The effect is short-term, and there is no way of knowing how long it will last. Nevertheless, it is interesting that a relatively brief encounter with pictures of attractive fashion models can have such an effect on body satisfaction, suggesting that body image is indeed "elastic" as suggested by Phillip Myers and Frank Biocca (1992).

Other studies that have shown men muscular images have tended to find that men can be made to feel significantly less satisfied with their bodies after viewing muscular images. Duane Hargreaves and Marika Tiggemann (2009) showed male Australian university students either advertisements showing muscular men or advertisements not typifying the muscular ideal, and measured body image before and after viewing the images. Men who saw the idealized images were more likely to report feeling insufficiently muscular afterwards and felt less attractive than those who had seen the non-idealized images. In another study (Leit et al., 2002), male US students were shown pictures of muscular men taken from magazine advertisements. On average, these men reported greater dissatisfaction with their own muscularity than men shown images of clothing advertisements. There was no effect on their satisfaction with their fat levels. Other work has also found that dissatisfaction is increased after viewing muscular images compared with thin, normal weight images and plump images (Lorenzen et al., 2004).

In one Canadian study Kelly Arbour and Kathleen Martin-Ginis (2006) investigated the effects on men's body image of the degree of muscularity of images displayed in the realistic context of a nutrition and weight-training seminar. Seventy-four men completed body dissatisfaction and muscularity dissatisfaction measures before and after attending the seminar, in which either muscular or hypermuscular (bodybuilder) images were viewed. Men who had pre-existing muscularity dissatisfaction had increased body dissatisfaction after viewing the muscular, but not hypermuscular, images. The authors conclude that exposure to the lean, muscular ideal promoted in the media leads to increased body dissatisfaction in men with pre-existing muscularity concerns. Hypermuscular (bodybuilder) images did not have any significant effect, possibly because this was perceived as unattainable (and so not a relevant comparison), or because the moderately muscular images were perceived as more "ideal" than the hypermuscular images.

Video games enable players to use avatars to represent themselves in the game as well as interacting with virtual figures of other women and men, and there is evidence that direct exposure to the kinds of idealized bodies that are found in video games affects body satisfaction in both men and women. Experimental research by Christopher Bartlett and Richard Harris (2008) found that men and women had lowered body satisfaction after playing fifteen minutes of a game with idealized bodies, and more recent research (Sylvia et al., 2014) demonstrated that men who experienced forty-five minutes of realistic gaming with a hypermuscular avatar experienced lower body satisfaction than controls.

In 2008 Christopher Bartlett and colleagues carried out meta-analyses to determine the impact of pressure from the media on men's body satisfaction, body esteem and self-esteem. Analyzing twenty-five correlational and experimental studies, they concluded that there was convincing evidence that pressure from the mass media was significantly related to men feeling worse about their own bodies:

> Results from both Study 1 and Study 2 suggest that as men felt pressure from the mass media (in correlational and experimental designs) they felt worse about their bodies. Results showed that pressure from the mass media was related to body satisfaction, body esteem, self-esteem, psychological disorders (e.g. depression), and behavioral outcomes (e.g. excessive exercising).
>
> (Bartlett et al., 2008: 279)

Studies of media effects have generally found that idealized images impact negatively on viewers' body images and that these effects are similar for men and women. Social comparison seems to mediate the process, and women who have internalized the thin ideal and who have a greater discrepancy between their actual body and their internalized ideal body seem most at risk of experiencing negative effects. In men, existing muscularity dissatisfaction may predispose to more negative effects of media images.

Interview studies

Authors of intervention studies tend to assume that results obtained in the laboratory can be generalized to real-life situations. However, results obtained in the somewhat sterile laboratory situation may not be generalizable to more realistic viewing situations for several reasons. Experiments carried out in university laboratories (as most of the above have been) place participants in a strange, unfamiliar situation in which they are given something specific to observe (rather than choosing it themselves), they are (usually) observed while they view, and they are (usually) asked to pay attention to particular details of the material they view. None of these factors are likely to be common in participants' everyday life, so results obtained in the laboratory may be different from those that would be obtained if we observed the participants in their everyday environment. These studies are also open to demand characteristics (people respond as they think they should respond in that particular unfamiliar situation). Survey studies have the advantage of observing naturally occurring media exposure, but they do not enable us to know enough about the causal direction of effects.

An alternative and fruitful approach is to interview people about their experience of media exposure, to help us to understand more about the experience of viewing these images from the viewer's perspective. In our interviews with women (reported in Chapter 3) participants did not accept the media images offered to them uncritically. They were highly critical of the fact that "skinny" models and actresses were represented as "normal" body shapes in magazines and on film. They saw fashion models as being too thin, representative of an unrealistic ideal. Data from these interviews will be discussed further in the section on body image role models later in this chapter.

Other recent data also suggest that women may be well aware of the idealized nature of images presented to them in the media, and know how to decode and criticize media imagery aimed at them (Engeln-Maddox, 2005). A good example of this is video gameplay. Studies have shown that video gameplay under experimental conditions can lead to reduced body satisfaction in women chosen at random from student populations who are not experienced gamers (probably as a result of social comparison with the viewed images) as shown above. However, there is evidence that experienced gamers may not make these kinds of social comparisons, possibly because the images shown are seen as fantasy images and therefore they are not relevant comparison targets. In one UK study (Cole and Grogan, in preparation), thirty-two women who identified as 'women gamers' answered open-ended questions on the portrayal of women's bodies in video games. Women presented complex accounts where they constructed themselves as informed gamers who were not duped into wanting to emulate the sexualized images on display. The idealized bodies in games were constructed as pandering to the sexual fantasies of male gamers, who were seen as malleable and naïve. Participants reported that they were frustrated by the prevalence of hyper-sexualized bodies in games, but emphasized their mastery over the gaming environment and their ability to dismiss the images as fantasy. Participants associated their resistance to being affected by the idealized images seen in video games with experience of, and understanding of, the medium, supporting suggestions from other studies that media literacy can reduce the negative impacts of exposure to idealized images (e.g. Ridolfi and Vander Wal, 2008).

The twenty-first century has seen a huge increase in tattooing and body piercing, and these practices have become mainstream and acceptable across the social spectrum, at least for the young (Heywood et al., 2012; Swami, 2012). Tattoo prevalence has been estimated to range from 10 per cent for adolescents to 25 per cent for the general population (Heywood et al., 2012). The numbers of physical locations of body art are also increasing. Piercings of the face (for example, nose, eyebrow, lip, tongue and upper ear) and body (for example, nipple, navel or genitals) have become increasingly popular in recent years, and studies have found that between 10 and 56 per cent of respondents now have a piercing in a site other than the earlobe (Swami and Harris, 2012).

Motivations for body modifications are complex and person-specific, but exposure to media images of pierced and tattooed celebrities may be triggers. Media imagery is replete with images of men and women with body art, and television programmes such as *Tattoo Fixers* have brought body art into the mainstream. Interview work has suggested that exposure to media images of celebrities with body art can be a factor in people's decisions to get a tattoo or piercing, but is probably less important than peer influence. For instance, Beth Rhodes at Staffordshire University in the UK interviewed British women and men about motivations for piercings (Rhodes, 2004). Nineteen pierced and non-pierced participants (seven men, twelve women) aged 18 to 28 years took part in focus groups discussing experiences of, and motivations for, body piercing. Knowing that celebrities had had a particular piercing was a significant incentive to get the same part of the body pierced. However, peer pressure was the main influence on deciding to get a piercing in this young adult group. Participants argued that it was often the suggestion of a particular piercing by a friend that led them to make the final decision to get the piercing, and that friends often went together to get the piercing done. Knowing someone else had had a particular piercing done at a particular studio would often lead to the decision to have the same piercing done themselves, as they would feel confident that it was safe.

Interview research has also focused on impacts of taking and posting "selfies" on body image. Selfies are usually understood to be photographs of the self, typically taken with a smartphone or webcam and shared via social media (Oxford Dictionaries Online, 2015). The role of selfies in relation to body image is unclear, with some arguing that they encourage body objectification, distorting women's body image and encouraging unhealthy eating (Briggs, 2014; Mabe et al., 2014), and linking posting and viewing selfies with low body esteem and insecurity in teenage girls (Chua and Chang, 2016), and others such as Katrin Tiidenberg (2014) suggesting that selfies can boost self-esteem and empower women through enabling control over the body aesthetic, and by showcasing variations in beauty and celebrating uniqueness.

Recently, Leonie Rothery ran an interesting study where self-professed UK women selfie users were interviewed about their experiences of selfie-posting (Rothery, 2015). Eighteen self-professed selfie users aged 19 to 22 were interviewed about their experiences of taking and posting selfies, and possible impacts on their body image. Participants reported that "likes" on social media boosted their body confidence, and that other people's selfies were seen as over-idealized images, so not relevant social comparison targets. Most felt some social pressure to post flattering selfies, and participants sometimes posted explicitly unflattering or amusing photographs to try to avoid critique through projecting a "laugh with me not at me" attitude. Women objectified both their own and others' selfies and were dismissive of sexually explicit selfies. Results queried constructions of these women as empowered and self-determined selfie posters who are engaging in a self-affirming and awareness-raising pursuit as suggested by Katrin Tiidenberg and Edgar Gomez Cruz (2015). Most of the participants felt constrained in what was appropriate to post, talked in objectifying ways about their bodies, felt pressure to post flattering and non-sexualized selfies, and were highly aware of the likely impact on their perceived audience, so that posting was more objectifying than empowering.

Theories of media influence

Psychologists have developed three main theories to explain how media images might affect body image, and who might be particularly vulnerable to these effects. The most influential psychological theories of media effects are adaptations of Leon Festinger's (1954) social comparison theory, Tory Higgins's (1987) self-discrepancy theory and Hazel Markus's (1977) self-schema theory.

Social comparison theory

In 1954 Leon Festinger published his landmark theory on social comparison processes. According to his social comparison theory, we desire accurate, objective evaluations of our abilities and attitudes. When unable to evaluate ourselves directly, we seek to satisfy this need for self-evaluation through comparison with other people. Unfavourable comparisons (where the other is judged to score higher in the target attribute than oneself) are known as "upward comparisons". Favourable comparisons (where the other is judged as lower on the target attribute) are known as "downward comparisons". This social comparison process may be unconscious, and may be outside volitional control (Miller, 1984). Most people are expected to prefer to make self-enhancing downward comparisons with others where possible (Wilson and Ross, 2000), although Rebecca Collins (1996) argues that some may choose to make upward comparisons in the hope of using the target to guide self-improvement (see also Strahan et al., 2006).

Social comparison theory predicts that people might use images projected by the media as standards for comparison. Upward comparisons with models' bodies (slim and carefully arranged in the most flattering poses) would be expected to lead to unfavourable evaluation of the body of the perceiver, so long as participants considered models to be sufficiently similar to them on relevant dimensions and body image to be self-relevant (Major et al., 1991). Even if images are not similar on all relevant dimensions, and if they are potentially damaging to self-esteem, they may still be chosen for comparison if the information they provide is high in perceived self-relevance. Renee Engeln-Maddox (2005) shows that even though comparisons with beautiful models may not seem logical for most women due to lack of similarity, and may be damaging due to potential to reduce body satisfaction, this needs to be understood within a context in which these images provide valuable information about social evaluation of one's own appearance, and may be seen as inspirational images and comparison targets for self-improvement (see also Halliwell and Dittmar, 2005).

Effects on body satisfaction may be most marked if participants are encouraged to engage in overt comparison between their own bodies and those of the media models (Cattarin et al., 2000), although Stephen Want (2009) has suggested that social comparisons are automatic and may actually be disrupted by experimental suggestions to perform them. Some authors have suggested that men are less likely to make upward comparisons with images of men's bodies than are women because men's bodies have less sociocultural importance than women's (Wykes and Gunter, 2005). However, although men's bodies may still be less salient to them, experimental studies have shown clearly that body dissatisfaction can be increased shortly after viewing idealized models in men (Arbour and Martin-Ginis, 2006; Hargreaves and Tiggemann, 2009; Leit et al., 2002; Lorenzen et al., 2004).

In 2009, Tarin Myers and Janis Crowther conducted a meta-analysis of 156 studies on social comparison and body dissatisfaction. They found strongest evidence for an impact of social comparison in women and in younger people, and most effect when social comparison was measured directly rather than inferred. They conclude that comparing oneself unfavourably to another on the basis of appearance may lead to dissatisfaction with one's own appearance. Social comparison effects are complex, and Emma Halliwell (2012) notes that it is important that researchers capture this complexity in social comparison studies, through focusing on motivations for comparisons as well as measuring comparison processes directly rather than inferring them. She concludes that interventions to improve body image need to address social comparison processes directly, and that we can use what we have learned about how these processes work to promote body satisfaction.

Self-schema theory

Self-schema theory was developed by Hazel Markus in 1977. A self-schema is a person's mental representation of those elements that make him/her distinctive from others, those aspects that constitute a sense of "me". According to Markus, people develop their sense of self through reflecting on their own behaviours, from observing reactions of others to the self, and through processing social information about which aspects of the self are most valued. Self-schemas influence how new incoming information is processed by organizing and guiding the processing of this new information (Hogg and Vaughan, 1995). Self-schema theory predicts that people who were schematic for appearance would be particularly sensitized to body-related media messages, and that information contained in media images would be incorporated into, and would affect, that person's concept of self (Markus et al., 1987).

One of the key aspects of self-schema theory is that it leads to the prediction that particular people may be more sensitive than others to body-related imagery, and more likely to internalize the slender body ideal. According to Markus et al. (1987), body image can become a central defining feature of self-concept for some people, meaning that they become extremely sensitive to additional incoming information about weight, shape and size (including media information and imagery). Thomas Cash and Andrew Labarge's (1996) Appearance Schema Inventory enables researchers to assess the degree of centrality of appearance to people's self-concepts, including items such as "What I look like is an important part of who I am". Women who are high on schematicity for appearance have been shown to have a more negative body image (and also to score lower on self-esteem and mood) than those who are aschematic on appearance (Jung and Lennon, 2009).

Women who are high on appearance schematicity have been found to be particularly sensitive to media imagery relating to the body. Duane Hargreaves and Marika Tiggemann (2002) presented evidence that adolescent girls high in schematicity may be affected more negatively by exposure to appearance-related television advertisements than those lower in this trait. They exposed 195 female and 206 male Australian adolescents to either appearance-related or non-appearance-related television commercials. They found that viewing appearance commercials led to increased schema activation and body dissatisfaction in women compared to the viewing of non-appearance commercials, and the effect was more marked in those higher in appearance schematicity. Male participants showed evidence of increased schema activation, but no significant change in body dissatisfaction. The results of this study provide support for the idea that schema activation may be the underlying process by which the media can increase body dissatisfaction in young women, and for appearance schematicity as a viable explanation for why some women may be more vulnerable to impacts of the media than others. The role of schematicity on men's responses to idealized images is unclear at present, though existing studies suggest that this may not be such an important factor for men. For instance, Daniel Agliata and Stacey Tantleff-Dunn (2004) exposed 158 males to television advertisements containing either ideal male images or neutral images. Participants exposed to ideal images of men's bodies had significantly higher levels of muscle dissatisfaction than those exposed to neutral advertisements, but there was no evidence that schematicity had an impact on body image changes.

Self-discrepancy theory

Self-discrepancy theory (Higgins, 1987) proposes that people's emotional vulnerabilities and motivations result from discrepancies in their patterns of beliefs about themselves. In order to reduce distress and discomfort, individuals are motivated to match their perceived actual self with an ideal self (the person they would ideally like to be) and an ought self (the person they believe that they ought to be through obligation to others). Tory Higgins proposes that a discrepancy between the actual and ideal/ought selves leads to discomfort and body dissatisfaction. Media imagery is conceptualized as part of the range of influences that can mould the ideal self, along with the influence of romantic partners, peers, parents and other significant others in the person's social world (Tantleff-Dunn and Thompson, 1995; Vartanian, 2012).

The main focus of self-discrepancy theory is the emotional reaction caused by lack of match between a person's perceived actual self and what are known as self-guides (ideal and ought selves), and this theory has been related more frequently and successfully to studies of eating disorders than to body image per se (e.g. Higgins et al., 1992). However, some studies have looked at body dissatisfaction within a self-discrepancy framework and have suggested that media imagery may form part of the information used to formulate the ideal self in relation to appearance, and that lack of match with this ideal may cause distress.

Madelaine Altabe and Kevin Thompson (1996) have shown that media imagery can produce emotional reactions in people with greater perceived discrepancies between actual and ideal body image characteristics, and Helga Dittmar and Sarah Howard (2004) have found that body-focused anxiety reactions to thin media images are conditional on having a body ideal that is thinner than one's actual body. Other authors have found that actual-ideal discrepancies are correlated with body dissatisfaction as well as eating disorder symptoms (Strauman *et al.*, 1991; Forston and Stanton, 1992), and that women with high levels of body image self-discrepancy are most likely to engage in social comparison with media images (Bessenoff, 2006). There is good evidence that internalization of the thin ideal, which is likely to coincide with a discrepancy, predicts a negative response to media imagery in terms of body dissatisfaction and concern (Cattarin et al., 2000; Halliwell and Dittmar, 2004; Yamamiya et al., 2005).

Self-discrepancy theory is useful in helping us to understand how and why particular body-related media images may trigger emotional reactions such as distress and body concerns, and how this may in some cases lead to appearance-fixing behaviours to try to rectify the perceived disparity between people's perceived current bodies and their ideal. Unfortunately, most evidence suggest that self-discrepancies result in negative health-related behaviours such as desire for cosmetic surgery and emotional (rather than intuitive) eating. Although self-discrepancies have been linked to exercise motivations, they have not been shown to predict exercise behaviour (Vartanian, 2012).

Body shape role models

It is important to investigate the relative importance of media imagery compared to other sources of social influence; other sources may be more or less salient at particular times, and to particular individuals. Lori Irving (1990), in a study of female college students scoring high on bulimic symptoms, asked her participants to rate the importance of different sources of social pressure. When she ordered their responses by rank, she found that the most powerful source of perceived social pressure for this group was "media", followed by "peers", followed by "family".

Leslie Heinberg and Kevin Thompson (1992) looked specifically at this issue of relevant body image comparison groups. They asked 297 women and men to rate the importance of six different groups. These ranged from particularistic (family and friends) to universalistic (celebrities and US citizens). Women and men put the comparison groups in the same order of importance. The most important group was friends; then came celebrities, classmates, and students; and then US citizens and family. Women with "eating disorders" or body image disturbance were most likely to compare their appearance with that of celebrities. Heinberg and Thompson used these data to argue that media figures are most likely to be used for body image evaluation in women with body image disturbance.

In the 1990s, in a study reported in the original edition of this book (Grogan, 1999), two hundred US college students (and friends of college students) aged 16 to 48 were asked to nominate their body image role models ("Who would you like to look like?"). The sample was made up of equal numbers of men and women. Their responses were content analyzed and coded into four categories: actor, model, sports person, and family member. Participants were split into four age groups: 16 to 19, 20 to 29, 30 to 39, and 40 to 49. Of the men, 23 per cent of the 16- to 19-year-olds had role models who were actors, and 3 per cent had role models who were sportsmen. The rest of the group reported having no role models for body shape. Of the 20- to 29-year-olds, 13 per cent cited actors, 2 per cent sportsmen, and 2 per cent family members (brothers) as role models. In the 30- to 39-year-olds, 31 per cent cited actors as role models, while the rest reported no body image role models. The older men (40 to 49) also reported that they had no particular body image role models. Some of the men reported wanting to look like well-muscled Hollywood actors and sportsmen with high media profiles. Men in the 20- to 29-year-old age group differed from the other groups in proposing family members (usually their older brother, but in some cases their father) as models of how they would like to look.

Of the women, 10 per cent of the 16- to 19-year-olds cited fashion models as role models, 5 per cent cited actresses, 3 per cent cited sportswomen, and 3 per cent a family member (usually the mother). Of the women in their twenties, 9 per cent had role models who were fashion models and 9 per cent named role models who were actresses, while 2 per cent cited sportswomen and 2 per cent cited a friend they would like to look like. The actresses, models and sportswomen chosen were the same as those for the younger women. For women in their thirties, actresses represented role models for 13 per cent of the group, with 7 per cent citing sportswomen and 7 per cent a family member (mother or sister). Of the women in their forties, 17 per cent cited a family member (mother or sister), and the remaining 83 per cent cited no particular role model.

These results suggest that media figures (fashion models, actors/actresses and sports persons) provide body image role models for a significant proportion of men and women under forty. Well-muscled Hollywood actors such as Jean-Claude Van Damme were the chosen model for many men under forty. More men in their thirties cited these actors as role models than in any other age group. For a significant proportion of women in their teens and twenties, fashion models represented how they would like to look. Women in their thirties chose actresses rather than fashion models. As the age of the participants increased they were more likely to choose a family member, such as a sister or their mother, as their role model, rather than a media figure. Clearly, media role models are more important to men and women in the younger age groups. It was also interesting that many participants in each age group did not cite any particular person that they would like to look like. Between 40 and 50 per cent of each group gave "like myself" or "no one in particular" as their response to the question "Who would you like to look like?" Perhaps there was some social desirability effect in operation here. It may be that participants wanted to appear satisfied with the way that they looked, with no need for a media role model. Perhaps they were concerned about not being seen to be unduly influenced by anyone else – or perhaps they really had no particular physical role model to which they compared themselves.

In interview work, this issue was explored further. It is much easier to investigate such issues when people can be asked to detail the reasons for their choices. In interview, girls aged 8 and 13 years reported that they thought that fashion models in magazines were too thin to be attractive (Grogan and Wainwright, 1996):

Girl 1: They look horrible. They're ugly half the time.
Girl 2: Yeah, they are.
Girl 1: I think they do sometimes look too thin. They look anorexic.

Older women aged 16 to 60 also cited fashion models and actresses as their ideal (see Chapter 3), although they also thought that fashion models were too thin. For instance:

They make me sick. They are too thin. But I would kill for one of their bodies.

Most of the women we interviewed present complex views relating to the influence of media models; they aspired to being slim and shapely (like the models) but generally felt that extreme thinness was inappropriate and unhealthy. Women were critical of media portrayal of skinny models and wanted to see more realistic images of models with average-sized bodies in magazines. They were particularly critical of what they saw as double standards projected by magazines:

This is the image you are trying to attain, in every women's magazine. I get [a women's magazine] ... and every month there is an article saying you should like the way that you look. It is OK. But then on the next page there is someone who weighs 120 lb and who is 6 feet tall, and that is not normal. Actually, they are the freaks of nature because that is not normal. And every single month they get all these letters, and they print a lot of them saying, "Why do we never see average-sized models?" Every month there is a letter like that.

It was striking, when listening to women talking in interview about media representations of the female body, how angry and dissatisfied many were with the way that the female body is portrayed in the media. They perceived that the fashion industry tries to manipulate them into feeling insecure about the way that they look.

In general, the women we interviewed want "skinny curves", as one woman put it (Grogan et al., 2013). They want to look slim but curvy, with an "hourglass" shape. Women are also extremely critical of clothes sizing systems that mean that they have to shop in different stores, and of media imagery that pressures them into feeling bad about their bodies. We have found a similar pattern of dissatisfaction in women aged 16 to 60 in interviews in Britain and in the USA between 1990 and 2015. Their experiences challenge conceptions of women as passive "victims" of a system of oppression. The women we have interviewed are aware that the images presented are unrealistic and unhealthy (although they still aspire to look like fashion models in magazines) and are often angry at what they see as the media manipulating them into feeling bad about the way that they look. Women (even the 13-year-olds we interviewed) are critical of the unrealistic images portrayed to them. However, most women still aspire to a very slim ideal, leaving a wide gap between ideal and current body shape for most women. This ambivalence is clear in our interviews with women of all ages. If social comparisons are largely automatic (e.g. Want, 2009), then women may not be making an active choice to make these comparisons. In environments where idealized images are highly prevalent, it might take more cognitive effort to avoid making comparisons than to make them. This may explain the conflicting evidence from interviews and experimental studies, although it requires further research to understand more fully these complex processes.

Boys aged 8 and 13 reported in interview (Grogan and Richards, 2002) that they aspired to the bodies of muscular men on television and in movies. In interview and questionnaire work with male bodybuilders (see Chapter 4) we also found that these men often describe making unfavourable comparisons between the media images of highly muscled men on television and in bodybuilding magazines and their own bodies. In some cases, this was cited as a catalyst in the decision to take anabolic steroids:

> The more I trained, the more magazines I looked at, the bigger I wanted to be ... and there was a TV programme and when I watched these people it made me feel really depressed, I didn't look as good as them, and it had a massive effect on my decision to take steroids.

However, most adult men we have interviewed report a minimal effect of media imagery on their body esteem (Grogan and Richards, 2002). Adults and 16-year-olds were more likely to report that they compared themselves with male friends and wanted to match those who were more muscular. An interesting difference between interviews with men and with women is that adult men tended to see media images as realistic goals. There was a general feeling that they could look like the media images if they wanted to, but that they did not care enough about the way they looked to spend time weight training. Spending time trying to look good was generally thought to be feminine – and therefore inappropriate – behaviour (see Chapter 4). A similar pattern emerged from interviews with 16-year-old boys, who reported that they would like to look more muscular but were insufficiently motivated to change their behaviour to try to become more muscular. The implication was that they had more important things to do:

> I wouldn't mind looking like that. But I wouldn't put myself out to look like it, you know.

Data from interviews, when combined with questionnaire data, suggest that men and women do use media images as standards for comparison to evaluate their own body shape and size. However, women (even young girls) may be critical of the limited range of images, and (usually) see them as unrealistic. Men may aspire to emulate the muscular form of men who represent their body shape ideal, but they are unwilling to admit to putting their energies into trying to build a muscular physique. Bodybuilders (who are seen as inappropriately narcissistic by many) are exceptional in putting time, energy and money (especially those who take anabolic steroids) into the quest for a well-muscled body that matches more closely the media ideal portrayed on television and in bodybuilding magazines. For both men and women, friends and family may be used as body image role models. In interviews women explicitly reported comparing themselves unfavourably to peers. For instance:

> I don't look at movie stars or anything like that. I look at the average person who is smaller than me. Even when I think, "She's really not that pretty," the first thing that hits me is, "She is little," and to me it is like, I would rather look like her. I don't even think she is pretty, but I just want to be slender.

Similar experiences were described by men, although in contrast they wanted to be at least as big as their friends:

> If you've got friends who are, like, quite big in build, you want to be the same as them. Although you might not be able to do anything about it, it's on your conscience all the time. You want to be that sort of size.

Our questionnaire work suggests that media models often become less important standards for comparison, and friends and family more important, as people reach their thirties and forties. Social comparison theory predicts that in order to be effective standards for comparison, people must see the bodies of models and actors/ actresses as in some way similar to their own (Major et al., 1991). Since most fashion models are in their teens and twenties, they would be expected to be less influential on other women once those women are out of that age range. This is borne out by our questionnaire data, in which actresses in the thirty-year-old age range are seen as role models for women in their thirties. Once people are in their forties, family role models become more relevant. Similarly for men, actors in their thirties are most frequently used as role models by men in their thirties. Above that range, no particular role models for body shape are cited. These data suggest that media models are used as standards for comparison for both men and women, but usually only by those who identify in some way with the person whose body is portrayed.

Recent developments

In the mid-1990s there was an interesting new trend for media to discuss their use of slender models. This reflects (or, possibly, has created) a cultural awareness of the potential dangers of presenting young women with images of very thin models. In 1996 the watch manufacturer Omega made headline news in Britain by withdrawing its advertising from *Vogue* magazine, complaining that the models used in the fashion pages were so thin as to appear anorexic. *The Guardian* newspaper of 31 May 1996 quoted the brand manager at Omega as saying:

> I thought it was irresponsible for a leading magazine which should be setting an example to select models of anorexic proportions. It made every effort to accentuate their skeletal appearance. Since Vogue presumably targets an audience which includes young and impressionable females, its creators must surely be aware that they will inevitably be influenced by what laughably passes for fashion in these pages.
>
> (Boseley, 1996: 1)

This trend continued in 1998 when the US media pilloried Calista Flockhart and Sarah Jessica Parker for being what were termed "lollipops" (having heads that looked too large for their thin bodies), and in the UK, in 2000 Victoria Beckham was criticized for looking too thin to be healthy and promoting starvation diets in young women who wanted to look like her (Reid, 2000). This coincided with the *Body Summit* in Britain, set up to discuss the potential link between eating disorders and magazine images of slender women. Around this time newspapers in Britain carried stories about this link ("Thin stars on TV put pressure on the young", *Daily Telegraph*, 31 May 2000; "Thin end of the wedge", *The Guardian*, 21 June 2000). In 2001 various newspaper journalists were discussing the "new athleticism" exemplified by the toned bodies of Beyoncé Knowles, Kelly Rowland and Michelle Williams of the singing group Destiny's Child, noting that there had been a significant change in the acceptability of the extremely thin body shape for women. It was reported that the new aesthetic favoured the muscular, worked-out, strong-looking body rather than a waifish, weak-looking, very thin body. For instance, in Britain Polly Vernon wrote in *The Independent on Sunday* in June 2001:

> The lollipop silhouette long-favoured by the female stars of American sitcoms, which involves disproportionately large heads wobbling atop

stick-thin bodies, does not say rich and it doesn't say clever. It says take me to a clinic. The New Athleticism, however, sends out a rather different set of messages: strong, confident, independent woman.

(Vernon, 2001: 1)

In 2016 the Pirelli Calendar (a trade calendar produced by a UK subsidiary of the Italian Pirelli company, famed for its portrayal of near-naked or naked models) has moved to quite different kinds of models, prompting a great deal of media attention in the UK. The 2016 calendar features fully- or partially-dressed images of women of outstanding professional, social, cultural, sporting and artistic accomplishment, including Amy Schumer, Serena Williams, Yoko Ono and Patti Smith.

This has been hailed as a significant move away from the traditional focus on slender models and actresses (e.g. London, 2015; Sowray, 2015). In 2016 the producers of Barbie dolls have also expanded their range to include "curvy", "tall" and "petite" dolls that represent a wider, and more realistic, range of body types than the traditional thin and busty doll (Sheffield, 2016).

However, it is important not to overestimate the extent of any change. Although some marketing campaigns have challenged the thin, youthful ideal (such as the *Campaign for Real Beauty* sponsored by Dove), magazines continue to use very thin and youthful-looking models (Tiggemann, 2014). Images of men are also as lean and muscular as they were in the 1980s and 1990s, and it has become normal and expected that models and men in glamorous roles in movies and music videos are toned and muscular (Diedrichs, 2012). The disparity between levels of muscularity among British male actors in James Bond films in the 1960s (for instance, Sean Connery in *Thunderball* in 1965 and *Dr No* in 1962) compared with Daniel Craig in *Skyfall* (2012) and *Spectre* (2015) illustrates this point.

In 1997 the model Sophie Dahl made headlines because she modelled designer fashion and she was a (UK) size 14 – the average size for British women. The fact that this was newsworthy shows that the fashion industry had a long way to go before it accepted models that represented realistic images of women's bodies. By 2004 Sophie Dahl had dieted down to a UK size 10, apparently due to embarrassment at being known as the "fat model" (Kay, 2004). Crystal Renn then made headlines for being a size 16 supermodel (Winter, 2014), but has now dieted down to a US size 8 (UK 12).

Most female models and actresses in the twenty-first century are still extremely thin (National Eating Disorders Association, 2013), and those who do not conform to the thin ideal are still criticized as being overweight, even directly following childbirth (Fern et al., 2012). There is growing concern that models are under increased pressure than previously to reduce their weight. Viren Swami and Emilia Szmigielska (2013) compared a sample of fifty-one UK models with a matched sample of non-models, and found that the models evidenced higher drive for thinness than the controls, and that duration of engagement as a professional model was associated with increased drive for thinness.

Clearly, media portrayals of the slender (and muscular, for men) body reflect the current cultural ideology of the body as well as promoting these ideals. However, since the portrayal of such imagery has been shown to reduce body satisfaction and create body concerns, this is surely sufficient reason for advertisers to opt for the use of models in a range of sizes. Although advertisers may argue that only thin models sell products, recent British evidence from a study by Emma Halliwell and Helga Dittmar demonstrates that it is attractiveness, rather than size of models, that is crucial in making associated products attractive to consumers (Halliwell and Dittmar, 2004).

Data collected from a variety of participants, including men and women university students, teachers, advertising professionals, and women with a history of eating disorders shows that average-size female models are rated as equally effective in advertisements as thin models traditionally seen in the media (Halliwell and Diedrichs, 2012). For instance, Philippa Diedrichs and Christina Lee (2011) explored the advertising effectiveness of average-size female fashion models and their impact on the body image of both women and men. A sample of 171 women and 120 men were assigned to conditions where they viewed no models, thin models, or average-size models. Findings showed that both women and men rated average-size models as equally effective compared to thin models. Importantly, for women with average and high levels of internalization of cultural body ideals, exposure to average-size female models was associated with significantly more positive body image compared to exposure to thin models. The authors conclude that their findings suggest that average-size female models can promote positive body image as well as appealing to consumers.

Many feminist writers believe that women (as a group) should reject traditional media conceptions of body image completely (Bordo, 2003) and challenge traditional conceptions of "slim as beautiful". Our interviews with women suggested that many women (who may not consider themselves radical or feminist) are dissatisfied with, and angry about, the narrow range of images portrayed in the popular media.

Various activists and academics are challenging media institutions to try to force change. Singers such as Adele and Beyoncé, actors such as Octavia Spencer and Rebel Wilson, and sports personalities with a high public profile such as Serena Williams (Figure 5.1) have shown how alternative images of beauty can be brought into the mainstream.

Various countries (e.g. Australia, France, the UK) have recommended that consumers should be made aware of digital enhancement of images, and that airbrushing should be avoided where possible (e.g. *Campaign for Body Confidence*, 2016). Activist feminist artists such as the "Guerrilla Girls" in New York (Ryzik, 2015) have attacked the traditional position of women within visual culture as objects of male gaze. The rise of online "girl gamer" communities in the last decade provides additional support for women gamers and possibly protects against negative impacts of idealized models in video games.

Figure 5.1 Serena Williams.

In the UK, the *Campaign for Body Confidence* (2016) is designed to work with advertisers and publishers to convince them to use more realistic images. In the US, Sara Ziff has set up a non-profitmaking organization called the Model Alliance to improve working conditions for models working in the modelling industry. Models Crystal Renn, and others such as modelling agent Chris Gay and Ashley Mears (a former model and now an academic sociologist), are actively involved in trying to force change in the modelling industry (e.g. National Eating Disorders Association, 2013). They suggest moving towards standard samples for fashion shoots that are larger than a US size 0 (UK size 4), ideally to a US size 8. They are also suggesting that customers boycott brands who promote extremely thin ideals in their advertising. Exerting change from within the fashion industry may be a positive way to build a pathway for change, and the next ten years will be a crucial time for observing effects.

Summary

- Western media present the male and female body quite differently. Men tend to be portrayed as slender and muscular whereas women tend to be portrayed as underweight.
- Data from studies of the effects of media images have tended to show that both women and men can feel less good about their bodies after viewing these idealized media images.
- Media figures (fashion models, actors, sports persons) provide role models for a significant proportion of men and women under forty. Young men's body shape role models tended to be well-muscled actors. Women's vary with age, with women in their teens and twenties choosing fashion models and those in their thirties choosing actresses.
- Interview work suggests that women are critical of the narrow range of body shapes presented in the media (which are viewed as unrealistic and unhealthy), and angry at the ways in which they perceive that the media (and in particular the fashion industry) sets up unrealistically thin ideals.
- Most men report that they would not exercise or diet to try to emulate the bodies of slender, muscular actors. Men who bodybuild are exceptional, reporting that unfavourable comparisons with media images of highly muscled men often resulted in increases in weight training as they try to become more like their role models.
- Existing data challenge images of the viewer as primarily passive. Viewers engage critically with media imagery, and are educated consumers of magazine, movie, internet and video-game imagery.
- Despite a critical engagement with appearance ideals, experimental studies indicate that these images still have an immediate negative impact on a large proportion of women and men.
- Research has identified factors that increase women's resilience to appearance ideals.
- Recent moves to challenge media institutions to try to force change are positive, though significant change is yet to be seen.

Bibliography

Agliata, D. and Tantleff-Dunn, S. (2004) 'The impact of media exposure on males' body image', *Journal of Social and Clinical Psychology*, 23 (1), 7–22.

Altabe, M. and Thompson, J.K. (1996) 'Body image: A cognitive self-schema construct?' *Cognitive Therapy and Research*, 20 (2), 171–93.

Andrew, R.J., Tiggemann, M. and Clark, L.S. (2015) 'The protective role of body appreciation against media-induced body dissatisfaction', *Body Image*, 15, 98–104.

Arbour, K.P. and Martin-Ginis, K. (2006) 'Effects of exposure of muscular and hypermuscular images on young men's muscularity dissatisfaction and body dissatisfaction', *Body Image*, 3 (2), 153–62.

Baker, P. (1994) 'Under pressure: What the media is doing to men', *Cosmopolitan*, November, 129–32.

Bartlett, C.P. and Harris, R.J. (2008) 'The impact of body emphasizing video games on image concerns in men and women', *Sex Roles*, 59 (7), 586–601.

Bartlett, C.P., Vowells, C.L. and Saucier, D.A. (2008) 'Meta-analyses of the effects of media images on men's body image concerns', *Journal of Social and Clinical Psychology*, 27 (3), 279–310.

Bessenoff, G. (2006) 'Can the media affect us? Social comparison, self-discrepancy, and the thin ideal', *Psychology of Women Quarterly*, 30 (3), 239–51.

Bordo, S. (2003) *Unbearable weight: Feminism, Western culture, and the body* (10th anniversary edition), Berkeley, CA: University of California Press.

Boseley, S. (1996) '"Anorexic" models cost "Vogue" ads', *The Guardian*, 31 May, 1.

Botta, R.A. (2000) 'The mirror of television: A comparison of black and white adolescents' body image', *Journal of Communication*, 50 (3), 144–59.

Botta, R.A. (2003) 'For your health? The relationship between magazine reading and adolescents' body image and eating disturbances', *Sex Roles*, 48 (9), 389–99.

Briggs, H. (2014) *Selfie body image warning issued*, available online at: http://www.bbc.co.uk/news/health-26952394 [accessed 21 August 2015].

Campaign for Body Confidence (2016) *Our pledge*, available online at: https://campaignforbodyconfidence.wordpress.com/ [accessed 19 January 2016].

Cash, T.F. and Labarge, A.S. (1996) 'Development of the Appearance Schemas Inventory: A new cognitive body-image assessment', *Cognitive Therapy and Research*, 20 (1), 37–50.

Cash, T.F., Cash, D.W. and Butters, J.W. (1983) 'Mirror, mirror on the wall...? Contrast effects and self-evaluations of physical attractiveness', *Personality and Social Psychology*, 9 (3), 359–64.

Cattarin, J., Thompson, J.K., Thomas, C.M. and Williams, R. (2000) 'Body image, mood and televised images of attractiveness: The role of social comparison', *Journal of Social and Clinical Psychology*, 19 (2), 220–39.

Chapkis, W. (1986) *Beauty secrets*, London: Women's Press.

Chapman, R. (1988) 'The great pretender: Variations on the new man theme', in R. Chapman and J. Rutherford (Eds) *Male order: Unwrapping masculinity* (pp. 225–48), London: Lawrence and Wishart.

Chua, T.H.H. and Chang, L. (2015) 'Follow me and like my beautiful selfies: Singapore teenage girls' engagement in self-presentation and peer comparison on social media', *Computers in Human Behaviour*, 55, 190–7.

Cole, J. and Grogan, S. (in preparation) *Women gamers' accounts of the portrayal of female bodies in video games: A qualitative analysis.*

Collins, R. (1996) 'For better or worse: The impact of upward social comparison on self-evaluations', *Psychological Bulletin*, 119 (1), 51–69.

Diedrichs, P.C. (2012) 'Media influences on male body image', in T.F. Cash (Ed.) *Encyclopedia of body image and human appearance* (pp. 547–53), London: Elsevier.

Diedrichs, P.C. and Lee, C. (2011) 'Waif goodbye! Average-size female models promote positive body image and appeal to consumers', *Psychology and Health*, 26 (10), 1273–91.

Dittmar, H. and Howard, S. (2004) 'Thin-ideal internalisation and social comparison tendency as moderators of media models' impact on women's body-focused anxiety', *Journal of Social and Clinical Psychology*, 23 (6), 768–91.

Dittmar, H., Halliwell, E. and Ive, S. (2006) 'Does Barbie make girls want to be thin? The effect of experimental exposure to images of dolls on the body image of 5- to 8-year-old girls', *Developmental Psychology*, 42 (2), 283–92.

Elliot, S. (1994) 'Hunks in trunks hit a gap in the sports market', *The Guardian*, 17 February, 14.

Engeln-Maddox, R. (2005) 'Cognitive responses to idealized media images of women: The relationship of social comparison and critical processing to body image disturbance in college women', *Journal of Social and Clinical Psychology*, 24 (8), 1114–38.

Entertainment Software Association (ESA) (2015) *2015 sales, demographics and usage data: Essential facts about the computer and video game industry*, available online at: www.theesa.com/wp-content/uploads/2015/04/ESA-Essential-Facts-2015.pdf [accessed 11 June 2015].

Ferguson, M. (1985) *Forever feminine: Women's magazines and the cult of femininity*, Aldershot, UK: Gower.

Fern, V.A., Buckley, E. and Grogan, S. (2012) 'Womens' experiences of body image and weight loss after childbirth', *British Journal of Midwifery*, 20 (12), 860–5.

Festinger, L. (1954) 'A theory of social comparison processes', *Human Relations*, 7 (2), 117–40.

Forston, M.T. and Stanton, A.L. (1992) 'Self-discrepancy theory as a framework for understanding bulimic symptomatology and associated distress', *Journal of Social and Clinical Psychology*, 11 (2), 103–18.

Ghaznavi, J. and Taylor, L.D. (2015) 'Bones, body parts, and sex appeal: An analysis of #thinspiration images on popular social media', *Body Image*, 14, 54–61.

Grabe, S., Ward, L.M. and Hyde, J.S. (2008) 'The role of the media in body image concerns among women: A meta-analysis of experimental and correlational studies', *Psychological Bulletin*, 134 (3), 460–76.

Groetz, L.M., Levine, M.P. and Murnen, S.K. (2002) 'The effect of experimental presentation of thin media images on body satisfaction: A meta-analytic review', *International Journal of Eating Disorders*, 31 (1), 1–16.

Grogan, S. (1999) *Body image: Understanding body dissatisfaction in men, women and children*, London: Routledge.

Grogan, S. and Richards, H. (2002) 'Body image: focus groups with boys and men', *Men and Masculinities*, 4 (3), 219–32.

Grogan, S. and Wainwright, N. (1996) 'Growing up in the culture of slenderness: Girls' experiences of body dissatisfaction', *Women's Studies International Forum*, 19 (6), 665–73.

Grogan, S., Williams, Z. and Conner, M. (1996) 'The effects of viewing same gender photographic models on body satisfaction', *Women and Psychology Quarterly*, 20 (4), 569–75.

Grogan, S., Gill, S., Brownbridge, K., Kilgariff, S. and Whalley, A. (2013) 'Dress fit and body image: A thematic analysis of women's accounts during and after trying on dresses', *Body Image*, 10 (3), 380–8.

Halliwell, E. (2012) 'Social comparison theory and body image', in T.F. Cash (Ed.) *Encyclopedia of body image and human appearance* (pp. 751–7), London: Elsevier.

Halliwell, E. (2013) 'The impact of thin idealized media images on body satisfaction: Does body appreciation protect women from negative effects?' *Body Image*, 10 (4), 509–14.

Halliwell, E. and Diedrichs, P. (2012) 'Influence of the media', in N. Rumsey and D. Harcourt (Eds) *The Oxford handbook of the psychology of appearance* (pp. 217–38), Oxford: Oxford University Press.

Halliwell, E. and Dittmar, H. (2004) 'Does size matter? The impact of model's body size on women's body-focused anxiety and advertising effectiveness', *Journal of Social and Clinical Psychology*, 23 (1), 104–22.

Halliwell, E. and Dittmar, H (2005) 'The role of self-improvement and self-evaluation motives in social comparisons with idealised female bodies in the media', *Body Image*, 2 (3), 249–62.

Hargreaves, D. and Tiggemann, M. (2002) 'The effect of television commercials on mood and body dissatisfaction: The role of appearance-schema activation', *Journal of Social and Clinical Psychology*, 21 (3), 287–308.

Hargreaves, D.A. and Tiggemann, M. (2009) 'Muscular ideal media images and men's body image: Social comparison processing and individual vulnerability', *Psychology of Men and Masculinity*, 10 (2), 109–19.

Heinberg, L. and Thompson, J.K. (1992) 'Social comparison: Gender, target importance ratings, and relation to body image disturbance', *Journal of Social Behavior and Personality*, 7, 335–44.

Heinberg, L. and Thompson, J.K. (1995) 'Body image and televised images of thinness and attractiveness: A controlled laboratory investigation', *Journal of Social and Clinical Psychology*, 14 (4), 325–38.

Heywood, W., Patrick, K., Smith, A.M.A. et al. (2012) 'Who gets tattoos? Demographic and behavioural correlates of ever being tattooed in a representative sample of men and women', *Annals of Epidemiology*, 22 (1), 51–6.

Higgins, E.T. (1987) 'Self-discrepancy: A theory relating self and affect', *Psychological Review*, 94 (3), 319–40.

Higgins, E.T., Klein, R. and Strauman, T. (1992) 'Self-concept discrepancy theory: A psychological model for distinguishing among different aspects of depression and anxiety', *Social Cognition*, 3 (1), 51–76.

Hogg, M.A. and Vaughan, G.M. (1995) *Social psychology*, Hemel Hempstead, UK: Prentice-Hall Europe.

Irving, L. (1990) 'Mirror images: Effects of the standard of beauty on the self- and body-esteem of women exhibiting varying levels of bulimic symptoms', *Journal of Social and Clinical Psychology*, 9 (2), 230–42.

Jung, J. and Lennon, S.J. (2003) 'Body image, appearance self-schema, and media images', *Family and Consumer Sciences Research Journal*, 32 (1), 27–51.

Kay, R. (2004) 'Now it's size six Sophie', *Daily Mail*, 23 August, 1.

Leit, R.A., Gray, J.J. and Pope, H.G.J. (2002) 'The media's representation of the ideal male body: A cause for muscle dysmorphia?' *International Journal of Eating Disorders*, 31 (3), 334–8.

Levine, M.P. (2012) 'Media influences on female body image', in T.F. Cash (Ed.) *Encyclopedia of body image and human appearance* (pp. 540–6), London: Elsevier.

London, B. (2016) *A Pirelli calendar with no nude models?* Available online at: www.dailymail.co.uk/femail/article-3339518/Serena-Williams-Patti-Smith-Amy-Schumer-star-Pirelli-Calendar-ditches-models-history-making-2016-edition-highlights-inspiring-women.html [accessed 1 December 2015].

Lorenzen, L.A., Grieve, F.G. and Thomas, A. (2004) 'Exposure to muscular male models decreases men's body satisfaction', *Sex Roles*, 51 (11–12), 743–8.

Mabe, A.G., Forney, K.J. and Keel, P.K. (2014) 'Do you "like" my photo? Facebook use maintains eating disorder risk', *International Journal of Eating Disorders*, 47 (5), 516–23.

Major, B., Testa, M. and Bylsma, W. (1991) 'Responses to upward and downward social comparisons: The impact of esteem relevance and perceived control', in J. Suls and T. Wills (Eds) *Social comparison: Contemporary theory and research* (pp. 237–60), Hillsdale, NJ: Erlbaum.

Markus, H. (1977) 'Self-schema and processing information about the self', *Journal of Personality and Social Psychology*, 35 (2), 63–78.

Markus, H., Hamill, R. and Sentis, K. (1987) 'Thinking fat: Self-schemas for body-weight and the processing of weight-relevant information', *Journal of Applied Social Psychology*, 17 (1), 50–71.

Martins, N., Williams, D.C., Harrison, K. and Ratan, R.A. (2009) 'A content analysis of female body imagery in video games', *Sex Roles*, 61 (11), 824–36.

Miller, C.T. (1984) 'Self schemas, gender and social comparison: A clarification of the related attributes hypothesis', *Journal of Personality and Social Psychology*, 46 (6), 1222–9.

Mishkind, M., Rodin, J., Silberstein, L. and Striegel-Moore, R. (1986) 'The embodiment of masculinity: Cultural, psychological, and behavioral dimensions', *American Behavioral Scientist*, 29 (5), 545–62.

Mort, F. (1988) 'Boys' own? Masculinity, style and popular culture', in R. Chapman and J. Rutherford (Eds) *Male order: Unwrapping masculinity*, London: Lawrence and Wishart.

Myers, P. and Biocca, F. (1992) 'The elastic body image: The effects of television advertising and programming on body image distortions in young women', *Journal of Communication*, 42 (3), 108–33.

Myers, T.A. and Crowther, J.H. (2009) 'Social comparison as a predictor of body dissatisfaction: A meta-analytic review', *Journal of Abnormal Psychology*, 118 (4), 683–98.

National Eating Disorders Association (2013) *Panel highlights wide range of reforms needed in the modeling industry*, available online at: www.nationaleatingdisorders.org/blog/panel-highlights-wide-range-reforms-needed-modeling-industry [accessed 20 December 2015].

Oxford Dictionaries Online. (2015) *Definition of Selfie*, available online at: www.oxforddictionaries.com/definition/english/selfie [accessed 25 August 2015].

Reid, S. (2000) 'Spot the lollipop ladies', *The Sunday Times Style Magazine*, 7 May, 10–11.

Rhodes, E. (2004) *Investigating body piercing: Lived experience and the theory of planned behaviour*, unpublished MSc Health Psychology thesis, Staffordshire University.

Ridolfi, D.R. and Vander Wal, J.S. (2008) 'Eating Disorders Awareness Week: The effectiveness of a one-time body image dissatisfaction prevention session', *Eating Disorders*, 16 (5), 428–43.

Rothery, L. (2015) *An investigation into young people's experiences of selfies in relation to Self-esteem and body image*, unpublished undergraduate dissertation, Manchester Metropolitan University, UK.

Ryzik, M. (2015) *The Guerrilla Girls: After 3 decades, still rattling art world cages*, available online at: www.nytimes.com/2015/08/09/arts/design/the-guerrilla-girls-after-3-decades-still-rattling-art-world-cages.html?_r=0 [accessed 15 December 2015].

Salter, A. and Blodgett, B. (2012) 'Hypermasculinity and dickwolves: The contentious role of women in the new gaming public', *Journal of Broadcasting and Electronic Media*, 56 (3), 401–16.

Schulman, R.G., Kinder, B.N., Powers, P.S., Prange, M. and Glenhorn, A. (1986) 'The development of a scale to measure cognitive distortions in bulimia', *Journal of Personality Assessment*, 50 (4), 630–9.

Sheffield, H. (2016) *Barbie adds 'tall', 'curvy' and 'petite' body styles*, available online at: www.independent.co.uk/news/business/news/barbie-adds-tall-curvy-and-petite-body-styles-a6839001.html [accessed 28 January 2016].

Sherman, A.M. and Zurbriggen, E.L. (2014) '"Boys can be anything": Effect of Barbie play on girls' career cognitions', *Sex Roles*, 70 (5), 195–208.

Smith D., Rutty, M.C. and Olrich, T. (in press) 'Muscle dysmorphia and anabolic-androgenic steroid use', in M. Hall, S. Grogan and B. Gough (Eds) *Chemically modified bodies: The use of diverse substances for appearance enhancement*, London: Palgrave Macmillan.

Smolak, L. (2004) 'Body image in children and adolescents: Where do we go from here?' *Body Image*, 1 (1), 15–28.

Sowray, B. (2015) *Meet the not-so-naked Pirelli Calendar girls for 2016*, available online at: www.telegraph.co.uk/fashion/people/2016-pirelli-calendar/ [accessed 1 December 2015].

Stice, E., Spangler, D. and Agras, S. (2001) 'Exposure to media-portrayed thin-ideal images adversely affects vulnerable girls: A longitudinal experiment', *Journal of Social and Clinical Psychology*, 20 (3), 270–88.

Strahan, E.J., Wilson, A.E., Cressman, K.E. and Buote, V.M. (2006) 'Comparing to perfection: How cultural norms for appearance affect social comparisons and self-image', *Body Image*, 3 (3), 211–28.

Strauman, T.J., Vookle, J., Berenstein, V. and Chaiken, S. (1991) 'Self-discrepancies and vulnerability to body dissatisfaction and disordered eating', *Journal of Personality and Social Psychology*, 61 (6), 946–56.

Sylvia, Z., King, T.J. and Morse, B.J. (2014) 'Virtual ideals: The effect of video game play on male body image', *Computers in Human Behavior*, 37, 183–8.

Swami, V. (2012) 'Written on the body? Individual differences between British adults who do and do not obtain a first tattoo', *Scandinavian Journal of Psychology*, 53 (5), 407–12.

Swami, V. and Harris, A.S. (2012) 'Body art: Tattooing and piercing', in T.F. Cash (Ed.) *Encylopedia of body image and human appearance* (pp. 58–65), London: Elsevier.

Swami, V. and Szmigielska, E. (2013) 'Body image concerns in professional fashion models: Are they really an at-risk group?' *Psychiatry Research*, 207 (1–2), 113–17.

Tantleff-Dunn, S. and Thompson, J.K. (1995) 'Romantic partners and body image disturbance: Further evidence for the role of perceived-actual disparities', *Sex Roles*, 33 (9), 589–605.

Tiggemann, M. (2006) 'The role of media exposure in adolescent girls' body dissatisfaction and drive for thinness: Prospective results', *Journal of Social and Clinical Psychology*, 25 (5), 523–41.

Tiggemann, M. (2014) 'The status of media effects on body image research: Commentary on articles in the themed issue on body image and media', *Media Psychology*, 17 (2), 127–33.

Tiggemann, M. and Miller, J. (2010) 'The internet and adolescent girls' weight satisfaction and drive for thinness', *Sex Roles*, 63 (1), 79–90.

Tiggemann, M. and Slater, A. (2013) 'NetGirls: The internet, Facebook, and body concern in adolescent girls', *International Journal of Eating Disorders*, 46 (6), 630–3.

Tiggemann, M. and Slater, A. (2014) 'NetTweens: The internet and body image concerns in preteenage girls', *The Journal of Early Adolescence*, 34 (5), 606–20.

Tiidenberg, K. (2014) 'Bringing sexy back: Reclaiming the body aesthetic via self-shooting', *Cyberpsychology: Journal of Psychosocial Research on Cyberspace*, 8, 1.

Tiidenberg, K. and Cruz, E.G. (2015) 'Selfies, image and the re-making of the body', *Body and Society*, 21 (4), 77–102.

Vartanian, L.R. (2012) 'Self-discrepancy theory and body image', in T.F. Cash (Ed.) *Encylopedia of body image and human appearance* (pp. 711–17), London: Elsevier.

Vernon, P. (2001) 'Lean, clean and maybe a little mean – 21st century woman is kicking sand in the face of the waif', *The Independent on Sunday: Life Etc. Supplement*, 24 June, 1.

Viner, K. (1997) 'The new plastic feminism', *The Guardian*, 4 July, 5.

Want, S (2009) 'Meta-analytic moderators of experimental exposure to media portrayals of women on female appearance satisfaction: Social comparisons as automatic processes', *Body Image*, 6, 257–269.

Williams, D., Martins, N., Consalvo, M. and Ivory, J. (2009) 'The virtual consensus: Representation of gender, race and age in video games', *New Media and Society*, 11, 815–34.

Wilson, A.E. and Ross, M. (2000) 'The frequency of temporal self and social comparisons in people's personal appraisals', *Journal of Personality and Social Psychology*, 78 (5), 928–42.

Winter, K. (2104) *I wanted people to question the dangerous lengths people go to to attain beauty*, available online at: www.dailymail.co.uk/femail/article-2727727/-Former-anorexic-turned-plus-size-model-Crystal-Renn-wrote-memoirs-23.html#ixzz3u17pehYS [accessed 14 August 2014].

Wykes, M. and Gunter, B. (2005) *The media and body image*, London: Sage.

Yamamiya, Y., Cash, T.F., Melnyk, S.E., Posavak, H.D. and Posavac, S.S. (2005) 'Women's exposure to thin-and-beautiful media images: Body image effects of media-ideal internalisation and impact-reduction interventions', *Body Image*, 2 (1), 74–80.

6

AGE, ETHNICITY, SOCIAL CLASS, AND SEXUALITY

Previous chapters have identified gender-related differences in body image, and specifically in body dissatisfaction. The participants in most studies have been groups of young, white college students of unspecified socioeconomic status and sexuality. Although most psychological research relies on this age group due to convenience for the academic investigator (Henrich et al., 2010), the results are necessarily limited in generalizability.

This chapter focuses on studies that have compared groups differing in age, social class, ethnicity and sexuality. First, evidence for changes in body dissatisfaction throughout the life span will be explored, to identify critical periods for dissatisfaction and to look at development and change in body dissatisfaction for women and men. This will be followed by a discussion of the historical links between "slenderness" and the middle and upper classes, with a review of studies of social class differences in body dissatisfaction. Following this, work on the associations of ethnicity with body satisfaction will be evaluated, considering in particular the negative effects of white Western values on body image in other subcultures. Next the impact of sexuality on body image will be investigated, looking at differential pressures on men and women to be sexually attractive and establishing links between heterosexual, gay and lesbian subcultures and body image. Finally, some of the intersections between these key demographic variables will be explored.

Body image across the life span

Preadolescence

Research from psychology, sociology and gender studies has suggested that boys and girls become dissatisfied with their bodies before adolescence, that girls use similar discourses of embodiment to adult women, and that, given a free choice, girls from age 5 years choose thinner ideal body sizes than their perceived current size. In recent work John and Harriet Worobey (2014) have shown that US girls aged 3½ to 5½ years assigned more positive characteristics to a thin or average-sized doll than to a plumper doll, suggesting significant preferences for slenderness even at pre-school age. In her classic work on the "culture of slenderness", Kim Chernin (1983) reports that preadolescent girls imitate the discourse of older women, expressing body dissatisfaction and concern over weight gain.

In a British study conducted in the 1990s, Nicola Wainwright and I found that girls as young as 8 years old reported body dissatisfaction (Grogan and Wainwright, 1996). We had been unable to find any study in the literature that asked girls and female adolescents to describe their experiences of dissatisfaction with their body shape and size. It seemed to us that this was the most valid way to try to understand how girls and female adolescents felt about their bodies. Our experience of talking with adult women had suggested that many women remembered feeling under pressure to be slim from primary school onward. We wanted to explore body image with young women who could share their experiences with us, rather than investigating memories of such experiences with adult women. In our study we carried out two focus groups – one with a group of 8-year-olds, and one with a group of 13-year-olds. The results provided some interesting insights into these young women's experiences and beliefs about their bodies, dieting, exercise and food.

The 8-year-olds agreed that they wanted to be thin, both now and when they grew up. When asked whether they worried about how they looked, they said that they worried about getting fat. When they were asked how they would like to look when they were older, they were quite clear that they wanted to be thin. When asked about their satisfaction with their present body shape, two of the 8-year-old girls said that they felt thin (and were satisfied with their weight), and two felt fat (and were dissatisfied). When asked what they would change about their bodies, both the girls who expressed dissatisfaction said they would want to lose weight.

> Interviewer: Is there anything you would like to do to change your body shape?
> Girl 3: Lose weight.
> Interviewer: Would you like to lose weight?
> Girl 3: Yeah.
> Girl 1: Lose weight.
> Girl 3: You're thin enough.
> Girl 1: I'm fat.
> Girl 2: Look at your legs.
> Girl 1: They're fat.

These results provided direct evidence that these young women were dissatisfied with their body shape and size, and showed that girls as young as 8 years old reported dissatisfaction with their body weight and shape and had a preference for an acceptably slim body. Their accounts suggested that they objectified and criticized their bodies, and that girls from primary-school age onward are sensitive to cultural pressures to conform to a limited range of acceptable body shapes.

Gemma Tatangelo and Lina Ricciardelli (2015) have suggested that girls expect to be evaluated on their appearance and are often self-critical when comparing themselves with their peers. Although the majority of the 8- to 10-year-old girls who took part in their interviews said that they did not make comparisons between their bodies and the bodies of others, about half made explicit social comparisons between their attractiveness and the appearance of other girls, including reference to their weight and body shape. When talking about the impacts of these kinds of body-related social comparisons for other girls, the majority reported that making these kinds of comparison would be negative, and likely to make the other girl sad, jealous or unhappy. These appearance-related comparisons were more common than in focus groups and interviews with boys in the same age group.

In work where girls have been asked to choose "ideal" and "current" figures from age-appropriate figure drawings, researchers based in Britain, Australia and the USA have found that girls from the age of 9 years old tend to choose thinner ideals than their current figures (e.g. Tiggemann and Pennington, 1990). More recently Helen Truby and Susan Paxton (2002) used the Children's Body Image Scale which comprises age-appropriate photographic images rather than silhouette figures, and found that 48 per cent of the 7- to 12-year-old girls in their Australian sample wanted to be thinner compared to only 10 per cent who wanted to be heavier.

It has been suggested that body dissatisfaction and desire to be thinner may start even younger. Williamson and Delin (2001) have presented evidence that girls as young as 5 years show a significant tendency to prefer thinner figures than their current size and to be significantly less satisfied with their body size than are 5-year-old boys, and there is growing evidence that 5-year-old girls are aware of calorie counting as a means to lose weight (Wheatley, 2006).

There are some difficulties associated with measuring body satisfaction through figure preferences in children younger than 8 years, making it difficult to draw conclusions with confidence about children in the 5- to 8 age group. Many studies have failed to find the expected correlation between children's "current" figure choice and their objectively measured size, casting doubt on the validity of this task with children in this younger age range (Smolak, 2004), so although figure and photographic rating scales produce an indication of girls' body satisfaction from age 7 years (Truby and Paxton, 2002; Ricciardelli, McCabe, Mussap and Holt, 2009), work on younger girls is less convincing.

Recently there has been an increase in work on body image in boys, partly fuelled by concern about increases in eating problems in men and potential health risks associated with the drive to become more muscular (Cafri et al., 2005; Ricciardelli and McCabe, 2004). Studies have also shown that as many as 50 per cent of preadolescent boys, aged as young as 8 years old, are concerned about both leanness and muscularity and place importance on having a fit-looking body (Ricciardelli and Williams, in press).

In an early study of boys' body image published in the 1980s, Michael Maloney and colleagues (1989) at the University of Ohio carried out an interesting study on a large sample of US boys and girls. Of the boys, they found (based on questionnaire data) that 31 per cent of 9-year-olds, 22 per cent of 10-year-olds, 44 per cent of

11-year-olds and 41 per cent of 12-year-olds wanted to be thinner. They found that 31 per cent of boys had tried to lose weight (36 per cent at the 9-year level), 14 per cent had dieted (27 per cent at the 9-year level), and 37 per cent had exercised to try to lose weight (44 per cent at the 9-year level). They concluded that for many boys and girls, body shape concerns start before adolescence. This work has been supported by other research suggesting that dieting is common in boys as young as 8 years old (Robinson et al., 2001).

The extent and direction of body dissatisfaction may be different in boys and girls; although some boys may want to be thinner (following the same pattern as girls), some may want to be broader and more muscular. For instance, one study found that although 35.5 per cent of boys wanted to be thinner, 19.4 per cent wanted to be heavier (Schur et al., 2000).

Lina Ricciardelli and Marita McCabe (2001) found that there is some variation in numbers of boys who are dissatisfied with their bodies, ranging from 30 per cent to 78 per cent, and that the majority wanted a larger body size. In a further review of literature published since 2001, Lina Ricciardelli and colleagues have reported that specific estimates of the numbers of preadolescent boys who desire a thinner body range from 27 to 47 per cent, while the number of boys who want to be larger ranges from 15 to 44 per cent (Ricciardelli, McCabe, Mussap and Holt, 2009). Ricciardelli et al. report that estimates of the numbers of boys desiring a larger body size were similar to those reported in their 2001 review, whereas a lower number of boys wanted to be thinner than in their previous review.

Interview work has allowed us to explain in more detail which aspects of body shape and size provoke most concern. This work has demonstrated that young boys represent adult body shape ideals, and present negative accounts of overweight. In the late 1990s Nicola Wainwright ran focus groups with boys aged 8 in which they were asked about their body shape ideals (Grogan et al., 1997; see also Grogan and Richards, 2002). She found that the 8-year-old boys wanted to be muscular when they grew up, and had role models who were well-muscled:

Interviewer: When you are in your twenties, how would you like to look?
All: Muscly!

This supports more recent survey work by Lina Ricciardelli and colleagues suggesting that boys are likely to attribute importance to muscles (Ricciardelli and McCabe, 2001; Holt and Ricciardelli, 2002). None of the boys had dieted, although they were clear what it meant to diet:

Interviewer: Do you know what it means to be on a diet?
Boy 4: Yeah, you don't eat as much.
Boy 2: And you don't eat any fat.
Interviewer: Have any of you lot been on a diet?
Boy 3: No way.
Boy 2: No.

They all exercised to some extent, and saw exercise as a way to avoid getting fat:

Interviewer: So do you exercise?
Boy 1: Um, sometimes.
Boy 3: A bit.
Boy 4: I always do it.

These results suggest that these 8-year-old boys shared body shape ideals with teenagers and young men in their early twenties. They wanted to be slim (they were fearful of being fat) and muscular (but not too muscular). The focus groups supported suggestions that body shape concerns start before adolescence. None of the boys had dieted, but they would diet or exercise to lose weight should weight become a problem. Body shape role models for these boys were television and movie celebrities, rather than their friends (who presumably were still too young to sport the culturally favoured, postpubertal muscular body).

In 2006 Vivienne Hopkins carried out individual interviews and focus groups with preadolescent and postadolescent boys in the UK, exploring body satisfaction, body idealization, attributional style and sociocultural influences on body image (Hopkins, 2006). She found that the preadolescent boys are generally positive about being moderate sized (rather than plump or thin), and that muscularity is linked with being fit and "cool". Plump and skinny boys were perceived negatively. In one group, the most "uncool" boy in their class at school is described as "[o]verweight. He might not do as much sport because he is lazy and a bit overweight". In another group, the least "cool" boy is described as "very weedy" and lacking in muscles:

Likes trying to show off his muscles when he really doesn't have any. Like his shoulders ... he says, "Look at my shoulders" ... and then they are like pancakes.

Clearly, muscularity was important to these preadolescent boys, supporting other work suggesting that boys in this age range idealize a muscular body shape (e.g. Grogan and Richards, 2002). However, there is a limit to the degree of muscularity that is acceptable, and extremely muscular body types are not idealized because of fears that these would make them look fat: "not too much though, or you will look like ... fat". Body satisfaction was linked by these boys to body function and specifically to sporting ability, supporting suggestions from other authors that sport provides a socially appropriate context for boys to talk about their bodies (e.g. Ricciardelli et al., 2006). For instance:

Interviewer: So can you describe your bodies now?
Boy A: Well, I am not exactly slim. I'm quite good at tackling. I'm not that good at playing rugby. I'm quite good at knocking people over, but I'm not overweight, but I...
Boy B: I'd say I was reasonably fit.

More recently, Gemma Tatangelo and Lina Ricciardelli (2013) ran interviews and focus groups with Australian boys between 8 and 10 years old (mean age 9.2 years). They found that sport and fitness were an important part of the boys' body ideals, supporting previous work. Boys made frequent use of sports and physical ability-related social comparisons when talking about their bodies and the bodies of others. Tatangelo and Ricciardelli argue that this focus on sport and physical abilities reflects gendered trends in children's social comparison that are promoted through socialization processes; boys are trained to expect to be evaluated in relation to strength and athleticism, whereas girls are socialized to expect to be evaluated on their appearance. In a more recent study the same authors have shown that when viewing media images, preadolescent boys tended to view them as inspiring rather than deflating, identifying with their favourite celebrities and wanting to emulate them. For instance, one of their participants says that looking at pictures of favourite celebrities "would make you feel good because you could be slowly looking like the person, just say it's the person you want to look like, well you're starting to look like them" (Tatangelo and Ricciardelli, 2015: 8).

Taken together, results from preadolescent boys and girls suggest that both genders are fearful of becoming fat and want to conform to the slender ideal (although girls want to avoid muscularity and boys aspire to a muscular ideal). Accounts from boys and girls are very similar to the accounts from adults reported in Chapters 3 and 4. Body shape ideals are similar to adults, as are role models.

Adolescence

There has been a lot of interest in body satisfaction in adolescence. Adolescent girls in Western societies are subject to powerful cultural pressures to be very thin (O'Dea and Cinelli, in press), and many authors have argued that adolescence is a time when body image concern in young women is at its peak due to physical changes in shape that may move girls away from a slender ideal (Burgess et al., 2006). Researchers working in this area have tended to infer body satisfaction from surveys of dieting or from discrepancy between current and ideal shape on age-relevant silhouette figures. It has been suggested that many adolescent girls say that they feel fat and want to lose weight (e.g. Nichter, 2000). Body dissatisfaction does not seem to motivate healthy weight management behaviours in adolescent girls, but it has been linked with very unhealthy weight control behaviours and low levels of physical activity. Dianne Neumark-Sztainer and colleagues (2006) followed a group of 2,516 adolescents over a five-year period, finding that, for young women, lower body satisfaction predicted higher levels of dieting, binge eating, lower levels of exercise, and very unhealthy weight control behaviours. When they had controlled for weight (BMI) they found that dieting, very unhealthy weight control practices and low levels of exercise were still predicted by low body satisfaction (also see O'Dea and Cinelli, in press).

In focus groups with adolescent girls (Grogan and Wainwright, 1996), we found that they expressed a desire to be of average size, neither too thin nor too fat:

Adolescent girl 3: Not too fat.
Adolescent girl 4: Not too thin.
Adolescent girl 2: Normal.

However, they were envious of those of their friends who were skinny and who ate "fattening" foods like chocolate and did not put on weight. They shared stories about skinny people they knew who could eat anything they liked and how they envied them:

Adolescent girl 3: Well, my friend used to come round all the time, but she's a right fussy eater and she's right skinny, but she eats a right lot of chocolate bars and everything.
Adolescent girl 2: I hate it when really skinny people say, "Oh, I'm fat." They just do it to annoy you.

These 13-year-olds expressed a dislike for muscles, which they saw as inappropriate for women because they made women look too masculine:

Adolescent girl 4: I don't like women bodybuilders 'cos they're right...
Adolescent girl 1: Fat and uhhh.
Adolescent girl 2: It's all right for them to have a few muscles, but not like...
Adolescent girl 4: Be like a man.
Adolescent girl 2: Just looks totally...
Adolescent girl 1: Out of shape.

The findings suggest that these young women have learned about the acceptability of the slim body in Western society (and the unacceptability of having a body that does not fit the slim ideal). What struck us most when reading the transcripts was the similarity between the accounts given by these 13-year-olds and those given by the adults in the interviews cited in Chapter 3. Adolescent women and girls may find it particularly difficult to challenge dominant cultural representations of femininity at a time when they are still learning about what it means to be a woman in Western society, and when they are experiencing changes in body shape and size as they move into adulthood. Of course, talking about being fat can be a mechanism for gaining social approval and reassurance among girls and adult women (Martz, Curtin and Bazzini, 2012).

In *Fat Talk*, Mimi Nichter (2000) reports results of interviews and focus groups carried out with 240 14- to 15-year-old girls in the USA as part of the Teen Lifestyle Project. She discusses patterns of talk in which the statement from one girl that she is fat can act as a bonding mechanism between adolescent girls, and also prompt reassurance from other girls that she is not fat:

Participation in fat talk was a critical component of peer-group membership and made girls appear no better than their friends. By affirming that their friends were not fat, girls helped one another keep their self-effacing thoughts about their bodies in check.

(Nichter, 2000: 183)

However, the existence of "fat talk" does not mean that the concerns expressed are not real concerns for these young women. Mimi Nichter (2000) reports that her young women respondents engaged in continual personal surveillance to check how they matched up to the cultural ideal, which had a significant impact on the rest of their lives:

As a result of being preoccupied with their physical selves, particularly during early adolescence, girls often fail to understand that they are far more than how they look. The comparisons that they draw between themselves and imagined or real others direct their energy away from more meaningful pursuits.

(Nichter, 2000: 183–4)

There has been a significant increase in studies investigating body image in adolescent boys in the twenty-first century, linked with concerns about unhealthy body-change behaviours such as anabolic steroid use in adolescents. It is estimated that between 40 per cent and 70 per cent of adolescent boys are dissatisfied with some aspect of their bodies (Ricciardelli and Williams, in press). Estimates of the percentage of boys who have used anabolic steroids range from 1 per cent to 12 per cent (Ricciardelli and McCabe, 2004), depending on where and when the study was undertaken. Matthew Dunn and Victoria White (2011) found that 2.4 per cent of their Australian sample of 12- to 17-year-olds had used steroids. Marla Eisenberg and colleagues (2012) studied a similar sample of 2,793 US adolescent boys (mean age 14.4 years) and found that 5.9 per cent had used steroids. As discussed in Chapter 4, anabolic steroid use is linked with serious health problems (see also Cafri et al. (2005) and Ricciardelli and Williams (in press) for reviews).

Studies of figure choices have shown that about a third of boys want to be larger and about a third want to be thinner (Ricciardelli and McCabe, 2003). One of the problems with most figure choice work is that it is not possible for boys to indicate whether they would like to be more muscular or to have more body fat (although the latter is rare). Harrison Pope et al.'s (2000) somatomorphic matrix (see Chapter 4) has made it possible to differentiate between wanting to be plumper and wanting to be more muscular, and work thus far has shown that a significant proportion of boys want to be more muscular. In *The Adonis Complex*, Harrison Pope reports results of a study with 11- to 17-year-old boys at a summer camp in the USA. On average, boys of all ages chose an ideal with about 35 lb more muscle than their current body size. Other work has also shown that many adolescent boys are dissatisfied with their muscle size, strength, shoulders, biceps and chests, and generally desire more muscle in these areas while maintaining a generally lean physique (McCabe and Ricciardelli, 2001).

In interviews with 13-year-old boys, we found that their body shape ideals are very similar to adult men's ideals (Grogan et al., 1997; Grogan and Richards, 2002). Thirteen-year-old boys said that their ideal body shape for a man was of average build and fairly muscular, bringing their ideal into line with that of the adult men whose accounts are reported in Chapter 4:

Interviewer: What is your ideal shape for a man, say, when you are in your twenties?
Adolescent boy 1: Muscular legs.
Adolescent boy 2: Muscular.
Adolescent boy 3: Good tan, like.
Adolescent boy 4: Like a footballer. Just medium build.
Adolescent boy 1: Not fat, not right thin, just medium.

They did not want to become too muscular because they believed that this could lead to getting fat in later life:

Adolescent boy 1: [Bodybuilders] will get fat anyway 'cos when you get older all muscles turn to fat. … If you have too much muscle, you're gonna be fat when you're older unless you can get rid of it.

Friends with muscular bodies were mentioned explicitly as a relevant comparison group, and unfavourable comparisons were said to lead to unhappiness. This suggests that body image is important for these young men's self-esteem:

Adolescent boy 3: And if you're hanging around with a mate who is right muscular and stuff and he's got a right good body shape, all women are hanging round him, that would depress you a bit, that would.

None of them had tried dieting, although they knew about the different diets available and three of them had family members who had dieted, but if they became overweight, two of them would diet:

Interviewer: So, would any of you do step-ups?
Adolescent boy 2: Not unless I were right fat, about 20 stone [280 1b].
Adolescent boy 1: I wouldn't exercise to lose weight then…
Adolescent boy 2: I'd just diet.
Adolescent boy 3: I wouldn't, I'd exercise.

These data suggest that adolescents present a slender, muscular ideal that is very similar to the adult male ideal, as suggested by Marita McCabe and Lina Ricciardelli (2001). They are fearful of becoming fat, and would diet or exercise to avoid becoming overweight. Looking good is linked with happiness, and adolescents explicitly compare their body shapes with those of their friends (who were one of their body shape comparison groups, along with well-muscled actors). Clearly, body image is important to young men as well as young women. These adolescents have a clear ideal that corresponds to the adult male ideal that we identified in interview work with men (see Chapter 4). These boys resist representing men's bodies, including their own bodies, as objects of aesthetic interest by deflecting discussion of how bodies looked into discussion of what they can do (looking "athletic" or "fit"). They are generally reticent about talking about the ways that their bodies look and are much more comfortable when talking about what a fit-looking body can do. These findings are supported by interviews with Australian adolescent boys reported by Lina Ricciardelli and colleagues (2006), who suggest that sport provides a context for discussing body image, and that the attributes boys like about their bodies are synonymous with those they associate with being successful at sport.

Vivienne Hopkins (2006) found that her adolescent respondents (mean age 14 years 7 months) described similar ideals to the young British men in the focus groups described above. They wanted to be muscular but not too muscular, and to reduce their body fat. For instance:

Interviewer: Is there anything you would like to change?
Adolescent boy 5: I'd like to lose a bit of fat and get more muscly. My legs aren't bad, but maybe lose something off my stomach. Get a six pack. Bigger legs and arms.

The degree of muscularity exemplified in bodybuilders was seen as too big and to be avoided:

Adolescent boy 6: It looks completely unnatural, even if they are about to pop out of his body. Looks, because I think there's like a balance, so, you know [the bodybuilder in picture] is too, um, muscly and overweight and everything.

Duane Hargreaves and Marika Tiggemann (2006) interviewed Australian boys aged 14 to 16, attempting to gain access to the boys' own ideas and terminology about their bodies and body image. Their participants reported that talking about the look of their bodies was seen as inappropriate for heterosexual boys. Young men are socialized into not talking about their bodies from an aesthetic point of view, and being concerned about the look of the body is often seen as feminine-appropriate in Western societies (Gough et al., 2014), so this reluctance is perhaps not surprising. In our interviews with men described in Chapter 4 it was only bodybuilders, well-practiced in objectifying and criticizing their own and other men's bodies, who appeared to feel comfortable talking about the look of their bodies. This needs to be taken into account in future work in which young men are asked to talk about body image as they may not feel able to express their concerns, leading to an overestimation of degree of satisfaction in young men compared with young women.

Adolescent boys and girls share body shape ideals and discourses relating to body image with adults of the same gender. In adolescent girls the ideal is slender (though not too thin), and for boys, slender and muscular (but not too muscular). The boys generally want to be more muscular (though not so muscular as bodybuilders), whereas the girls believe muscularity is inappropriately "masculine" and want to be slender. The area of the body that presents most concern to girls is the "stomach", whereas the boys want to be more muscular in general, and particularly in the upper body. Being fat is feared by both boys and girls, in line with adult concerns.

Body image throughout adulthood

Most psychological research on body image in adults has focused on samples of young women and men, partly because most work has been done in US or Australian universities or high schools where students (who may be co-opted into research as part of a course requirement) are usually young adults and are a convenient participant sample. Work that has looked at body image concerns in older adults has produced some interesting findings which will be discussed below, after a consideration of differential social pressure on men and women of different ages in relation to body image.

The idealized slender body shape is generally associated with youth. Women in particular are expected to try to maintain a youthful appearance. Diane Cepanec and Barbara Payne (2000) argue that there is significant social pressure on women to maintain a youthful look, pressure that is not imposed on men to the same extent, and that this fuels the cosmetic surgery industry:

> As a woman ages, failure to replicate society's ideal becomes all the more apparent. Beauty and youth tend to be seen as synonymous in our society. In short, surgical alteration of the face and body is a procedure that women in many cultures undergo in order to improve and transform their bodies to meet the cultural requirements of youth and femininity.
>
> (Cepanec and Payne, 2000: 122)

Many researchers have noted a "double standard" of aging, whereby women are judged more harshly than men in terms of physical attractiveness as they show signs of ageing. Signs of aging in men may be seen to make them look "distinguished", whereas in women (who are often judged in terms of physical attractiveness rather than in terms of abilities or experience) signs of aging may be seen negatively both by others and by themselves. Susan Bordo notes that for older actresses "facelifts are virtually routine" (Bordo, 2003: 25) as they attempt to make themselves acceptable to an audience critical of any signs of aging in women.

Men in their forties and fifties are frequently portrayed on film as attractive and sexual, and as having sexual relationships with much younger women. It is easy to think of examples of Hollywood actors who still play "love interest" roles in their sixties (Richard Gere, Harrison Ford, Pierce Brosnan, Bruce Willis), and it is not uncommon for men to be portrayed as lovers of women twenty years younger than themselves. Studies of media portrayal of men over sixty-five have tended to find that they are rarely portrayed on television (on average, about 5 per cent of characters on television fall into this age range), although older men are represented significantly more frequently than older women. When they are portrayed in films, they have historically been portrayed as incapacitated, incompetent, pathetic and the subject of ridicule, and older men's or women's bodies are rarely seen on film, except when they are represented in roles where their bodies might be expected to be exposed (e.g. as hospital patients).

Researchers who have analyzed media representations of women have reliably found that the predominant image of "woman" in the media is of a young, conventionally attractive, usually white model. Maggie Wykes and Barrie Gunter (2005) argue that although equality in the workplace is portrayed in twenty-first century television comedy dramas, the women characters are portrayed by similar-looking, slender, young actresses and the underlying message is that women need to be thin and beautiful to be successful and happy. Older women are rarely portrayed in movies, and when they are they are often portrayed in stereotypical roles (the lonely ageing female boss; the cruel stepmother; the doting grandmother). Older women are hardly ever portrayed as romantic leads, and sexual desire in older women is often a point of ridicule. When older women are portrayed in sexual roles they are usually women who have a youthful appearance, and the director often avoids exposing the body of the actress by implying sexual activity rather than actually filming the actors naked, by using body doubles, or by filming from a distance (e.g. Meryl Streep in *It's Complicated* in 2009).

Susan Bordo (2003) notes that although some older women are presented sexually in films, these tend to be those who have had cosmetic surgery to make their bodies acceptable to a critical audience. She argues that cosmetic surgery has shifted cultural expectations of how women are expected to look in their forties, fifties, sixties and beyond to a more youthful-looking image, and that this is not positive:

> These actresses, whose images surround us on television and in videos and films, are changing cultural expectations of what women "should" look like at forty-five and fifty. This is touted in the popular culture as a liberating development for older women; in the nineties, it is declared, fifty is still sexy. But in fact, Cher, Jane Fonda, and others have not made the ageing female body sexually more acceptable. They have established a new norm – achievable only through continual cosmetic surgery – where the female body ceases to age physically as the body grows chronologically older.
>
> (Bordo, 2003: 25–6)

Research on body image has suggested that women's dissatisfaction with their appearance does not vary significantly across the life span. Studies using figure choices and the questionnaire measures discussed in Chapter 3 suggest a remarkable uniformity in dissatisfaction relative to men of similar ages, and a general desire to be thinner across the age range (Grogan, 2012; Tiggemann and Slevec, 2012). One crucial time point for body image change seems to be the post-natal period, where many women report increased dissatisfaction. Although women may feel more positive about the look of their bodies during pregnancy when increased weight may be seen as legitimate (Skouteris, 2012), increased weight and body changes in the post-natal period are often experienced much more negatively (see Chapter 3). In our interviews, having a "flabby belly" and "droopy breasts" (which they believed had resulted from breastfeeding) were mentioned as a specific cause of dissatisfaction. The post-natal period may be challenging for many women who may feel under pressure to regain their pre-pregnancy appearance as soon as possible after the birth.

Emma Hodgkinson and colleagues (2014) conducted a systematic review of seventeen qualitative studies of women's experiences of body image post-partum and concluded that body dissatisfaction dominates the post-partum period, primarily linked to women's unrealistic expectations about their post-partum body, and they suggest that women are given support in body acceptance. Media representations of celebrity women's post-partum bodies tend to focus on "bouncing back" to pre-pregnancy body shapes and may contribute to this perceived pressure (Fern et al., 2012), though there is some evidence that breastfeeding may be somewhat protective in focusing attention on the functional (rather than aesthetic) aspects of post-natal body changes (Fern et al., 2014).

Women over forty might be expected to suffer from higher levels of body dissatisfaction than younger women, since they may be even further from the youthful, slim ideal than younger women. Hormonal changes associated with the menopause can lead to weight gain, and other changes such as undesirable reductions in skin elasticity and changes in hair quality take women's bodies away from the youthful ideal. However, most research has found that there is no change with age in terms of body satisfaction in women. In our interviews with women (see Chapter 3), we found that women aged 16 to 63 reported similar levels of dissatisfaction. Areas of the body that were a cause for concern did not differ in relation to the age of the interviewees. Women reliably reported dissatisfaction with stomach, hips and thighs, irrespective of their age. Most were motivated to lose weight and represented an ideal that was tall and slim with firm breasts, again irrespective of their age. The main motivator for women of all ages was being able to get into their favourite clothes (Grogan, 1999; Grogan et al., 2013), all were able to identify a part of their body that they would like to change, and almost all wished to be slimmer if possible. This may also be true for women over sixty. In Laura Hurd Clarke's (2002) interviews with Canadian women aged 61 to 92, she found that women were dissatisfied with their weight and reported that a key motivator for weight loss was an expected positive impact on their appearance:

Many of the women suggest that while the health benefits of weight loss are often the stated reason for losing weight, the perceived appearance dividends are the key motivation behind altering one's body weight in later life.

(Clarke, 2002: 751)

In a useful review of relevant work in this area, Marika Tiggemann (2004) showed that women's body dissatisfaction does not differ with age until they become quite elderly. Ageing, then, can become positive for women in terms of body image. Reviewing work in women over the age of 60, she found increased body satisfaction in women in this older age group with a shift in focus toward body function and health, and similar levels of body satisfaction to men of the same age. She also noted that the "invisibility" of older women described by feminist writers (e.g. Bordo, 2003) can mean that the importance of body size and weight decreases with age for women, as they are able to relinquish the internalized observer's perspective on their bodies. This can result in lowered self-objectification, reduced body monitoring and less appearance anxiety. This freedom from self-consciousness and pressure to aspire to the slender, youthful, sexually available ideal has been largely overlooked in previous work that has focused on body dissatisfaction and on the potential negative effects of youth-obsessed media imagery:

As women (and perhaps men) age, they place less emphasis on the importance of the body's appearance. Physical appearance is no longer such a central part of who they are. This allows a greater acceptance of the otherwise socially undesirable and largely uncontrollable age-related body changes which, in turn, means that older women are somewhat able to protect their self-concept and self-esteem from their increasing deviation from the thin and youthful ideal.

(Tiggemann, 2004: 38)

Research on age-related changes in men's body image have produced complex patterns of results. However, studies have suggested that when men are asked specifically about body weight, older men tend to have more concerns than younger men. Sue Lamb and colleagues (1993) administered silhouette scales to older and younger women and men. The older women and men (aged about 50) were objectively heavier and considered themselves to be heavier than the younger groups (aged about 20). Younger and older women, and older men, presented body ideals that were much thinner than their perceived size. Only the younger men were satisfied with their bodies.

Marita McCabe and Lina Ricciardelli (2004) suggest that men tend to focus on different aspects of their bodies at different ages. Young men and adolescents tend to be primarily focused on muscle development, but adult men are focused on increasing muscle tone and losing weight, particularly as they become older. Marika Tiggemann and colleagues (2007) compared body ideals and body dissatisfaction among 134 gay and 119 heterosexual men aged 18 to 60 years. In order to ensure that the desires for both slenderness and muscularity were considered, silhouette drawings varying on both adiposity (fatness) and muscularity were used. Gay and heterosexual men desired to be more slender and more muscular at all ages, although the discrepancy between "current" and "ideal" figures was greater for gay men. Interestingly, dissatisfaction with adiposity increased with age for both heterosexual and gay men, but there was no change in satisfaction with muscularity. Studies focusing on age differences in men need to take into account the possibility that men's dissatisfaction may be linked to lack of muscle or perceived overweight. Current work suggests that dissatisfaction with body weight may increase as men get older, though men may have other appearance concerns (such as lack of muscularity) at all ages.

One of the most consistent findings across body image studies is that men are generally more satisfied with their bodies than women (Tiggemann and Slevec, 2012). However, there is some evidence that this gap in satisfaction shrinks as men and women move into their sixties and beyond, and may even reverse when people are over eighty years, when women may be more satisfied than men. For instance, Lucie Baker and Eyal Gringart (2009) have shown that the women in the age range of 79 to 85 years in their Australian sample were significantly more satisfied than the men in the same age group – the reverse pattern to that found consistently in younger groups. They concluded:

> Whilst women appear to develop various strategies to counter the effects of ageing, men seem to be more negatively affected, particularly in relation to body functioning.
>
> (Baker and Gringart, 2009: 977)

To conclude, current data suggest that women are likely to be more dissatisfied than men among individuals aged between 18 and 60. There are no significant differences in satisfaction between different age groups of women, irrespective of how body satisfaction is measured, despite suggestions that media imagery focuses on the importance of youth. This may be because women choose age-appropriate models for body image comparisons as they age, and/or because appearance becomes less important as they age. Women seem to be as satisfied as men in the over-sixty group, when body function may become more important than body appearance for both men and women, and they may even be *more* satisfied when they are over eighty years of age. Older men are likely to be less satisfied with their body size than younger men, though men are likely to have concerns other than weight at all ages, including concerns about insufficient muscularity. Future research in this area needs to look at the process of body change with age in longitudinal studies that follow the same cohort through the various ages, to control for the effects of historical changes in body shape ideals on the development of both men's and women's body image.

Ethnicity and body image

Some variations in preferred body size have been documented in people from different ethnic groups in Western countries. Most studies have focused on anti-fat prejudice, body satisfaction and frequency of dieting in different ethnic groups, and most have concentrated on women. Research has found that body dissatisfaction is most frequent in British and US white women, and less frequent among African-Americans and women from the British Afro-Caribbean community. Although research published in the 1990s reported that Hispanic and Asian women are generally more satisfied with their bodies than white women, new evidence suggests that Hispanic and Asian women are becoming less satisfied in the twenty-first century, bringing them in line with white women in terms of dissatisfaction. This evidence is reviewed below. There is less work on ethnic differences in men's body image, although there is general agreement that African-American men report higher levels of satisfaction than white men, and have heavier body ideals for women and men than do white men.

Research conducted in the USA in the 1990s produced convincing evidence that obesity and overweight are viewed least positively in white groups. Harris et al. (1991) reported that African-American participants (both men and women) were more positive about overweight in women than white Americans. Black US men were more likely than white US men to want to date overweight women, and to consider them sexually attractive. Harris et al. also found that obese African-American women had a more positive body image than obese white US women, and were less likely to want to lose weight. These findings suggested less negative attitudes to overweight in the African-American community. Another study investigated ethnic and gender differences in perceptions of ideal body size in 9-year-olds (Thompson et al., 1997). In a random sample of 817 children, half white and half female, the researchers found that African-American children selected significantly heavier ideal body sizes than white children for the categories of self, male child, female child, adult male and adult female. Black boys selected significantly heavier figures for ideal girl and ideal woman than the white boys. They concluded that ethnic differences in ideal body sizes are apparent by age 9 years, with black boys and girls selecting significantly heavier figures than white boys and girls.

These differences in body ideals were correlated with differences in body satisfaction and dieting in women and girls. Studies undertaken in the 1990s suggested that African-American, Asian and Hispanic women were likely to report higher desired body weights, larger desired body shapes and fewer weight concerns than white women (Harris, 1994; Crago et al., 1996). Studies of girls and adolescents produced similar findings, showing that African-American girls reported less dieting than white US girls. For instance, Neff et al. (1997) looked at body size perceptions and weight management practices in both black and white adolescent women. They selected their sample through a randomized sampling procedure designed to ensure that the sample was statistically representative of high-school students in South Carolina. The resulting sample was made up of

1,824 black and 2,256 white girls aged 14 to 18. They found that significantly more (41 per cent) white girls than black girls (28 per cent) considered themselves overweight. White girls were six times more likely to use diet pills and vomiting to control weight, and four times more likely to diet or exercise as a way to manage their weight. The authors concluded that white adolescent girls were significantly more likely to consider themselves overweight, and were more likely to engage in unhealthy weight management practices than black girls of the same age.

Similar results were found in British work conducted in the 1990s. In one British study, Jane Wardle and Louise Marsland (1990) found that fewer Afro-Caribbean and Asian British girls than white girls wanted to lose weight. In another study Jane Wardle et al. (1993) studied body image and dieting concerns in a sample of 274 white and Asian British women aged 14 to 22. The Asian women were less likely to describe themselves as too fat, less dissatisfied with their body size, less likely to want to lose weight, and less likely to diet. Some of these differences were the result of generally lower body weight in the Asian group. However, when the researchers controlled for the effects of body size, they found that white women rated their stomach, thighs and buttocks as significantly larger than those of Asian women of the same size. The authors concluded that white women felt larger than Asian women of the same size, and suggested that these results may demonstrate cultural differences between the two groups as body shape may be a less emotive issue for the Asian group and/or obesity may not be such a stigma as in the white group.

More recent work has suggested that women from Asian and Hispanic communities may be less satisfied with their bodies than suggested in previous studies. Work conducted in the twenty-first century has found that Hispanic, Asian and white adolescents do not differ significantly in terms of their body satisfaction (e.g. Nishina et al., 2006), and the existence of differences between Hispanic, Asian and white women has also been questioned (e.g. Shaw et al., 2004). Kathleen Kawamura (2011) argues that although plumpness has traditionally been seen to be an indicator of prosperity, good health and beauty in Asian culture, it is no longer so regarded; Chinese and Japanese women now show a similar desire to white women for a slender body size, and Korean and Chinese women may have higher levels of body dissatisfaction than those in the US. Madeline Altabe and Keisha-Gaye O'Garo (2002) have also argued that Hispanic/ Latina women are heavily exposed to idealized, slender media imagery, and have adopted a thin ideal, although Deborah Schooler and Lynda Lowry (2011) suggest that ideals may vary between different sub-groups of Latina women and that acculturation processes (and body image) vary between those immersed in a primarily white environment and those who live, work and study within a predominantly Latina environment.

Shelly Grabe and Janet Hyde (2006) conducted a meta-analysis of ninety-eight studies looking at body dissatisfaction in Asian-American, black, Hispanic and white women. They found that white women were only marginally less satisfied than other groups, noting that:

The findings directly challenge the belief that there are large differences in body dissatisfaction between White and all Non-White women and suggest that body dissatisfaction may not be the golden girl problem promoted in the literature.

(Grabe and Hyde, 2006: 622)

Although Hispanic and Asian groups have been found to be similarly dissatisfied to white groups in the twenty-first century, African-American women and girls still seem to be marginally more satisfied than girls and women from other groups (e.g. Franko and Roehrig, 2011; Gillen and Lefkowitz, 2012; Kronenfeld et al., 2010; Nishina et al., 2006). For instance, LaShanda Jones and colleagues (2007) focused on gender and ethnic differences in body dissatisfaction, body size discrepancy and current and ideal figure ratings in 384 African-American and Caucasian US adolescents. Caucasian females reported significantly greater body dissatisfaction than African-Americans, and had significantly thinner ideals.

Debra Franko and James Roehrig (2011) note that black girls and women are more likely than other groups of women to be comfortable with their bodies at higher weights. These differences in body concern may relate to subcultural differences in pressures on women to be slender. In ethnic groups where overweight is less stigmatized, healthier, more satisfied attitudes to larger body shape and size may develop. African-American culture has privileged plumpness in women, representing the voluptuous female body as being sexual and powerful (Cachelin et al., 1998). This is displayed in the writings of Alice Walker, Maya Angelou and other black women writers, and in traditional African-American jazz, blues and rap music, which have represented the full-figured female as a symbol of sexuality and power. This is in marked contrast to the negative images of plumpness in mainstream (white) media.

Subcultural pressures may be more important than mainstream media images in influencing the value attached to body size. There are many reasons why African-American and British Afro-Caribbean women might reject mainstream media images as being offensive or (at best) irrelevant. It has been argued that positive images of black women's and men's bodies have historically been rare in mainstream Western media (Doy, 1996; Shilling, 1993). Advertising has used images of black bodies as sensual and dangerous, in order to advertise products aimed at the white consumer. Anoop Nayak (1997) shows how a Häagen-Dazs ice cream advertisement from the 1990s uses a black male model to contrast the "purity" of the white ice cream daubed on his back with the sensuality implied by his black skin. The utilization of the contrast between black skin and white product was also represented in Naomi Campbell's advertisements for milk in the USA, and for Müller yogurt in Britain in the 1990s. Some authors have suggested that the negative portrayal of black bodies in mainstream media may lead to privileging paler skin colour within the black community (Lopez et al., 2012), and to dissatisfaction with skin colour and features that do not conform to a Eurocentric ideal (Ashikari, 2005; Glenn, 2008).

There is a noticeable absence of African-American and Afro-Caribbean models in cosmetics advertisements. Hadley Freeman (2014) notes the "blatant racism" of the fashion industry, noting that black model Jourdan Dunn was told that portraying a black model on the front page of a fashion magazine means that it will not sell. She reports that models at New York Fashion Week in 2014 were 78.69 per cent white, 7.67 per cent black, 9.75 per cent Asian and 2.12 per cent Latina – an improvement from 2008 when 87 per cent were white, but still a significant imbalance. The rarity of positive black images in mainstream media may alienate African-American and British Afro-Caribbean viewers. This (along with conflicting values attached to plumpness) may make it likely that black viewers will reject the underlying values implied by mainstream media images.

Rejection of white Western values in relation to the idealization of slenderness may lead to less prejudice against overweight in men and women who identify with other ethnic groups. The degree of adoption of white Western body shape ideals has been shown to influence body image, and it has been found that higher acculturation levels relate to increased body dissatisfaction and more negative attitudes to overweight (Franco and Herrera, 1997; Cachelin et al., 2006), although Angela Celio et al. (2002) argue that the exact role of ethnic identity in body image development is unknown due to some conflicting findings in this area and problems in defining and measuring ethnic identity in African-American groups.

Relatively few studies have considered ethnic differences in body image in boys and men. Studies that have investigated body image in African-American groups have tended to find that black men are more satisfied with their bodies than white men (e.g. Miller et al., 2000; Aruguete et al., 2004) and prefer a larger body size than white men (Welch et al., 2004; Yates et al., 2004), although some have failed to find differences between ethnic groups (Nishina et al., 2006). Studies of Hispanics have tended to find no differences in body size preferences (e.g. Ericksen et al., 2005) or body satisfaction (e.g. Miller et al., 2000) from white groups. Studies with Asian men are inconsistent, with some authors reporting no differences in satisfaction (Franzoi and Chang, 2002) and some finding that Asian men are less satisfied than white men (Kowner, 2002; Neumark-Sztainer et al., 2002). Clearly there are complex relationships here, and the picture is further complicated in that although African-Americans are generally more satisfied with their bodies than white men, they also tend to place more importance on their bodies than white men and are more likely to engage in chronic dieting and use diet pills, laxatives/diuretics and vomiting than white groups (Barry and Grilo, 2002). In a review of the role of ethnicity and culture on men's body image, Ricciardelli and colleagues (2007) conclude that men from non-white ethnic groups engage in more extreme body change strategies than white men. They suggest that a number of factors are important in moderating and/or mediating the relationship between ethnicity and body image in men, including body build, level of acculturation, socioeconomic status, media exposure, and internalization of the lean body ideal.

To summarize, current data suggest that white women are currently at more risk of "feeling fat" and are more likely to diet than British Afro-Caribbean and

African-American women. There is some evidence of recent increases in dissatisfaction in Asian-American and Hispanic women and girls, bringing their concerns in line with white women, possibly as a result of the adoption of dominant white sociocultural values in relation to body image.

Data for men are less consistent. However, African-American men have generally been found to have higher levels of satisfaction than white men, and to attach more importance to their bodies. Studies with Hispanic men have tended to find no differences from white men, and there is some indication that Asian men may be less satisfied than white men.

Further work is needed to clarify these differences and their aetiology, although the availability of alternative, more flexible subcultural body shape ideals seems to protect against body dissatisfaction for both women and men. Future studies need to go much further in differentiating between subcultural groups, particularly within the wide bands conventionally defined as "Asian" and "Hispanic", to recognize the potential importance of differences between subgroups within these communities. These subgroups are likely to vary in important ways in terms of ideology around the body, body build, socioeconomic status and ethnic identity. Religious belief may also impact on body image. Viren Swami and colleagues (2014), in a survey of 587 British Muslim women, found that women who wore the hijab had more positive body image, lower internalization of media ideals and were less invested in appearance than women who did not wear the hijab. Hijab use also predicted weight discrepancy and body appreciation over and above the effects of religiosity. Also, Daniel Akrawi and colleagues (2015), in an extensive review, found that 80 per cent of the articles reviewed reported positive associations between body image and aspects of religiosity and spirituality. The authors suggest that having strong and internalized religious/spiritual beliefs may be linked with having fewer body concerns. Studies of impacts of ethnicity on body image tend not to discuss intersections between ethnicity and religiosity/ spirituality, but this is an important omission given possible variations in religion and spirituality (and linked expectations relating to clothing and eating/fasting) within different ethnic communities.

Social class and body image

Differences in body satisfaction in people from different social classes have rarely been addressed in research. Most psychology researchers do not even indicate the social classes of participants in their studies. Those that do indicate the socioeconomic status (SES) of their participants do not usually analyze the effects of SES on body image. Also, definitions of SES vary between studies, and researchers use quite different kinds of measures such as occupational status, income, education and social position (Bojorquez and Unikel, 2012) which can make it difficult to compare between studies.

Researchers who have compared body satisfaction in participants from different social groups have produced mixed results. Some studies have found SES differences in body concern in women. For instance, Wardle and Marsland (1990) interviewed 846 girls, aged 11 to 18 years and from different socioeconomic backgrounds, about weight and eating. They found higher levels of weight concern in girls from schools catering for higher social class backgrounds. Dieting was also more common in girls from these schools. They concluded that there are social class differences in body concern, with higher levels of concern among girls from higher social class backgrounds. This was supported by Australian work showing that physical self-esteem was lowest among 6- to 19-year-old overweight girls of middle/upper SES, and highest in boys of lower SES, despite the latter being more likely to be overweight (O'Dea and Caputi, 2001). Other work with women of differing social classes has also found that those in the higher social class bands are more dissatisfied with their bodies (Striegel-Moore et al., 1986).

Other studies have failed to find social class differences in body dissatisfaction. Robinson and colleagues (1996) asked 939 US girls aged 12 to 13 to complete scales including parental education levels (the authors' definition of SES) and body dissatisfaction. They found that parent education level did not correlate significantly with body dissatisfaction, and concluded that there is no link between SES and body concern among young women. They suggested that pressures to be thin are spreading beyond the upper and middle classes, producing increased body concern among working-class girls, and that body dissatisfaction was no longer associated with SES in women. This was supported by Story et al. (1995), who assessed dieting behaviours and body perceptions in adolescents of different socioeconomic subgroups and found greater weight satisfaction and lower rates of unhealthy weight control behaviours in boys and girls higher in SES.

Western cultures are becoming more homogeneous in terms of pressures to be thin (Bordo, 2003). Many social commentators have suggested that the popular media have created more similar cultural pressures on people of different social classes. Developments in mass communications in the twenty-first century mean that most people have access to the same body shape ideals via magazines, the internet, video games, movies and television (Wykes and Gunter, 2005). Through this democratization of vision, people of all social classes are presented with the same kinds of pressures to conform to the idealized images presented in the media. Indeed, studies have tended to find that body shape ideals are very similar in people of different social classes in affluent Western cultures. In one UK study (Hodkinson, 1997), ten men and ten women from Occupational Class 2 (Intermediate: teachers, nurses and managers) and Class 3 (shop assistants) on the UK Registrar General's scale were asked about body shape beliefs in relation to work. Participants (irrespective of their own occupational group) believed that overweight people were slow workers, that slim people did the most work, that employers preferred slim staff, that people had a better chance of getting a job if they were slim, that slim people were more successful at work, and that they would be more successful in their jobs if they were slimmer. All groups associated positive characteristics (self-discipline, health, fitness and being energetic) with slenderness, and all agreed that overweight people are kind and caring. Slimness was also associated with youthfulness by all occupational groups, and all groups (on average) believed that they would look younger if they became slimmer. Obviously, these data come from only a limited range of occupational groups. Nevertheless, they are interesting in demonstrating similarities in beliefs and preferences in people from a variety of occupational groups.

Susan Bordo (2003) notes that up until the nineteenth century, body size was an indication of social class: the middle classes opted to display their wealth ostentatiously by eating enough to attain a corpulent form, whereas the upper classes attempted to attain a slender form, rejecting the need for an outward show of wealth. Bordo shows how corpulence went out of fashion for the middle classes at the turn of the century, when social power became linked with the ability to control and manage the labour of others. A slender ideal in men and women started to be associated with success and willpower, and overweight with lack of self-control.

Bordo argues that slenderness has retained some of its high-class associations, although the link has become weaker over the years. Overweight and being working class are often associated, and often the overweight person is represented as lazy and to blame for lack of upward mobility. Popular Western culture is full of symbols of upward mobility through mastery and control of the body (e.g. the *Rocky* films, in which Sylvester Stallone is shown enduring pain to build up his strength and become successful, and – of course – to become wealthy and attain the trappings of the middle classes):

> To the degree that the question of class still operates in all this, it relates to the category of social mobility (or lack of it) rather than class location. So, for example, when associations of fat and lower class status exist, they are usually mediated by moral qualities – fat being perceived as indicative of laziness, lack of discipline, unwillingness to conform, and absence of all those "managerial" abilities that, according to the dominant ideology, confer upward mobility.
>
> (Bordo, 2003: 195)

Susie Orbach (1993) shows how fashion trendsetters have generally come from the middle and upper social classes, because they have the economic means to experiment with different kinds of fashion images. This was particularly the case in the UK in the 1960s. Jean Shrimpton, the first model to be represented as angular and thin, came from the upper-middle class, and was photographed in magazines catering for the upper classes (*Vogue* and *Harper's Bazaar*) wearing clothes designed by upper-middle-class designers, whose message was that women should break out from the confines of convention. The so-called "Jet Set", the wealthy young, produced a trend representing freedom and adventure. Tied in with this new image was the idea of thinness, which came to signify freedom and the rejection of convention. Thinness was seen as the key to enable working-class women to transcend the barriers of class and to emulate the "Jet Set" life. The emergence of Twiggy, a working-class model who did not attempt to hide her background, signalled to other young women that freedom and elegance could be achieved through thinness. In the USA, thinness became part of the "American dream", apparently achievable by anyone.

This apparent democracy is an illusion because, as we have seen, for most people the attainment of a fashionable body image requires economic power. Fashion designers and those in the slimming and cosmetics industries ensure that the fashionable "look" is constantly changing, and that its achievement requires time and money. It is often costly to attain a fashionably slender but muscular body. Sufficient resources are not equally available to everyone, thus effectively keeping the ideal at arm's length for most people. There are well-documented social class differences in the incidence of overweight; working-class women and men are more likely to fall into the "obese" category than those in the middle classes (Bojorquez and Unikel, 2012; Campos, 2004; Monaghan, 2005). The current slender, toned and muscular Western ideal requires time and resources for most people (unless they have a job which requires heavy manual labour). This ideal may be easier to attain for people who have the resources to spend time in the gym (or to have cosmetic surgery) to become fashionably lean and toned.

In summary, research linking social class to body image suggests that social class is not related to body shape ideals, since people from different social classes present similar ideals. Studies comparing body shape ideals and body satisfaction between men and women of varying social classes cast doubt on the now outmoded assumption that body dissatisfaction is a middle-class phenomenon. Much more work is needed in this area, looking specifically at income and class differentials in body image, to extend the current literature and to develop work on body satisfaction beyond the traditional middle-class student group that is usually chosen for study by psychologists.

Body shape, sexual attractiveness and sexuality

Most of this text has considered body image in terms of aesthetics rather than sexual attractiveness. Body shape and size have important implications for sexual attraction. Some researchers have focused on the relationship between body shape and size and perceived sexual attractiveness, and have produced some interesting findings. There is some debate in the literature as to the basis for opposite-sex attraction in body shape and size. Social psychologists and sociologists have generally argued that sexual preferences in body shape and size are largely learned, and are affected by the value that a particular culture attaches to that kind of body shape. They have stressed the cultural relativity of body shape features that signal sexual attractiveness, and have focused on same-sex, as well as opposite-sex, attraction. On the other hand, evolutionary psychologists have argued that people have an inherent preference for sexual partners who are biologically "fit" (healthy and able to reproduce), and that body shape features, such as being of normal weight and having a pronounced waist (in women), or no pronounced waist (in men), serve as biological indicators of "mate value" to the opposite sex. Here we will consider arguments from these two perspectives, evaluating the usefulness of each approach in explaining the available data in relation to body shape ideals and body satisfaction. For convenience, this section is divided into four sections, looking separately at the specific social pressures on heterosexual women, lesbians, gay men and heterosexual men.

Heterosexual women

Many researchers, particularly within the feminist tradition, have focused on the social pressures experienced by women to conform to a particular body shape in order to be attractive to men. Nickie Charles and Marilyn Kerr (1986), in interviews with two hundred British women, found that sexual attractiveness was cited as one of the major reasons why women desired to conform to the slim ideal. For most of the women they spoke to, this was phrased in terms of the necessity of staying (or getting) slim to maintain their current (heterosexual) sexual relationship. Many women reported that their sexual partners monitored their "fatness" and told them when they needed to lose weight. Charles and Kerr concluded that body image is closely linked with sexual attractiveness, and that particularly after childbirth women feel pressure from their sexual partners to regain their figures and to be slender, in order to maintain their sexual relationship. They concluded that the unnaturally thin feminine ideal leads women to be constantly dissatisfied with their bodies, and that perceived pressure from sexual partners is a key factor in this dissatisfaction.

In our interviews with women (reported in Chapter 3), many women reported that they felt their sexual relationships had suffered because they were self-conscious about their bodies, usually feeling too fat. They were clear that they had more desire to be sexually active when they felt good about themselves (including good about their bodies). Ironically, many women reported that their sexual partners thought they were attractive and had not commented negatively on their bodies, yet they still felt fat. For instance, one 23-year-old woman said:

> I'm off [on vacation] for a week, and I want to wear little sexy things and all that, and my sex life is suffering because of my body image. There are a lot of times that I would like to and he would like to, but I just can't bring myself to undress. I don't want him to see how fat I am.

The relationship between body image and satisfaction with sexual relationships is well documented (see Wiederman and Pryor, 1997). Tom Cash and colleagues (2004) have reported that women low in body satisfaction experience fear of intimacy in sexual relationships, replicating other work suggesting that women low in body satisfaction report concerns about the appearance of their body in sexual interactions with their partners (e.g. Ackard et al., 2000). Werlinger and colleagues (1997) reported a significant increase in sexual desire among US women who had lost weight and developed a more positive body image as a result. The reasons why such a relationship exists are complex, and seem to relate to increased self-esteem (which may result from, or produce, body satisfaction) resulting in positive impacts on all aspects of life, including sexual performance and desire.

Many of the women we interviewed reported that it was important that their male sexual partner should be heavier and generally bigger, to make them feel relatively small and slender, and they cited occasions when they were made to feel really good because they felt that their partner was much larger. For instance:

I have to look for someone with a certain body image that will make me feel better, feel small. I had this boyfriend in college who was huge, he was 6 feet 4 and he was a tanker. And I would put his jacket on and the sleeves would fall over my hand and I loved it. I mean, I loved it.

These experiences may be most relevant to women with traditional views of male–female relationships in terms of dependence–independence, who tend to be more concerned with body image than those with less traditional views (Cash et al., 1997).

Some interesting work has compared women's perceptions of men's ideal body size for women with men's actual preferences. Sue Lamb and colleagues (1993) found that women tended to believe that men preferred much thinner body shapes than the men themselves actually chose. They also found that women's ideal was actually thinner than the size that they thought men preferred. It seems likely that women are sensitive to pressure from men to be thin, but also that they are sensitive to more general cultural pressures – from the dieting industry, for instance – which may set up an even slimmer ideal, and pressure from other women to conform to a thin ideal.

Gail Huon and colleagues (1990) asked forty men and forty women in the first year of a Psychology course at the University of New South Wales in Australia to select a photograph showing their ideal female figure, their actual size (or, for men, the size of their best female friend), the one they thought most men would prefer, and the one that most women would prefer. The choice was from twelve projected photographs of two female models, adjusted to different sizes by a device that systematically varied the images about the vertical axis. The men were accurate in predicting women's preferred size. The women's preferred female size was the thinnest, followed by what they believed to be men's preferred female size, followed by their own ideal, followed by their actual size. The authors concluded that women's body image is affected by general social pressure, from women as well as from men.

Evolutionary psychologists suggest that there are biological reasons for body shape and size preferences in potential sexual partners. Devendra Singh (1993) suggests that men's preferences for women's shapes are determined by the woman being of normal weight and having a waist-to-hip ratio (WHR) that signals fertility.

At puberty, women typically gain weight around the waist and hips. Singh suggests that the curves created by this "reproductive fat" provide men with a gauge of reproductive potential. According to Singh, healthy, fertile women typically have WHR of 0.6–0.8, meaning that their waists are 60–80 per cent the size of their hips, whatever their weight. When women go through the menopause they generally become heavier in the waist, so that the WHR becomes similar to the male range of 0.85–0.95. He suggests that women with higher WHR report having their first child at a later age than women with lower WHR. He also argues that low WHR relates to better general health, as defined by the absence of major diseases such as diabetes, heart attack and stroke, which are all less common when people carry more fat in the lower body (Singh, 1993: 295). He concluded that WHR reliably signals degree of sexual maturity, reproductive potential and good health.

In a study of *Playboy* centrefolds and "Miss America" contest winners, Singh found that women whose bodies were considered appropriate in the 1980s were measurably leaner than the women chosen in previous decades, yet their WHRs were still around 0.7. When he asked male volunteers to rate line drawings of female figures for attractiveness, sexiness, health and fertility, the preferred figure (irrespective of the culture or age of the participants) was the figure with the 0.7 WHR (which was the figure with the lowest WHR that he presented). Singh concluded that the distribution of body fat plays a crucial role in judgements of women's physical attractiveness, health, youth and reproductive potential; and that to be perceived as attractive by male judges, women must be of normal weight and have a low WHR – neither factor alone is sufficient to predict attractiveness, since being either underweight or overweight reduces perceived attractiveness and also perceived healthiness.

Singh suggested that WHR may be involved in the initial stages of physical attraction when men may be more likely to initiate contact with women with low WHR, so that this would lead to a filtering out of women with high WHR. Then a second filter would take account of culturally defined standards of attractiveness for that particular culture (for instance, overall plumpness or slenderness, facial features etc.). However, all societies (whether they generally preferred plumpness or slenderness) would favour women of low WHR, because of its association with fertility and health.

Singh did not offer his participants the choice of the full range of WHRs (i.e. including WHRs of less than 0.7). The range of figures that he used (0.7–1.0) gave participants a restricted choice, and did not allow an assessment of the effects of very low WRH on perceived sexual attractiveness. Presumably there may be an optimum WHR below which men no longer find the figure attractive. Although very few women have WHR below 0.5, it would nevertheless have been interesting to see how figures of 0.6 and 0.5 were rated. Following Singh's logic, these should be perceived as more sexually attractive than the 0.7 figure, which was the lowest he presented. Indeed, the corset and bustle combination that he mentioned (Singh, 1993: 296) would have produced a WHR below 0.7 in many women, through constricting the rib cage to give a tiny waist in relation to the hips (see Brownmiller,

1984). Although Singh assumed that the female body with low WHR is more sexually attractive to men than one with high WHR, it would have been informative to have investigated the limits of this effect in order to try to identify an optimum WHR (as he did for women's judgements of men).

Although Singh investigated the consistency of the WHR effect in men of different ages, his biological argument would be more convincing if it were based on cross-cultural data. His participants were all US (white and Hispanic) males, so they were all likely to be experiencing similar cultural influences (television, magazines etc.). It could be that he was observing a learned preference for a "slender but curvy" shape. Sixty-five per cent of men rated normal weight figures most attractive, and 35 per cent underweight ones. The "overweight" woman (irrespective of WHR) was not found "most attractive" by any man, despite the fact that she was not sufficiently overweight to represent a threat to reproductive status or health (the figure is designed to represent a 5 foot 5 inch tall woman weighing 150 lb, who is not obese as judged on the Metropolitan Life Insurance Tables). What strikes the reader is the fact that the 0.7 and 0.8 WHR bodies look very familiar on the page (i.e. they are similar to body shapes represented in the media), whereas the others do not. If, as Singh said, models tend to conform to the 0.7 WHR, then perhaps the findings reflect a familiarity effect – a learned preference for this kind of body shape. It would be interesting to show his line drawings to heterosexual women (or gay men) to see which pictures are chosen as "most attractive". If the preferences he observed reflect learned social preferences rather than biological mate value, we would predict the same pattern of preferences in women as those seen in Singh's male participants. In Singh's study, the impact of men's sexuality was not reported.

In one recent study (Grogan et al., 2013) we asked twenty women aged 18 to 45 years to try on a number of dresses, and we photographed them in their chosen dress. Women were also whole-body scanned (see Chapter 3). We recorded their spontaneous speech while trying on the dresses (with their permission), and we discussed both the scan and the photograph in semi-structured interviews. Most women aspired to a slim "hourglass" ideal (with fuller breasts and hips and a small, defined waist) and used well-fitting clothes to try to attain a slender hourglass look. This would seem to support Singh's arguments. However, in Chapter 3 we saw that the area of the body that presents most concern for women is the very area (hips and thighs) where women store the reproductive fat that is supposed to make them attractive to men. Nearly all the women we interviewed, whatever their body type and weight, wanted to lose weight around their hips (i.e. to increase their WHR). This would not be predicted from Singh's model, although our finding that women want a defined waist would be predicted. Women generally also want to be as slim as possible (rather than of normal weight).

There is clearly a conflict between the factors identified by evolutionary psychologists as being high in "mate value" and women's desire to attain the slender, slim-hipped ideal. It seems likely that there may be a difference between heterosexual men's body shape preferences for women and women's own preferences, which (according to interview data in Chapter 3) may relate more to a fashion for a particular body type than to being sexually attractive to men, although this may be a secondary concern. Recent work has tended to find that BMI is a much better predictor of both men's and women's attractiveness ratings for women's bodies than WHR (Tovee and Cornelissen, 2001: Swami et al., 2006; Swami and Harris, 2012).

Viren Swami and Amy Harris (2012) argue that Singh's (1993) argument of temporal stability in the WHRs of *Playboy* centrefolds and "Miss America" winners does not stand up to scrutiny, and that "the narrow range reported by Singh does not encompass most of the members of either sample" (p. 408). They suggest that waist-to-hip ratio may act as a broad cognitive filter to differentiate male body shapes from female, so it is best understood as a cognitive process of social categorization used by both men and women rather than the result of "mate choice" adaptations unique to male psychology.

Social psychologists and evolutionary psychologists have generally been reticent about discussing the intersexual significance of breasts, even though there is no doubt that breast size and firmness are intimately tied to Western notions of heterosexual attractiveness in women. Evolutionary psychologists have generally argued that breast size is largely irrelevant to sexual attractiveness, since breast development does not reliably signal fertility. Women with adrenal tumours and true hermaphrodites have fully formed breasts, but they are infertile. Singh argues that these women have male-like WHRs, making WHR a more reliable indicator of fertility. Desmond Morris (1985) even argues that the breasts evolved to mimic buttocks (to make women's front view more attractive to men), and have no sexual significance of their own. However, most social psychologists would agree that moderate-to-large breasts on a slender frame are men's cultural ideal in Western societies. A cursory perusal of popular men's magazines, or an overview of images of female characters in video games marketed at young men, leaves the viewer in no doubt that the magazine editors and game designers expect their consumers to prefer women with firm, moderate-to-large breasts.

Kevin Thompson and Stacey Tantleff (1992) ran an interesting study in which they asked US men and women to categorize schematic male and female figures differing in breast or chest size as current, ideal, and the size that they thought was the opposite sex's and their own sex's ideal. Overall, results indicated a preference for large breast/chest sizes. Both sexes rated their own current size as smaller than ideal. Men's conception of ideal breast size was larger than women's. It was concluded that the findings explain the societal preoccupation with breasts, overall dissatisfaction with this area of the body in women, and the decision to seek cosmetic surgery for breast enlargement. Positive adjectives were associated with large breasts (particularly confidence, popularity and being likely to succeed) for both men and women judges. The only positive characteristics associated with small breasts were athleticism and intelligence. More recent research has generally supported this early work, though it also suggests that preferences for large breasts may be linked with the socioeconomic status of the men doing the judging and that higher SES men are more likely to show a preference for smaller breasts (Swami and Tovee, 2013).

Susan Brownmiller (1984) discusses the paradox for women of the possession of breasts that are intensely private (usually hidden from view), yet very public (evaluated socially by men and by women themselves). She is particularly interested in the ways that men fetishize, and claim ownership of, women's breasts, leading women to be self-conscious about perceived inadequacies (too large, too small, or not firm enough):

> No other part of the anatomy has such semi-public, intensely private status, and no other part of the body has such vaguely defined custodial rights. One learns to be selectively generous with breasts – this is the girl child's lesson – and through the breast iconography she sees all around her, she comes to understand that breasts belong to everybody, but especially to men. It is they who invent and refine their myths, who discuss breasts publicly, who criticize their failings as they extol their wonders, and who claim to have more need and intimate knowledge of them than a woman herself.
>
> (Brownmiller, 1984: 24)

Many studies have noted women's dissatisfaction with breast size and shape and their concern about their attractiveness to male partners. In interviews with women with large breasts, Rhona Reardon found that women reported hiding their breasts from male partners (Reardon and Grogan, 2010):

> I have never let my boyfriend see me with my bra off. I am so ashamed of them. I constantly worry about what he thinks and how much they get in the way (Catherine, considering surgery).

David Frederick and colleagues (2008) analyzed views of breast size and shape among 52,227 heterosexual adults aged 18 to 65. Although 56 per cent of men were satisfied with their partner's breasts, many women (70 per cent) were dissatisfied with the size or shape of their breasts. Younger and thinner women worried that their breasts were too small, whereas older and heavier women were more concerned with breast "droopiness". Dissatisfied women were less willing to undress in front of their partner and were more likely to conceal their breasts from their partner during sex than those who were more satisfied.

If men tend to prefer slenderness with largish firm breasts, this presents a conflict for women who wish to be attractive to men. Slenderness may be achieved through restriction of food intake. However, weight loss will also lead to breast shrinkage. Media images of women's bodies aimed at a male audience often present an unusual, slim-hipped, long-legged, large-breasted ideal (seen in its most extreme form in video game characters such as Lara Croft). This ideal is only possible for most women through a mixture of diet and exercise (to slenderize hips and thighs) and cosmetic surgery (to swell the breasts).

163

The popularity of cosmetic surgery to augment the breasts is increasing every year. Breast augmentations were first carried out in the 1950s in Japan, and by the 1960s silicone gel implants were being used more and more frequently to increase breast size, despite problems with rejection of the implants by the body's immune system (Meredith, 1988). By the 1990s concern over silicone leakage led to a preference for saline implants, which, if they leak, cause less damage. Despite wide publicity about health risks, it is estimated that over a million women in the USA had had breast implants by the mid-1990s (Davis, 1995). In 2014 breast enlargement was the most common cosmetic procedure carried out on women (International Society of Aesthetic Surgeons, 2016).

In conclusion, heterosexual women are clearly under pressure to conform to a very slender ideal. Most studies have shown that women prefer a thinner ideal for women's bodies than do men. Social and evolutionary psychologists have suggested that individual Western men report preferences for "normal weight" (rather than very slender) women's bodies. However, women operate within a cultural context where a very thin ideal is promoted by the beauty industry, and these pressures contribute to women's thin ideal. The recent increase in breast augmentations may also reflect perceived pressure from men. Although women tend to report that the decision to have cosmetic surgery was taken independently of pressure from sexual partners, it is difficult (or impossible) to separate women's choice in this matter from cultural influences (which include pressure from men).

Lesbians

There is very little research on the degree of pressure exerted on women who choose female sexual partners, although most authors tend to assume that lesbians are under less pressure to be slender and large-breasted from sexual partners than are heterosexual women (Huxley and Hayfield, 2012). Laura Brown (1987) argues that lesbian culture downplays the importance of conventional physical attractiveness, leading to higher levels of body satisfaction among lesbians than heterosexual women and lower levels of anorexia and bulimia. Interviews with bisexual women have also shown that women feel more pressure to conform to traditional beauty norms when in relationships with men than with women (Taub, 1999). However, Sari Dworkin (1988) argues that lesbians are socialized to conform to the same societal standards of physical attractiveness as heterosexual women, and must comply with socially accepted standards to be accepted within the lesbian community.

Most studies have failed to find differences in body image between lesbians and heterosexual women. A US study based on a small number of lesbian and heterosexual women concluded that the groups did not differ in degree of body dissatisfaction, although the lesbian group showed a lower frequency of dieting and had higher self-esteem (Striegel-Moore et al., 1990). Similarly, Brand et al. (1992) found no differences in body satisfaction between lesbians and heterosexual women, concluding that gender was a better predictor of body dissatisfaction than sexuality. Strong et al. (2000) also found no significant differences in body dissatisfaction between lesbians and heterosexual women, although they suggest that body image may be less important to lesbians than to heterosexual women. In work conducted with British samples (Grogan et al., 2006a) we have failed to find differences in body-image-related motivations for exercise between lesbian and heterosexual women. We had predicted that heterosexual women would be more likely than lesbians to be motivated to exercise for appearance and weight management. In fact, there was no significant difference between the two groups, suggesting that exercise motivations did not differ between these groups of lesbians and heterosexual women. In another recent study we also failed to find any significant difference between lesbians and heterosexual women in terms of dieting (Conner et al., 2004), concluding that both lesbians and heterosexual women are under mainstream social pressure to be thin, and that gender may be a better predictor of eating and exercise motives than sexuality in this context.

In a study that has identified differences, Michael Siever (1994) compared the importance placed on physical attractiveness in 53 lesbians, 62 heterosexual women, 59 gay men, and 63 heterosexual men. In a study at the University of Washington, Siever asked both men and women to complete a packet of self-report questionnaires, including the Franzoi and Shields (1984) Body Esteem Scale, the Cooper et al. (1987) Body Shape Questionnaire, and the Stunkard et al. silhouette drawings (see Chapters 3 and 4). He found that the lesbians who took part in his study placed significantly less emphasis on physical attractiveness in their sexual partners than did heterosexual women, and reported that their partners placed less emphasis on physical attractiveness than did all other groups. Lesbians were also more satisfied with their bodies than were heterosexual women (although this difference was not statistically significant on most measures). Some of the lesbian group indicated that they had suffered from body dissatisfaction and disordered eating before they "came out". Siever suggests that the lesbian subculture may have a protective function, in that lesbians may become more satisfied with their bodies as they become assimilated into the lesbian community. He proposes that the lesbian subculture places less emphasis on youth and beauty and does not promote the unrealistic ideals seen in mainstream heterosexual culture, leading to less objectification and higher body satisfaction. Siever's work has been highly influential but has been supported by very few studies, though Tamara Share and Laurie Mintz (2002) found some evidence of more positive body image in lesbians than heterosexual women.

In a meta-analysis of existing literature, Melanie Morrison and colleagues (2004) conclude that across studies there is some evidence that when samples are well matched, lesbians may be slightly more satisfied than heterosexual samples, although the size of this difference is not statistically significant and does not approximate to the difference between gay and heterosexual men. They argue that the low magnitude of this difference suggests that "the norms of lesbian subculture may be insufficient to counteract the types of messages that bombard all women from childhood onward" (p. 136), citing evidence that lesbians internalize societal standards of thinness, albeit not to the same extent as heterosexual women. Anne Peplau and colleagues (2009) compared body satisfaction and comfort with one's body during sexual activity among lesbian women, gay men, heterosexual women and heterosexual men through two large online surveys with 2,512 and 54,865 respondents. Results showed that "[t]here was little evidence that lesbian women experience greater body satisfaction than heterosexual women" (p. 713). More recently, Todd Morrison and Jessica McCutcheon (2011) also present a critical review of available evidence and conclude that "lesbian and heterosexual women are more similar than dissimilar in terms of their body image" (p. 215).

There are many unanswered questions in the existing literature on body image in lesbians. Studies have generally ignored the butch/femme gender style of participants. This is particularly important for studies of body image, where it could be expected that style of presentation could be salient in determining satisfaction with the body. It is possible that there is more social pressure for women presenting as "femme" to conform to prevailing social mores of slenderness (from their sexual partners, from lesbian subculture, and/or from mainstream culture). Laura Kelly (2007) interviewed twenty lesbians and concludes that women who are "femme-identified" may have less acceptance and support from within the lesbian community than those who present as "butch". There is some limited evidence that lesbians and bisexual women who present as "femme" may be lower in body satisfaction than those who present as masculine or androgenous (e.g. Ludwig and Brownell, 1999). This is a question requiring further research, which should be addressed through in-depth interviews with lesbians presenting as butch/femme to clarify the factors at work here.

The political climate within which lesbianism exists is also important in understanding lesbian body image. In a review of relevant literature, Esther Rothblum (2002) discusses the diverse social pressures that may be experienced by lesbians and gay men, where they are first socialized by mainstream culture and then by the lesbian and gay communities. She suggests that lesbians may be "torn between their beliefs and their interactions with mainstream media, families of origin, and the work setting" (p. 263), arguing that the experience of biculturality may explain the conflicting findings in the literature on lesbian body image. Laura Kelly (2007) also suggests that lesbians may be faced with conflicting sets of "oppressive mandates" relating to body image:

> The internalization of the dominant culture's beauty expectations coupled with the adoption of a lesbian identity caused the participants to contend with a multitude of oppressive mandates from both sociocultural contexts.
>
> (Kelly, 2007: 873)

Brian Zamboni and colleagues (2007) have suggested that lesbians and bisexual women who were more comfortable with their sexual orientation had more positive body image. Further work is needed to investigate sources of social support, the influence of ageing, and the effects of gender-style presentation and political orientation on body image in lesbians.

Gay men

Gay men may be under more extreme social pressure than heterosexual men in relation to body image in a context in which they are the objects of male gaze (Atkins, 1998), and studies of body dissatisfaction tend to suggest that gay men are less satisfied with their bodies in general than heterosexual men (Morrison and McCutcheon, 2011). It has frequently been argued that gay male subculture places an elevated importance on the appearance of the body. Jamie Gough (1989) argued that the 1980s had seen increased pressure on gay men to have a body that was toned and muscular, and that this was oppressive to men (Gough, 1989).

> Masculinity as a sexual fetish is, therefore, oppressive not simply for dictating a certain norm, but for demanding something that cannot be achieved. The new style of sexual attractiveness is all the more tyrannous in that, as we have seen, it prescribes not only social behaviour but also physiology.
>
> (Gough, 1989: 121–2)

Studies have tended to find higher levels of body concern in gay than in heterosexual men from the 1980s onwards. For instance, Marc Mishkind et al. (1986) found that gay men expressed greater dissatisfaction with body shape, waist, biceps, arms and stomach. They also indicated a greater discrepancy between their actual and ideal body shapes than did heterosexual men, and were more preoccupied with their weight and diet. The study was flawed in that the sample of "heterosexual" men was drawn from a group of undergraduate men in an introductory psychology class who were assumed to be heterosexual, but it presents some interesting findings in relation to differences in pressures from the gay male subculture to conform to the male body ideal.

Susan Beren and colleagues (1996) found that their sample of 58 gay Yale University undergraduate students reported significantly higher levels of body dissatisfaction than 58 heterosexual men. Using self-report measures, they were able to measure level of affiliation with the gay community. They expected that those who were more strongly affiliated with the gay community would indicate more body dissatisfaction, due to the high level of emphasis on body appearance in the gay community. Their results supported this hypothesis, finding that those who identified most strongly with the gay community were least satisfied with their bodies, and concluding that aspects of the gay community increase vulnerability to body dissatisfaction. Perhaps these data should be interpreted more cautiously since what they have actually demonstrated is merely an association between the two variables, meaning that the causal link may run in the opposite direction (so that men who are more satisfied with the way they look feel a closer link with the body-conscious gay culture). Still, the demonstration of a link is interesting and suggestive of social pressure within this community to have a "good" body.

In the 1990s, Michael Siever (1994) noted that many researchers have proposed that gay male subculture imposes pressure on gay men to be physically attractive, and that empirical data suggest that gay men generally value physical appearance more than heterosexual men do. He found that gay men and heterosexual women showed the highest levels of body dissatisfaction. Gay men were significantly more dissatisfied with their bodies than heterosexual men. In fact, in this study, gay men were less satisfied with their bodies than were heterosexual women. Siever suggested that this may be because gay men have the potential to be dissatisfied with their bodies on two dimensions. Like heterosexual men they may worry that their bodies are inadequate in terms of athletic prowess, and like heterosexual women they may rate themselves on an aesthetic dimension. Siever concluded that sexual objectification results in increased emphasis on physical attractiveness and body dissatisfaction in the recipients of the objectification, be they men or women. He argues that assimilation into the gay subculture may lead to gay men becoming less satisfied with their bodies, within a context where slenderness and muscularity are prized.

More recently, Christine Yelland and Marika Tiggemann (2003) investigated body concerns in a community sample of Australian participants: 52 gay men, 51 heterosexual men, and 55 heterosexual women. They found that gay men scored higher than heterosexual men and women on drive for muscularity, and higher than heterosexual men on drive for thinness. They did not differ from heterosexual men on body esteem, both groups of men scoring significantly above the sample of women. The authors concluded that gay men experience more body concern and disordered eating than heterosexual men, and that although gay men may not experience the same degree of body dissatisfaction as women, they experience a similar level of drive to reach their ideal body shape.

In British studies on eating and exercise motives we have found that gay men are more likely to diet (Conner et al., 2004) and more likely to exercise for appearance reasons (Grogan et al., 2006a) than heterosexual men. In both studies, gay men's behaviour and motivations did not differ from those of heterosexual women. In focus groups with a community-based sample of gay and heterosexual Australian men aged 18 to 52, Helen Fawkner (2004) also found that negative affect and behaviour change as a result of self–ideal comparison were more prevalent in gay than heterosexual men, and in questionnaire work with 106 gay men and 244 heterosexual men, that the gay men were less satisfied with their appearance and more preoccupied with overweight. Maurice Levesque and David Vichesky (2006) have also produced evidence that gay men in their sample expressed high levels of body dissatisfaction and weight concern, and were primarily concerned with developing bigger muscles.

In a meta-analysis of existing relevant literature, Melanie Morrison and colleagues (2004) conclude that existing evidence suggests that gay men are less satisfied with their bodies than heterosexual men, in parallel with increased pressure from the gay community to be slender and muscular. This is also supported through reviews by Todd Morrison and Jessica McCutcheon (2011, 2012).

It is important to place pressure from the gay community in its social context. Body-image-related pressures from the gay "scene" do not exist in a vacuum. They exist within mainstream culture in which young men generally have significant spending power, making them an attractive market for consumer goods. The 1990s and the twenty-first century have seen an opening of young men's markets generally, and particularly for young gay men (Hall, 2015; O'Kelly, 1994). It is clearly in the interests of purveyors of clothes, cosmetics and other body-related consumer goods to encourage body consciousness in the gay community and to capitalize on the resulting demand, and the spending power of affluent gay men (Clarke and Turner, 2007).

In addition to pressures from within the gay community to be attractive, gay men are also faced with the cultural stereotype that "gay men look after their bodies" and are "physically fit". Duane Hargreaves and Marika Tiggemann (2006) found that the Australian male adolescents who took part in their study were reticent about talking about their bodies and body image, as they perceived this to be a "gay issue". Mainstream media are full of examples of gay men's bodies being represented as attractive and "fit". For instance, in an *Independent on Sunday* article discussing the reasons why women were not buying the new soft pornography magazines aimed at them, one of the "problems" identified by the journalist was that magazines aimed at heterosexual women tended to use gay male models, since "gay men are the ones who tend to look after their bodies" (Forna, 1996: 3). Even feminist writers fall into the trap of objectifying gay men and expecting them to conform to the "fit gay" stereotype:

Many gay men, as straight women often observe, are very attractive. There's a lot to be said for tight pants on a good body in excellent condition.
(Brownmiller, 1984: 71)

As when women's and black men's bodies are objectified, the objectification of gay men's bodies is a way of disempowering the group. In a culture where the quest for beauty has been used for hundreds of years to control women's energies (Wolf, 1991), the expectation that gay men should be attractive can be conceptualized as a form of social control. Diana Fuss (1989) argues that gay men (and lesbians) are seen as a threat to public safety, and believes that gay men are persecuted by the state apparatus. The "gay man as fit body" stereotype is a potential source of social control, especially in a context where "heterosexism" is validated by the supposed risk of the spread of AIDS. Many authors have documented the rampant heterosexism that emerged in the 1980s with awareness of AIDS in both Britain (Kitzinger, 1987; Ellis and Heritage, 1989) and the USA (Yingling, 1991). External "fitness" can reassure the fearful both within and outside the gay community that the gay man (and his behaviour) does not represent a risk.

169

In conclusion, most studies have found that gay men are less satisfied with their bodies than heterosexual men. This may relate to pressures from the gay community to have an acceptably muscular body, within a mainstream cultural context where gay men are more "embodied" than heterosexual men, and where there is a cultural expectation of body consciousness in gay men from within and without the gay community. More work is needed in this area to compare men of different ages (since most of the existing work has focused on men under 30), and to compare men involved in the "gay scene" with others who do not identify with this community. Choosing samples from venues attended by gay men (as most researchers have done) may overestimate the extent of body dissatisfaction by producing a sample who identify most strongly with the "scene". We also need to know more about body image in minority sub-groups of gay men. For instance, there is evidence that heavier gay men report the development of more positive body image when they become involved in sub-groups that eroticize the "bear" (a heavier, hairier, normally older ideal; Gough and Flanders, 2009).

Heterosexual men

Despite recent media interest in the social pressure on heterosexual men to conform to the well-muscled slender ideal (e.g. Cruz, 2014), there is little evidence that most heterosexual men are responding to pressure from women by trying to attain a well-muscled look. Although many heterosexual men report some dissatisfaction with the way that they look, their levels of body concern are reliably lower than those reported for women and for gay men (Morrison and McCutcheon, 2011). Heterosexual men are also less likely to be motivated to engage in appearance-fixing behaviours such as dieting, or to exercise for reasons relating to appearance, than gay men or women (Conner et al., 2004; Grogan et al., 2006a).

Interview work with heterosexual men suggests that men believe that women prefer them to be toned and muscular, and they are aware of media pressure to be muscular, but mostly they are not motivated to try to achieve this look through exercise or diet. In focus groups men reported that most pressure came from male peers (rather than women), who criticized body shape and size especially if a man was considered to be overweight (Grogan and Richards, 2002). Some of the bodybuilders we interviewed have commented that the primary motivation to start bodybuilding was to be more sexually attractive to women (Grogan et al., 2006b). However, once they had started to bodybuild, competition with other men became a more important motivator. None of the men who were using steroids cited pressure from female partners as a motivator. Pressure from media models and other men training at the gym was a more significant factor here (see Chapter 4).

Michael Siever (1994) found that gay men, heterosexual women and heterosexual men did not differ significantly in their beliefs as to the degree to which their body mattered to potential sexual partners. Similarly, when asked about the importance of physical appearance to their own potential sexual partners, no significant differences in importance between heterosexual women, heterosexual men and gay men were cited. These data are important since they show that (according to their own reports) heterosexual men and gay men do not place a higher premium on physical attractiveness in their partners than heterosexual women.

Taken at face value, these findings might suggest that heterosexual men are under equivalent pressure to gay men and to heterosexual women to attain a slender and (in the case of men) muscled appearance to attract female sexual partners. However, although heterosexual men may receive, and perceive, pressure from women to look slender and muscular, existing data suggest that this is unlikely to motivate body change strategies (Grogan and Richards, 2002; Fawkner, 2004; Hargreaves and Tiggemann, 2006). This may be because pressure to look toned and muscular is to some extent counterbalanced by a general cultural attitude that attributes other than physical attractiveness are important in heterosexual men (Bordo, 2003), and because they function within a mainstream culture that does not openly sanction the objectification of heterosexual men (Davis et al., 2001; Morrison et al., 2004).

Evolutionary psychologists have generally failed to consider what women find attractive in men, largely because of their assumption that what women are looking for in a man is his ability to defend and support her financially. However, even Charles Darwin argued that women would choose men for the way they look (rather than for their abilities to support them financially, or for personality factors):

> Both sexes, if the females as well as the males were permitted to exert any choice, would choose their partners not for mental charms, or property, or social position, but almost solely from external appearance.
>
> (Darwin, 1871, cited in Singh, 1995: 1089)

Devendra Singh (1995) suggested that body shape may be important in determining how attractive women rate men to be. He suggests that body fat distribution is important in determining which men are judged sexually attractive by women. After puberty, men tend to lose fat from lower body parts and deposit fat on upper body parts (shoulders, nape of neck and abdomen). From an analysis of data from the US National Aeronautics and Space Administration, sampling from European, Asian, African and Latin American men, Singh argues that most men, irrespective of culture, have a WHR of between 0.8 and 0.87. He argues that men with WHR in this range are healthier than other men, and are likely to be of reproductive age. In a series of studies he found that white and Hispanic women of different ages found men with WHR in the average range most attractive when presented with male body shapes varying in WHR. This effect was maximized if the males were of higher financial status. Singh suggests that physical appearance is important in determining women's choice of sexual partner because it relates to health:

> Women may select mates who are healthy to ensure that their offspring inherit a predisposition for good health and that the man would be able to provide good quality parental care.
>
> (Singh, 1995: 1099)

171

There are similar problems associated with these arguments to those relating to the data on men's preferences for women's body types. Although these results could be affected by biological factors, they may also be influenced by learned preferences. Data come from US (white and Hispanic) women who share similar cultural influences. The results would be more convincing if they came from different cultures. He shows that women tend to prefer men who fall into the average (i.e. most familiar) range. Singh does not examine waist-to-shoulder ratios or waist-to-chest ratios, which may be more telling in terms of women's preferences for male body types. Also, explanations are post-hoc and could as easily be explained by social-cultural pressures as by evolutionary "mate value".

Chest size may be particularly important in women's ratings of men, and Kevin Thompson and Stacey Tantleff (1992) found that women showed a preference for large chest sizes in men when presented with male figures varying in chest size. Most men rated their current chest size as smaller than ideal on this scale. Women associated adjectives such as assertive, athletic, sexually active, confident and popular with large chest sizes for men. Thompson and Tantleff concluded that women (and the men themselves) show a distinct preference for large chest sizes.

Viren Swami and Amy Sunshine Harris (2012) review available literature and conclude that waist-to-chest ratio (WCR; the ratio of the circumference of the waist to the circumference of the chest) is the best predictor of women's ratings of male attractiveness. Studies using phorographic images (rather than line drawings) suggest that figures with large chest size and BMI towards the low end of the normal range are perceived as maximally attractive (Tovee et al., 2006).

To summarize, heterosexual men perceive some pressure from sexual partners, but expect that their current body shape and size are close to women's ideal, and are less likely than other groups to be motivated to exercise and diet to make themselves more attractive to potential sexual partners. Arguments from evolutionary psychologists suggest that women in heterosexual relationships look for characteristics indicating "fitness" in their partners. However, evolutionary psychologists have failed to demonstrate convincingly that preferences for particular body shapes are biologically based, and preferences are open to alternative, sociocultural interpretations.

Intersections between demographic categories

The term "intersectionality" (Crenshaw, 2015; Hill-Collins and Bilge, 2016) relates to the view that cultural pressures are bound together and influenced by the intersectional systems in society. So, women may be under societal pressure to look a particular way because of their gender, but they may also be influenced by sub-cultural pressures linked to social class, age and ethnicity. Individuals may also have several different body-related identities (e.g. "male", "heterosexual", "middle class", "white") which may be more or less important at different times in their lives, and may influence sensitivity to body-related cultural pressures.

Tracy Tylka and Rachel Calogero (2010) note that culturally prescribed appearance ideals for women and men combine with multiple individual variables and identities (including gender role identification, developmental stage, cultural identification and sexual orientation) to influence body image. Laura Kelly (2007) and Esther Rothblum (2002) also talk about ways that identifying as "woman"/"man" and "lesbian"/"gay" can be associated with conflicting sets of "oppressive mandates" relating to body image. Other work has shown that identifying as "sportsman" and "gay" also provides contradictory messages about the male body (Filiault and Drummond, 2008). It is important to keep these complexities in mind and to consider possible intersections between demographic categories, especially when developing the kinds of interventions that will be discussed in Chapter 7.

Summary

- This chapter has reviewed data from a variety of sources looking at the associations between age, ethnicity, social class, and sexuality and body image.
- Body dissatisfaction is evident from 8 years of age and possibly even earlier. Boys and girls express similar concerns to those voiced by adults in relation to their "fear of fat", and describe similar body shape ideals to those described by adults (slender for girls and slender but muscular for boys). Women do not appear to become less satisfied with age, and there is some indication that women's ideals may become heavier (in line with actual body size) as they become older. There is some evidence that older men are less satisfied with adiposity than younger men, though men of all ages seem to have muscularity concerns. Over 80, women may be generally more body-satisfied than men.
- Data in relation to ethnicity show that African-American and Afro-Caribbean British women have heavier body shape ideals and are less dissatisfied than white US or white British women. Recent work suggests that Hispanic and Asian women may be becoming less satisfied as a result of the spread of mainstream, white cultural prejudice against overweight beyond the white community; they are unlikely to differ from white women. Data from men are mixed, although African-American men may be more satisfied than white men and have heavier ideals for both men and women, and Hispanic men do not seem to differ from white men.
- Studies of sexuality and body image have shown that heterosexual women and gay men may be most dissatisfied with their bodies and heterosexual men most satisfied, due in part to differences in cultural pressures in relation to body shape and size. Lesbian subcultures may be protective against body dissatisfaction in women, although research results are mixed, with many studies showing no significant differences in satisfaction, possibly because of the overriding power of mainstream cultural pressure on all women.

- Data in relation to body image in people of differing age, class, ethnic group and sexuality emphasize the crucial importance of understanding sociocultural pressures on group members, and differential pressure linked with different sub-cultural identities, in order to make sense of variations in body image.

Bibliography

Ackard, D.M., Kearney-Cooke, A. and Peterson, C.B. (2000) 'Effect of body image and self-image on women's sexual behaviours', *International Journal of Eating Disorders*, 28 (4), 422–9.

Akrawi, D., Bartrop, R., Potter, U. and Touyz, S. (2015) 'Religiosity, spirituality in relation to disordered eating and body image concerns: A systematic review', *Journal of Eating Disorders*, 3, 39.

Altabe, M. and O'Garo, K.-G. (2002) 'Hispanic body images', in T.F. Cash and T. Pruzinsky (Eds), *Body image. A handbook of theory, research, and clinical practice* (pp. 250–6), New York: Guilford Press.

Aruguete, M.S., Nickleberry, L.D. and Yates, A. (2004) 'Acculturation, body image, and eating attitudes among black and white college students', *North American Journal of Psychology*, 6 (3), 393–404.

Ashikari, M. (2005) 'Cultivating Japanese whiteness: The "whitening" cosmetics boom and the Japanese identity', *Journal of Material Culture*, 10 (1), 73–9.

Atkins, D. (Ed.) (1998) *Looking queer: Body image and identity in lesbian, bisexual, gay and transgender communities*, New York: Harrington Park Press.

Baker, L. and Gringart, E. (2009) 'Body image and self-esteem in older adulthood', *Aging and Society,* 29(6), 977–95.

Barry, D.T. and Grilo, C.M. (2002) 'Eating and body image disturbances in adolescent psychiatric inpatients: Gender and ethnicity patterns', *International Journal of Eating Disorders*, 32 (3), 335–43.

Beren, S., Hayden, H., Wilfley, D. and Grilo, C. (1996) 'The influence of sexual orientation on body dissatisfaction in adult men and women', *International Journal of Eating Disorders*, 20 (2), 135–41.

Bojorquez, I. and Unikel, C. (2012) 'Body image and social class', in T.F. Cash (Ed.) *Encyclopedia of body image and human appearance* (pp. 153–9), London: Elsevier.

Bordo, S. (2003) *Unbearable weight: Feminism, Western culture, and the body* (10th anniversary edition), Berkeley, CA: University of California Press.

Brand, P., Rothblum, E. and Soloman, L. (1992) 'A comparison of lesbians, gay men, and heterosexuals on weight and restricted eating', *International Journal of Eating Disorders*, 11 (3), 253–9.

Brown, L. (1987) 'Lesbians, weight and eating: New analyses and perspectives', in Boston Lesbian Psychologies Collective (Eds), *Lesbian psychologies* (pp. 294–309), Urbana, IL: University of Illinois Press.

Brownmiller, S. (1984) *Femininity*, New York: Linden Press.

Burgess, G., Grogan, S. and Burwitz, L. (2006) 'Effects of a 6-week aerobic dance intervention on body image and physical self-perceptions in adolescent girls', *Body Image*, 3 (1), 57–67.

Cachelin, F.M., Monreal, T.K. and Juarez, L.C. (2006) 'Body image and size perceptions of Mexican-American women', *Body Image*, 3 (1), 67–76.

Cachelin, F.M., Striegel-Moore, R.H. and Elder, K.A. (1998) 'Realistic weight perception and body size assessment in a racially diverse community sample of dieters', *Obesity Research*, 6 (1), 62–8.

Cafri, G., Thompson, J.K., Ricciardelli, L., McCabe, M., Smolak, L. and Yesalis, C. (2005) 'Pursuit of the muscular ideal: Physical and psychological consequences and putative risk factors', *Clinical Psychology Review*, 25 (2), 215–39.

Campos, P. (2004) *The obesity myth: Why America's obsession with weight is hazardous to your health*, New York: Gotham Books.

Cash, T., Ancis, J. and Strachan, M. (1997) 'Gender attitudes, feminist identity, and body images among college women', *Sex Roles*, 36 (7–8), 433–47.

Cash, T.F., Theriault, J. and Annis, N.M. (2004) 'Body image in an interpersonal context: Adult attachment, fear of intimacy, and social anxiety', *Journal of Social and Clinical Psychology*, 23 (1), 89–103.

Celio, A.A., Zabinski, M.F. and Wilfley, D.E. (2002) 'African-American body images', in T.F. Cash and T. Pruzinsky (Eds), *Body image: A handbook of theory, research, and clinical practice* (pp. 234–42), New York: Guilford Press.

Cepanec, D. and Payne, B. (2000) '"Old bags" under the knife: Facial cosmetic surgery among women', in B. Miedema, J.M. Stoppard and V. Anderson (Eds) *Women's bodies, women's lives* (pp. 121–41), Toronto: Sumach Press.

Charles, N. and Kerr, M. (1986) 'Food for feminist thought', *Sociological Review*, 34, 537–72.

Chernin, K. (1983) *Womansize: The tyranny of slenderness*, London: Women's Press.

Clarke, L.H. (2002) 'Older women's perceptions of ideal body weights: The tensions between health and appearance motivations for weight loss', *Aging and Society*, 22 (6), 751–73.

Clarke, V. and Turner, K. (2007) 'Clothes maketh the queer? Dress, appearance and the construction of lesbian, gay and bisexual identities', *Feminism and Psychology*, 17 (2), 267–76.

Conner, M., Johnson, C. and Grogan, S. (2004) 'Gender, sexuality, body image and eating behaviours', *Journal of Health Psychology*, 9 (4), 505–15.

Cooper, P., Taylor, M., Cooper, Z. and Fairburn, C. (1987) 'The development and validation of the Body Shape Questionnaire', *International Journal of Eating Disorders*, 6 (4), 485–94.

Crago, M., Shisslak, C.M. and Estes, L.S. (1996) 'Eating disturbances among American minority groups: A review', *International Journal of Eating Disorders*, 19 (3), 239–48.

Crenshaw, K. (2015) *On intersectionality: The essential writings of Kimberle Crenshaw*, New York, NY: New Press.

Cruz, J. (2014) *Body-image pressure increasingly affects boys*, available online at: www. theatlantic.com/health/archive/2014/03/body-image-pressure-increasingly-affects-boys/283897/ [accessed 20 December 2014].

Davis, C., Dionne, M. and Schuster, B. (2001) 'Physical and psychological correlates of appearance orientation', *Personality and Individual Differences*, 30 (1), 21–30.

Davis, K. (1995) *Reshaping the female body: The dilemma of cosmetic surgery*, London: Routledge.

Doy, G. (1996) 'Out of Africa: Orientalism, "race", and the female body', *Body and Society*, 2 (4), 17–44.

Dunn, M. and White, V. (2011) 'The epidemiology of anabolic-androgenic steroid use among Australian secondary school students', *Journal of Science and Medicine in Sport,* 14 (1), 10–14.

Dworkin, A. (1988) 'Not in man's image: Lesbians and the cultural oppression of body image', *Women and Therapy,* 8 (1–2), 27–39.

Eisenberg, M.E., Wall, M. and Neumark-Sztainer, D. (2012) 'Muscle-enhancing behaviors among adolescent girls and boys', *Pediatrics,* 130 (6), 1019–26.

Ellis, S. and Heritage, P. (1989) 'AIDS and the cultural response: The normal heart and we all fall down', in S. Shephard and M. Wallis (Eds), *Coming on strong: Gay politics and culture* (pp. 39–53), London: Unwin Hyman.

Ericksen, A.J., Markey, C.N. and Tinsley, B.J. (2005) 'Familial influences on Mexican-American and Euro-American preadolescent boys' and girls' body dissatisfaction', *Eating Behaviours,* 4 (3), 245–55.

Fawkner, H. (2004) *Body image attitudes in men: An examination of the antecedents and consequent adjustive strategies and behaviors,* unpublished PhD thesis, University of Melbourne.

Fern, V.A., Buckley, E. and Grogan, S. (2012) 'Womens' experiences of body image and weight loss after childbirth', *British Journal of Midwifery,* 20 (12), 860–5.

Fern, V., Buckley, E. and Grogan, S. (2014) 'Postpartum body image and feeding choices: Dealing with the pressure to be slender', *British Journal of Midwifery,* 22 (11), 788–94.

Filiault, S.M. and Drummond, M.J.N. (2010) '"Muscular, but not 'roided out'": Gay male athletes and performance-enhancing substances', *International Journal of Men's Health,* 9 (1), 62–81.

Forna, A. (1996) 'For women, or for men only?' *The Independent on Sunday,* 28 April.

Franko, D.L. and Herrera, I. (1997) 'Body image differences in Guatemalan-American and white college women', *Eating Disorders,* 5 (2), 119–27.

Franko, D.L. and Roehrig, J.P. (2011) 'African American body images', in T.F. Cash and L. Smolak (Eds), *Body image: A handbook of science, practice and prevention* (pp. 221–8), London: The Guilford Press.

Franzoi, S. and Shields, S. (1984) 'The body esteem scale: Multidimensional structure and sex differences in a college population', *Journal of Personality Assessment,* 48 (2), 173–8.

Franzoi, S.L. and Chang, Z. (2002) 'The body esteem of Hmong and Causasian young adults', *Psychology of Women Quarterly,* 26 (1), 89–91.

Frederick, D.A., Peplau, L.A. and Lever, J. (2008) 'The Barbie mystique: Satisfaction with breast size and shape across the lifespan', *International Journal of Sexual Health,* 20 (3), 200–11.

Freeman, H. (2014) *Why black models are rarely in fashion,* available online at: www.theguardian.com/commentisfree/2014/feb/18/black-models-fashion-magazines-catwalks [accessed 20 January 2016].

Fuss, D. (1989) *Essentially speaking: Feminism, nature and difference,* New York and London: Routledge.

Gillen, M.M. and Lefkowitz, E.S. (2012) 'Gender and racial/ethnic differences in body image development among college students', *Body Image,* 9 (1), 126–30.

Glenn, E.N. (2008) 'Yearning for lightness: Transnational circuits in the marketing and consumption of skin lighteners', *Gender and Society,* 22 (3), 281–302.

Gough, B. and Flanders, G. (2009) 'Celebrating "obese" bodies: Gay "bears" talk about weight, body image and health', *International Journal of Men's Health,* 8 (3), 235–53.

Gough, B., Hall, M. and Seymour-Smith, S. (2014) 'Straight guys do wear make-up: Contemporary masculinities and investment in appearance', in S. Robertson (Ed.) *Debating modern masculinities: Change, continuity, crisis?* (pp. 106–24), Basingstoke: Palgrave Macmillan.

Gough, J. (1989) 'Theories of sexual identity and the masculinisation of the gay man', in S. Shepherd and M. Wallis (Eds), *Coming on strong: Gay politics and culture* (pp. 119–35), London: Unwin Hyman.

Grabe, S. and Hyde, J. (2006) 'Ethnicity and body dissatisfaction among women in the United States: A meta-analysis', *Psychological Bulletin*, 132 (4), 622–40.

Grogan, S. (1999) *Body image: Understanding body dissatisfaction in men, women and children*, London: Routledge.

Grogan, S. (2012) 'Body image development – adult women', in T.F. Cash (Ed.), *Encyclopedia of body image and human appearance* (pp. 201–6), London: Elsevier.

Grogan, S., Conner, M. and Smithson, H. (2006a) 'Sexuality and exercise motivations: Are gay men and heterosexual women most likely to be motivated by concern about weight and appearance?' *Sex Roles*, 55 (7–8), 567–72.

Grogan, S., Donaldson, C., Richards, H. and Wainwright, N. (1997) 'Men's body image: Body dissatisfaction in eight- to twenty-five-year-old males', paper presented to the European Health Psychology annual conference, Bordeaux, 3 September.

Grogan, S., Gill, S., Brownbridge, K., Kilgariff, S. and Whalley, A. (2013) 'Dress fit and body image: A thematic analysis of women's accounts during and after trying on dresses', *Body Image*, 10 (3), 380–8.

Grogan, S. and Richards, H. (2002) 'Body image: Focus groups with boys and men', *Men and Masculinities*, 4 (3), 219–32.

Grogan, S., Shepherd, S., Evans, R., Wright, S. and Hunter, G. (2006b) 'Experiences of anabolic steroid use: Interviews with men and women steroid users', *Journal of Health Psychology*, 11 (6), 849–60.

Grogan, S. and Wainwright, N. (1996) 'Growing up in the culture of slenderness: Girls' experiences of body dissatisfaction', *Women's Studies International Forum*, 19 (6), 665–73.

Hall, M. (2015) *Metrosexual masculinities*, London: Palgrave Macmillan, UK.

Hargreaves, D. and Tiggemann, M. (2006) '"Body image is for girls": A qualitative study of boys' body image', *Journal of Health Psychology*, 11(4), 567–76.

Harris, M.B., Walters, L.C. and Waschull, S. (1991) 'Gender and ethnic differences in obesity-related behaviors and attitudes in a college sample', *Journal of Applied Social Psychology*, 21 (19), 1545–66.

Harris, S. (1994) 'Racial differences in predictors of college women's body image attitudes', *Women and Health*, 21 (4), 89–104.

Harris, S. and Carr, A. (2001) 'Prevalence of concerns about physical appearance in the general population', *British Journal of Plastic Surgery*, 54 (3), 223–6.

Henrich, J., Heine, S.J. and Norenzayan, A. (2010) 'The weirdest people in the world?' *Behavioral and Brain Sciences*, 33 (2–3), 61–83.

Hill-Collins, P. and Bilge, S. (2016) *Intersectionality*, New York, NY: Polity Press.

Hodgkinson, E.L., Smith, D.M. and Wittkowski, A. (2014) 'Women's experiences of their pregnancy and postpartum body image: A systematic review and meta-synthesis', *BMC Pregnancy and Childbirth*, 14, 330.

Hodkinson, W. (1997) *Body image stereotypes: The idealisation of slimness and perceptions of body image and occupational success*, unpublished BSc dissertation, Manchester Metropolitan University.

Holt, K. and Ricciardelli, L.A. (2002) 'Social comparisons and negative affect as indicators of problem eating and muscle preoccupation among children', *Journal of Applied Developmental Psychology*, 23 (3), 285–304.

Hopkins, V. (2006) 'Understanding pre-pubescent and post-pubescent boys' body image: An interpretative phenomenological analysis', unpublished MSc Health Psychology dissertation, Staffordshire University.

Huon, G. (1988) 'Towards the prevention of eating disorders', in D. Hardoff and E. Chigier (Eds) *Eating disorders in adolescents and young adults* (pp. 447–54), London: Freund.

Huxley, C. and Hayfield, N. (2012) 'Lesbian, gay and bisexual sexualities: Appearance and body image', in N. Rumsey and D. Harcourt (Eds), *The Oxford handbook of the psychology of appearance* (pp. 190–202), Oxford: Oxford University Press.

International Society of Aesthetic Surgeons (2016) *ISAPS Global Statistics*, available online at: www.isaps.org/news/isaps-global-statistics [accessed 5 January 2016].

Jones, L.R., Fries, E. and Danish, S.J. (2007) 'Gender and ethnic differences in body image and opposite sex figure preferences of rural adolescents', *Body Image*, 4 (1), 103–108.

Kawamura, K. (2002) 'Asian-American body images', in T.F. Cash and T. Pruzinsky (Eds) *Body image: A handbook of theory, research, and clinical practice* (pp. 243–9), New York: Guilford Press.

Kawamura, K. (2011) 'Asian-American body images', in T.F. Cash and L. Smolak (Eds), *Body image: A handbook of science, practice and prevention* (pp. 229–36), New York: Guilford Press.

Kelly, L. (2007) 'Lesbian body image perceptions: The context of body silence', *Qualitative Health Research*, 17 (7), 873–883.

Kitzinger, C. (1987) *The social construction of lesbianism*, London: Sage.

Kowner, R. (2002) 'Japanese body image: Structure and esteem scores in a cross-cultural perspective', *International Journal of Psychology*, 37 (3), 149–59.

Kronenfeld, L.W., Reba-Harreleson, L., Von Holle, A., Reyes, M.L. and Bulik, C.M. (2010) 'Ethnic and racial differences in body size perception and satisfaction', *Body Image*, 7(2), 131–6.

Lamb, C.S., Jackson, L., Cassiday, P. and Priest, D. (1993) 'Body figure preferences of men and women: A comparison of two generations', *Sex Roles*, 28 (5–6), 345–58.

Levesque, M. and Vichesky, D. (2006) 'Raising the bar on the body beautiful: An analysis of the body image concerns of homosexual men', *Body Image*, 3 (1), 45–56.

Lopez, I., Gonzalez, A.N. and Ho, A. (2012) 'Skin color', in T.F. Cash (Ed.), *Encyclopedia of body image and human appearance* (pp. 730–7), London: Elsevier.

Ludwig, M.R. and Brownell, K.D. (1999) 'Lesbians, bisexual women and body image: An investigation of gender roles and social group affiliation', *International Journal of Eating Disorders*, 25 (1), 89–97.

McCabe, M.P. and Ricciardelli, L.A. (2001) 'Body image and body change techniques among young adolescent boys', *European Eating Disorders Review*, 9 (5), 335–47.

McCabe, M.P. and Ricciardelli, L.A (2004) 'Body image dissatisfaction among males across the lifespan: A review of past literature', *Journal of Psychosomatic Research*, 56 (6), 675–85.

Maloney, M., McGuire, J., Daniels, S. and Specker, B. (1989) 'Dieting behaviour and eating attitudes in children', *Pediatrics*, 84 (3), 482–9.

Martz, D., Curtin, L. and Bazzini, D. (2012) 'Fat talk and body image', in T.F. Cash (Ed.) *Encyclopedia of body image and human appearance* (pp. 120–7), London: Elsevier.

Meredith, B. (1988) *A change for the better*, London: Grafton.

Miller, K.J., Gleaves, D.H., Hirsch, T.G., Green, B.A., Snow, A.C. and Corbett, C.C. (2000) 'Comparisons of body image dimensions by race/ethnicity and gender in a university population', *International Journal of Eating Disorders*, 27 (3), 310–16.

Mishkind, M., Rodin, J., Silberstein, L. and Striegel-Moore, R. (1986) 'The embodiment of masculinity: Cultural, psychological, and behavioral dimensions', *American Behavioral Scientist*, 29 (5), 545–62.

Monaghan, L. (2005) 'Discussion piece: A critical take on the obesity debate', *Social Theory and Health*, 3 (4), 302–14.

Morris, D. (1985) *Bodywatching*, New York: Crown.

Morrison, M.A., Morrison, T.G. and Sager, C.-L. (2004) 'Does body satisfaction differ between gay men and lesbian women and heterosexual men and women?' *Body Image*, 1 (2), 127–38.

Morrison, T.C. and McCutcheon, J.M. (2011) 'Gay and lesbian body mages', in T.F. Cash and L. Smolak (Eds), *Body image: A handbook of science, practice and prevention* (pp. 214–220), London: The Guilford Press.

Morrison, T.C. and McCutcheon, J.M. (2012) 'Body image among gay, lesbian, and bisexual individuals', in T.F. Cash (Ed.), *Encyclopedia of body image and human appearance* (pp. 103–107), London: Elsevier.

Nayak, A. (1997) 'Frozen bodies: Disclosing whiteness in Haagen-Dazs advertising', *Body and Society*, 3 (3), 33–51.

Neff, L., Sargent, R., McKeown, R., Jackson, K. and Valois, R. (1997) 'Black-white differences in body size perceptions and weight management practices among adolescent females', *Journal of Adolescent Health*, 20 (6), 459–65.

Neumark-Sztainer, D., Croll, J., Story, M., Hanno, P.J., French, S.A. and Perry, C. (2002) 'Ethnic/race differences in weight-control concerns and behaviours among adolescent girls and boys: Findings from project EAT', *Journal of Psychosomatic Research*, 53 (5), 963–74.

Nichter, M. (2000) *Fat talk: What girls and their parents say about dieting*, Cambridge, MA: Harvard University Press.

Nishina, A., Ammon, N.Y., Bellmore, A.D. and Graham, S. (2006) 'Body dissatisfaction and physical development among ethnic minority adolescents', *Journal of Youth and Adolescence*, 35(2), 189–201.

O'Dea, J. and Caputi, P. (2001) 'Association between socioeconomic status, weight, age and gender, and the body image and weight control practices of 6- to 19-year-old children and adolescents', *Health Education Research*, 16 (5), 521–32.

O'Dea, J. and Cinelli, R.L. (in press) 'Use of drugs to change appearance in girls and female adolescents', in M. Hall, S. Grogan and B. Gough (Eds) *Chemically modified bodies: The use of diverse substances for appearance enhancement*, London: Palgrave.

O'Kelly, L. (1994) 'Body talk', *The Guardian*, 23 October, 30–2.

Orbach, S. (1993) *Hunger strike: The anorectic's struggle as a metaphor for our age*, London: Penguin.

Peplau, L.A., Frederick, D.A., Yee, C.K., Maisel, N., Lever, J. and Ghavami, N. (2009) 'Body image satisfaction in heterosexual, gay, and lesbian adults', *Archives of Sexual Behavior*, 38 (5), 713–25.

Pope, H.G., Phillips, K.A. and Olivardia, R. (2000) *The Adonis complex: The secret crisis of male body obsession*, New York: Free Press.

Reardon, R. and Grogan. S. (2011) 'Women's reasons for seeking breast reduction: A qualitative investigation', *Journal of Health Psychology*, 16 (1), 31–41.

Reboussin, B.A., Rejeski, W.J., Maryin, K.A., Callahan, K., Dunn, A. et al. (2000) 'Correlates of satisfaction with body function and body appearance in middle- and older-aged adults: The activity counselling trial (ACT)', *Psychology and Health*, 15 (2), 239–54.

Ricciardelli, L.A. and McCabe, M.P. (2001) 'Children's body image concerns and eating disturbance: A review of the literature', *Clinical Psychology Review*, 21 (3), 325–44.

Ricciardelli, L.A. and McCabe, M.P. (2003) 'A longitudinal analysis of the role of biopsychosocial factors in predicting body change strategies among adolescent boys', *Sex Roles*, 48 (7), 349–59.

Ricciardelli, L.A. and McCabe, M.P. (2004) 'A biopsychosocial model of disordered eating and the pursuit of muscularity in adolescent boys', *Psychological Bulletin*, 130 (2), 179–205.

Ricciardelli, L.A., McCabe, M.P. and Ridge, D. (2006) 'The construction of the adolescent male body through sport', *Journal of Health Psychology*, 11 (4), 577–87.

Ricciardelli, L.A., McCabe, M.P., Mussap, A.J. and Holt, K.E. (2009) 'Body image in preadolescent boys', in L. Smolak and J.K. Thompson (Eds) *Body image, eating disorders and obesity in youth*, 2nd edition (pp. 77–96), Washington, DC: APA.

Ricciardelli, L.A., McCabe, M.P., Williams, R.J. and Thompson, J.K. (2007) 'The role of ethnicity and culture in body image and disordered eating among males', *Clinical Psychology Review*, 27 (5), 582–606.

Ricciardelli, L.A. and Williams, R.J. (in press) 'Use of supplements and drugs to change body image and appearance among boys and male adolescents', in M. Hall, S. Grogan and B. Gough (Eds) *Chemically modified bodies. The use of diverse substances for appearance enhancement*, London: Palgrave.

Robinson, T., Killen, J., Litt, I., Hammer, L., Wilson, D., Haydel, F., Hayward, C. and Taylor, B. (1996) 'Ethnicity and body dissatisfaction: Are Hispanic and Asian girls at increased risk for eating disorders?' *Journal of Adolescent Health*, 19 (6), 384–93.

Robinson, T.N., Chang, J.Y., Haydel, K.F. and Killen, J.D. (2001) 'Overweight concerns and body dissatisfaction among third grade children: The impacts of ethnicity and socioeconomic status', *Journal of Pediatrics*, 138 (2), 181–7.

Rothblum, E.D. (2002) 'Gay and lesbian body images', in T.F. Cash and T. Pruzinsky (Eds), *Body image: A handbook of theory, research, and clinical practice* (pp. 257–68), New York: Guilford Press.

Schooler, D. and Lowry, L.S. (2011) 'Hispanic/Latino body images', in T.F. Cash and L. Smolak (Eds), *Body image: A handbook of science, practice and prevention* (pp. 237–243), London: Guilford Press.

Schur, E.A., Sanders, M. and Steiner, H. (2000) 'Body dissatisfaction and dieting in young children', *International Journal of Eating Disorders*, 27 (1), 74–82.

Share, T.L. and Mintz, L.B. (2002) 'Differences between lesbians and heterosexual women in disordered eating and related attitudes', *Journal of Homosexuality*, 42 (4), 89–106.

Shaw, H., Ramirez, L., Trost, A., Randall, P. and Stice, E. (2004) 'Body image and eating disturbances across ethnic groups: More similarities than differences', *Psychology of Addictive Behaviors*, 18 (1), 12–18.

Shilling, C. (1993) *The body and social theory*, London: Sage.

Siever, M. (1994) 'Sexual orientation and gender as factors in socioculturally acquired vulnerability to body dissatisfaction and eating disorders', *Journal of Consulting and Clinical Psychology*, 62 (2), 252–60.

Singh, D. (1993) 'Adaptive significance of female physical attractiveness: Role of the waist-to-hip ratio', *Journal of Personality and Social Psychology*, 65 (2), 293–307.

Singh, D. (1995) 'Female judgement of male attractiveness and desirability for relationships: Role of the waist-to-hip ratio and financial status', *Journal of Personality and Social Psychology*, 69 (6), 1089–1101.

Skouteris, H. (2012) 'Pregnancy: Physical and body image changes', in T.F. Cash (Ed.), *Encyclopedia of body image and human appearance* (pp. 664–8), London: Elsevier.

Smolak, L. (2004) 'Body image in children and adolescents: Where do we go from here?' *Body Image*, 1 (1), 15–28.

Story, M., French, S.A., Resnick, M.D. and Blum, R.W. (1995) 'Ethnic racial and socioeconomic differences in dieting behaviours and body image perceptions in adolescents', *International Journal of Eating Disorders*, 18(2), 173–9.

Striegel-Moore, R.H., Silberstein, L.R. and Rodin, J. (1986) 'Toward an understanding of risk factors for bulimia', *American Psychologist*, 41 (3), 246–63.

Striegel-Moore, R.H., Tucker, N. and Hsu, J. (1990) 'Body image dissatisfaction and disordered eating in lesbian college students', *International Journal of Eating Disorders*, 9 (5), 493–500.

Strong, S.M., Williamson, D.A., Netemeyer, R.G. and Geer, J.H. (2000) 'Eating disorder symptoms and concerns about body differ as a function of gender and sexual orientation', *Journal of Social and Clinical Psychology*, 19 (2), 240–55.

Swami, V. and Harris, A.S. (2012) 'Evolutionary perspectives on physical appearance', in T.F. Cash (Ed.), *Encyclopedia of body image and human appearance* (pp. 404–11), London: Elsevier.

Swami, V. and Tovée, M.J. (2013) 'Resource security impacts men's female breast size preferences', *PLoS ONE*, 8 (3), E57623.

Swami, V., Caprario, C., Tovee, M.J. and Furnham, A. (2006) 'Female physical attractiveness in Britain and Japan: A cross-cultural study', *European Journal of Personality*, 20 (1), 69–81.

Swami, V., Frederick, D., Aavik, T., Alcalay, L., Allik, J. et al. (2010) 'The attractive female body weight and female body dissatisfaction in 26 countries across 10 world regions: Results of the international body project I', *Personality and Social Psychology Bulletin*, 36 (3), 309–326.

Swami, V., Miah, J., Noorani, N. and Taylor, D. (2014) 'Is the hijab protective? An investigation of body image and related constructs among British Muslim women', *British Journal of Psychology*, 105 (3), 352–63,

Tatangelo, G.L. and Ricciardelli, L.A. (2013) 'A qualitative study of preadolescent boys' and girls' body image: Gendered ideals and sociocultural influences', *Body Image*, 10 (4), 591–8.

Tatangelo, G.L. and Ricciardelli, L.A. (2015) 'Children's body image and social comparisons with peers and the media', *Journal of Health Psychology*. [E-pub ahead of print; DOI:1359105315615409]

Taub, J. (1999) 'Bisexual women and beauty norms: A qualitative examination', *Journal of Lesbian Studies*, 3 (4), 27–36.

Thompson, J.K. and Tantleff, S. (1992) 'Female and male ratings of upper torso: Actual, ideal, and stereotypical conceptions', *Journal of Social Behavior and Personality*, 7 (2), 345–54.

Thompson, S., Corwin, S. and Sargeant, R. (1997) 'Ideal body size beliefs and weight concerns in fourth grade children', *International Journal of Eating Disorders*, 21 (3), 279–84.

Tiggemann, M. (2004) 'Body image across the adult lifespan: Stability and change', *Body Image: An International Journal of Research*, 1 (1), 29–41.

Tiggemann, M. and Pennington, B. (1990) 'The development of gender differences in body-size dissatisfaction', *Australian Psychologist*, 25 (3), 306–13.

Tiggemann, M. and Slevec, J. (2012) 'Appearance in adulthood', in N. Rumsey and D. Harcourt (Eds) *The Oxford handbook of the psychology of appearance* (pp. 142–59), Oxford: Oxford University Press.

Tiggemann, M., Martins, Y. and Kirkbride, A.B. (2007) 'Oh to be lean and muscular: Body image ideals in gay and heterosexual men', *Psychology of Men and Masculinity*, 8 (1),15–24.

Tovee, M.J. and Cornelissen, P.L. (2001) 'Female and male perceptions of female physical attractiveness in front-view and profile', *British Journal of Psychology*, 92 (2), 391–402.

Truby, H. and Paxton, S. (2002) 'Development of the Children's Body Image Scale', *British Journal of Clinical Psychology*, 41 (2), 185–203.

Tylka, T. and Calogero, R. (2010) 'Fiction, fashion, and function revisited: An introduction to the special issue on gendered body image, Part II', *Sex Roles*, 63 (9), 601–8.

Wardle, J. and Marsland, L. (1990) 'Adolescent concerns about weight and eating: A social-developmental perspective', *Journal of Psychosomatic Research*, 34 (4), 377–91.

Wardle, J., Bindra, R., Fairclough, B. and Westcombe, A. (1993) 'Culture and body image: Body perception and weight concern in young Asian and Caucasian British women', *Journal of Community and Applied Social Psychology*, 3 (3), 173–81.

Welch, C., Gross, S.M., Bronner, Y., Dewberry-Moore, P. and Paige, D.M. (2004) 'Discrepancies in body image perception among fourth-grade public school children from urban, suburban, and rural Maryland', *Journal of the American Dietetic Association*, 104 (7), 1080–5.

Werlinger, K., King, T., Clark, M., Pera, V. and Wincze, J. (1997) 'Perceived changes in sexual functioning and body image following weight loss in an obese female population: A pilot study', *Journal of Sex and Marital Therapy*, 23 (1), 74–8.

Wheatley, J. (2006) 'Like mother like daughter: The young copycat dieters', *The Times*, 11 August, 6–7.

Wiederman, M. and Pryor, T. (1997) 'Body dissatisfaction and sexuality among women with bulimia nervosa', *International Journal of Eating Disorders*, 21 (4), 361–5.

Williamson, S. and Delin, C. (2001) 'Young children's figural selections: Accuracy of reporting and body size dissatisfaction', *International Journal of Eating Disorders*, 29 (1), 80–4.

Wolf, N. (1991) *The beauty myth: How images of beauty are used against women*, New York: William Morrow.

Worobey, J. and Worobey, H.S. (2014) 'Body-size stigmatization by preschool girls: In a doll's world, it is good to be "Barbie"', *Body Image*, 11 (2), 171–4.

Wykes, M. and Gunter, B. (2005) *The media and body image*, London: Sage.

Yates, A., Edman, J. and Aruguete, M. (2004) 'Ethnic differences in BMI and body/self dissatisfaction among whites, Asian subgroups, Pacific Islanders, and African Americans', *Journal of Adolescent Health*, 34 (4), 300–7.

Yelland, C. and Tiggemann, M. (2003) 'Muscularity and the gay ideal: Body dissatisfaction and disordered eating in homosexual men', *Eating Behaviors*, 4 (2), 107–16.

Yingling, T. (1991) 'AIDS in America: Postmodern governance, identity and experience', in D. Fuss (Ed.) *Inside out: Lesbian theories, gay theories* (pp. 291–310), New York: Routledge.

Zamboni, B.D., Robinson, B.B.E. and Bockting, W.O. (2007) 'Body image and sexual functioning among bisexual women', *Journal of Bisexuality*, 6 (4), 7–26.

7

REDUCING BODY DISSATISFACTION AND PROMOTING POSITIVE BODY IMAGE

The preceding chapters have summarized existing work on men's and women's body image. From what we know about the impact of the effects of membership of particular subcultural groups (gender, class, ethnicity, sexuality and age), being white and being heterosexual are likely to predict body dissatisfaction in women. Age or social class are unlikely to have a significant impact on satisfaction, though there is some evidence that women over 60 years may be less invested in appearance and more in body function and health than younger women. Men in their middle years may be more dissatisfied with their body size than younger men, and heterosexual men may be more satisfied than gay men. Men are likely to be more satisfied than women in general, though this pattern may reverse over 80 years of age. The average woman could be expected to have dieted to try to lose weight, and the average man is probably not highly motivated to diet or exercise even if he perceives a mismatch between his current body and his ideal body image; if he does change his behaviour, he will probably exercise. Women are likely to want a slim "hourglass" shape, whereas men are likely to want an inverted triangle shape with broad shoulders and chest. Most women want to lose some weight, whereas men are equally likely to want to be heavier or lighter, and are likely to want to be more muscular at all ages.

Dissatisfaction exists in a context where body image is subjective and socially determined. The social relativity of body dissatisfaction has been demonstrated by illustrating how dissatisfaction varies by culture and subculture, and intersections between subcultures may also be important in predicting body image. Data from different social groups have shown that the same body shape may be perceived more or less positively depending on the gender and subculture of the person doing the perceiving. A person's body satisfaction can be easier to predict from what we know about that person's subjective evaluation of what it means to have that particular kind of body within a particular subculture (particularly if the person identifies strongly as a member of that group) than from actual body size as determined by BMI. This has led researchers from a range of disciplines to argue that body image is subjective, and open to change through social influences.

It is important to reduce body dissatisfaction, as even relatively minor body concerns may lead to exercise avoidance (Pridgeon and Grogan, 2012), use of anabolic steroids and other drugs to increase muscularity (Grogan et al., 2006; Hall et al., 2015), unhealthy eating behaviours such as binge eating, restrictive dieting and self-induced vomiting (Levine and Piran, 2004; Stice and Shaw, 2004), inability to quit smoking (King et al., 2005; Grogan, in press), greater incidence of risky UV exposure (Blashill et al., 2015), and desire for cosmetic surgery with its associated health risks (Calogero et al., 2014; von Soest et al., 2006). This may be a particular problem with vulnerable groups such as adolescents. On the basis of the results of a large-scale prospective study of body image and health-related behaviours, Diane Neumark-Sztainer and colleagues (2006) argue that body dissatisfaction puts adolescents at significant risk of weight gain and overall poor health. By identifying factors that predict dissatisfaction, we may be able to produce useful ideas for encouraging a more positive image of the body in those who are dissatisfied, to help improve health and well-being.

Psychological factors predicting body dissatisfaction

Psychologists have suggested various psychological factors that predict body dissatisfaction and that may reduce positive body image. Here we will examine proposed links between these psychological variables and body dissatisfaction, and look specifically at how this psychological knowledge can be useful in trying to reduce body dissatisfaction and promote positive body image in women and men.

Self-esteem

People who are low in self-esteem tend to be less satisfied with their bodies. This is the case for both men and women (O'Dea, 2012), although it has been suggested that there is a closer association of these two variables for women than for men (Avsec, 2006; Connors and Casey, 2006), probably because body dissatisfaction is generally more central to most women's sense of self than to men's (Orbach, 2010; Tiggemann, 2005). Some research has suggested that the relationship between self-esteem and body dissatisfaction may become weaker as women age and their appearance becomes less central to self-esteem (Webster and Tiggemann, 2003), and other studies have found that for adult men, low self-esteem is related to dissatisfaction with fatness but not with muscularity (Tiggemann et al., 2007).

Interview work has also supported the link between self-esteem and body image in both women and men. In interviews with women and men of different ages (Chapters 3 and 4), body dissatisfaction has been linked with negative feelings about the self, as well as lack of self-confidence and power in social situations. Although most authors have assumed that low self-esteem leads to body dissatisfaction rather than the reverse, recent evidence suggests that, at least for adolescent girls and late adolescent boys, body dissatisfaction may precede low self-esteem (Tiggemann, 2005; Paxton et al., 2006). Self-esteem may also precede changes in adult body satisfaction at some key points (for instance, women with higher self-esteem may find the physical changes associated with pregnancy and ageing easier to cope with and less damaging to body satisfaction than other women). Further work should enable a fuller understanding of the time course links between these two variables, and the ways that these links are gendered.

Research in Australia and the USA has shown that programmes designed to raise self-esteem in adolescents (O'Dea, 2007) and adults (Springer et al., 1999) can be effective in improving body image. The idea behind these programmes is that once self-esteem has improved, body image will also improve as a by-product of the self-esteem intervention. Jenny O'Dea (2004, 2012) argues that interventions that focus directly on body image may inadvertently raise body concerns. The advantage of programmes that do not focus directly on body image is that they may avoid increasing body concern in vulnerable people, and this may be particularly important in children who had not considered body image problematic prior to the intervention.

More work is needed in this area to determine the effectiveness of programmes that aim to build self-esteem and resiliency as an indirect method of improving body image, although existing US and Australian work with children and adolescents is producing very positive results (O'Dea and Abraham, 2000; O'Dea, 2007; O'Dea, 2012; Steese et al., 2006).

Internalization of the thin/muscular ideal

Women and men who internalize the mainstream thin/muscular ideal may be particularly sensitive to thin-ideal media cues and vulnerable to body dissatisfaction caused by self-ideal discrepancies (e.g. Jones, 2004; Ahern and Hetherington, 2006). The Tripartite Influence model (van den Berg et al., 2001) suggests that internalization of body ideals mediates between sociocultural messages and body image, and this is supported in empirical work with young men and women. Yuko Yamamiya and colleagues (2005) showed that body dissatisfaction can be increased by as little as five minutes of exposure to thin-and-beautiful images in women high in thin-ideal internalization, showing that social comparison with media ideals can produce particular risks for this group of women. Debra Franko and colleagues (2015) have also shown that internalization of body ideals was an important mediator between conformity to masculine norms and drive for muscularity and desire for leanness in young men from the US, Sweden and Australia.

Psychologists have suggested that people can be made resistant to the negative effects of media imagery by changing the ways that they interpret incoming social information. Studies using Heinberg et al.'s (1995) Sociocultural Attitudes Toward Appearance Questionnaire, which measures the degree of internalization and awareness of the thin/muscular ideal seen in mainstream media, find that women who score lower on internalization of the thin ideal are more satisfied with their bodies (e.g. Engeln-Maddox, 2005), and that men scoring lower on internalization of the slender and muscular ideal score significantly higher on body satisfaction (e.g. Jones, 2004). This raises the question of how some people resist internalizing the thin/muscular ideal and whether strategies used by them can be taught to others.

Most work on internalization of cultural ideals has been conducted with women, although Harrison Pope et al. (2000) focus on ways that individual men can challenge the muscular ideal through gaining an understanding of the ways that unrealistic images portrayed in the media are produced. A popular approach to resisting internalization of the thin ideal is to use psychoeducational interventions (known as "media literacy" programmes) to teach women (most studies have been conducted on women rather than men) to reject media images as appropriate targets for comparison. These techniques are based on the sociocultural model of body image (Chapter 1), which suggests that women are under significant pressure to be slender, mediated by media imagery and pressure from peers and family. Programmes stress the cultural relativity of slenderness ideals, and usually involve explanations of the variety of photographic techniques that can be used to bring pictures of models closer to the cultural ideal.

Although media literacy programmes have been found to be effective in reducing body concern in adult women with eating disorders and in adolescents, the effectiveness of these programmes with non-clinical adult groups has been mixed. Although such studies have generally been successful in training women to be sceptical about media images (e.g. Irving and Berel, 2001), they have mostly not been successful in reducing resulting body dissatisfaction. An exception is a study by Danielle Ridolphi and Jillion Vander Wal (2008) who allocated eighty-one US women undergraduates to either a media literacy or a control intervention, and found that the group exposed to the media literacy condition has significantly fewer body concerns at follow-up than the controls. Other studies have only shown a significant effect on body image in women either at risk of, or already experiencing, eating disorders. For instance, Janelle Coughlin and Cynthia Kalodner (2006) found that women at high risk of an eating disorder reported significant decreases in body dissatisfaction, drive for thinness, feelings of ineffectiveness and internalization of societal standards of beauty after participating in a media literacy intervention, but there was no significant change on any of these variables among low-risk participants. There is some evidence that media literacy programmes may be more effective with adolescents than with adults, and the Australian *Media Smart* programme has shown promise in reducing body concerns and body dissatisfaction in 13-year-old girls and boys (Wilksch and Wade, 2009).

Another approach that has enabled people to challenge unrealistic cultural messages and to rethink unrealistic body standards is cognitive-behavioural therapy (CBT). CBT is based on the idea that negative thoughts, feelings, behaviours and perceptions about the body are learned and can be unlearned (e.g. Cash, 2012). Researchers working within the cognitive-behavioural paradigm focus on the mental image that we have of our bodies. Rita Freedman (1990) suggests that CBT could be used on an individual level to train people to resist media pressure, through challenging "faulty cognitions" and developing new ways of conceptualizing incoming information.

187

CBT interventions tend to include cognitive restructuring and self-monitoring to change body-related thoughts, behavioural techniques such as desensitization to change body-dissatisfaction-linked behaviours such as avoidance of situations where the body might be exposed, and size estimation accuracy training to reduce size over- or underestimation (Jarry and Ip, 2005). CBT has been reported to be extremely effective in promoting positive body image in non-clinical populations (Cash, 2012; Cash and Hrabosky, 2004; Cash and Strachan, 2002). Reviews of the characteristics and effectiveness of body image interventions have concluded that CBT is a highly effective body image treatment producing long-term changes in body image (Jarry and Beraldi, 2004), and that interventions addressing the attitudinal, behavioural and perceptual components of body image were more effective than those that address only attitude and behaviour (Jarry and Ip, 2005).

Social comparison

Resistance to making unrealistic social comparisons may also reduce body dissatisfaction. As discussed in Chapter 5, upward social comparisons to thin/ muscular ideal imagery have been shown to increase body dissatisfaction in both men and women, and effects are not limited to young groups. For instance, Joy Kozar and Mary Damhorst (2009) examined the relationship between body image and proclivity to compare with fashion models in 281 women aged between 30 and 80 years. They found a significant positive relationship between social comparison behaviour and body dissatisfaction; the more women compared themselves with fashion models, the less satisfied they were. Older women were less likely to compare themselves with fashion models (as we found in work reported in Chapter 5), although "felt age" was also important, and women who felt younger were more inclined to compare themselves with models. Julie Slevec and Marika Tiggemann (2011) investigated the influence of media exposure on body dissatisfaction and disordered eating in 101 women aged between 35 and 55 years. They found that the tendency for social comparison predicted body dissatisfaction and disordered eating.

Reducing the tendency to make upward social comparisons may be challenging. It has been suggested that social comparison is largely automated, so asking participants to avoid comparing their bodies may increase tendencies to make these kinds of comparisons by drawing attention to them (e.g. Want, 2009). However, one viable strategy may be to train women to make downward comparisons. Renee Engeln-Maddox (2005) has suggested that since so many women make comparisons with media ideals, teaching women to focus on making downward comparisons with the parts of the body that they feel are superior to those of particular models may be helpful. In her study of 202 female students she notes that there were some aspects of the women's bodies that they felt were better than those of the models (one woman's elbows, another's navel), and she argues that getting women to focus on these positives may be an effective way to counter the negative effects of upward comparisons. Emma Halliwell and Helga Dittmar

(2005) have shown that women's motives when making upward comparisons are also crucial in determining their effect. If women are motivated to self-improve (rather than self-evaluate) then making upward comparisons with media models does not seem to increase body-focused anxiety as women may temporarily imagine themselves as the idealized image portrayed. The authors note that further work is necessary to establish how long-lasting this effect might be.

Some researchers have had success using media literacy techniques to reduce social comparisons. For instance, Emma Halliwell and colleagues (2011) ran an experimental study where they used a brief video intervention which explained the artificial nature of media images as a protective strategy to reduce social comparisons. A group of 127 British girls aged between 10 and 13 were assigned to one of four experimental conditions. Half the girls saw the video immediately before they viewed ultra-thin models or control images. In the absence of the intervention video, viewing thin idealized models was associated with greater lower body dissatisfaction than exposure to control images. However, viewing the video intervention immediately before exposure prevented this negative exposure effect. They concluded that the media literacy intervention prevented girls from making damaging social comparisons with media models. Unfortunately, questioning the validity of images may not be enough to produce this kind of effect in adult women. For instance, experimental studies where fashion magazine images have been labelled as either "retouch free" or unlabelled have tended to show that body dissatisfaction tends to increase with and without the label (e.g. Tiggemann et al., 2014b).

Self-objectification

Objectification Theory (Fredrickson and Roberts, 1997; see Chapter 1) suggests that existing in a sexually objectifying culture means that women may experience self-objectification resulting in body shame. Trait self-objectification, where women develop a chronic view of their bodies as objects, has been shown to be associated with body dissatisfaction in women of all ages (Grippo and Hill, 2008). Nita Mary McKinley (2011) links body surveillance, internalization of cultural body standards and body concern, and Rachel Calogero and colleagues (2014) have shown that exposure to sexually-objectifying cues in a scrambled sentence task increased both body shame and intentions to have cosmetic surgery in 18- to 21-year-old UK women, compared with women allocated to non-objectifying conditions.

Research has shown that women who hold feminist attitudes to body image are more satisfied than those who do not identify with feminist values. In a meta-analysis of twenty-six studies relating feminist identity to body dissatisfaction, Sarah Murnen and Linda Smolak (2009) found that feminist women reported higher levels of satisfaction. This has led some researchers to look at the effectiveness of incorporating feminist theory in programmes designed to prevent body dissatisfaction.

Feminist approaches such as those outlined in Chapter 3 have been applied in intervention programmes to enable women to change the ways that they interpret cultural messages through recognizing and challenging unhealthy female body ideals and objectifying practices (Murnen and Seabrook, 2012). In one study, Rachel Peterson and colleagues (2006) investigated whether exposure to feminist perspectives increases women's body satisfaction through increasing feminist identity. Peterson and colleagues suggest that a feminist schema may operate as a buffer through which societal messages may be filtered, to enable women to resist internalization of the thin ideal. Women in the feminist theory intervention condition (focusing on feminist theories of body image and eating disturbance, and delineation of feminist theories) were more likely to increase their identification as a feminist relative to those in the psychoeducation intervention condition (where women were exposed to a media literacy programme) or a control group who were not exposed to an intervention. Feminist identity predicted higher body satisfaction after the intervention. This study suggests that exposure to feminist theories may serve as an effective intervention to improve body image, at least in educated, university undergraduate samples similar to the women who took part in this study.

In a follow-up study focused specifically on Objectification Theory, Peterson and colleagues (2008) found that perceived empowerment was an important factor in reducing self-objectification in young women, and relatively more predictive of body image than was feminist identity. Work by Niva Piran and colleagues (e.g. Piran et al., 2004) is also informative in taking girls' and women's experiences as their starting point, enabling participants to evaluate critically the lived experience of being a female in a culture that objectifies women's bodies and promoting empowerment and positive body image.

Self-efficacy

Other work has suggested that those who feel greater physical self-efficacy are likely to be more body-satisfied. In interviews reported in Chapter 3, women bodybuilders indicated that bodybuilding had enabled them to take control of their bodies, and this had impacted positively on their body satisfaction, self-esteem and feeling of mastery over all aspects of their lives (Grogan et al., 2004). Stressing control over the body is a traditional "feminine" discourse, drawing on notions of restraint and control of the female body (Bordo, 2003), although in this case women were talking about increasing rather than reducing the size of their bodies.

Gail Huon (1994) suggests that engagement in group discussion about practical strategies for improving body satisfaction stressing "taking control" may lead to improved body image. She investigated the extent to which it is possible to change young women's attitudes to their bodies and to reduce dieting intentions. Twenty-four women aged 18 to 25 were assigned to four discussion groups. Discussions focused on ideas for helping others to give up dieting and to develop a more positive body image. She found that discussion of strategies for the development of a more positive body image and for giving up dieting was sufficient to produce highly significant changes in women's body satisfaction scores. Discussions of barriers to developing a positive body image produced no significant effects. Informal conversation after the interviews revealed that the women experienced the two kinds of discussion quite differently. Discussion of strategies to improve body satisfaction (taking up sports, identifying goals and learning to value individuality) was experienced as positive and motivating, because the women felt that they had some control over these things. Discussion of factors over which they felt that they had no control (barriers such as media promotion of the thin image and social attitudes to weight and shape, which are covered in media literacy programmes) was experienced as demotivating because of a perception of low control over these factors.

There is a growing body of evidence that moderate exercise, focusing on self-efficacy rather than aesthetics, can improve body satisfaction. Intervention studies where men and women have been randomly allocated to exercise and non-exercise conditions have shown that exercise programmes are effective in improving body image (e.g. Campbell and Hausenblas, 2009; Reel et al., 2007).

Gillian Burgess and colleagues (2006) investigated the effects on body satisfaction and physical self-perception of a six-week aerobic dance programme with fifty British female adolescents aged 13 to 14 years who were selected for the programme because they were dissatisfied with their bodies. Results revealed that participation in the aerobic dance programme significantly reduced body dissatisfaction and enhanced physical self-perception relative to controls. In Canada, in a study conducted by Kathleen Martin-Ginis and colleagues (2005), twenty-eight men and sixteen women completed a twelve-week, five-day-a-week strength training programme. Significant improvements in body image were found for both men and women. The authors conclude that both men and women benefit from subjective perceptions of increased strength, and that women also appear to benefit from objective improvements in strength.

Kathleen Martin-Ginis and Rebecca Bassett (2012) argue that exercise produces increased self-efficacy, and that these changes in self-efficacy are a better predictor of body image change than measurable changes in physical fitness:

> When it comes to using exercise to improve body image, actual changes in one's physical abilities are not nearly as important as the experience and interpretation of these changes.
>
> (Martin-Ginis and Bassett, 2012: 414)

These positive effects of exercise on body satisfaction suggest that people, and particularly women, should be encouraged to undertake exercise as a way of improving body image, as well as for the other positive impacts on mental and physical health.

Body appreciation

Although body image research has a history of prioritizing negative aspects of body image, a strong new focus within body image research is the move towards a positive psychology paradigm (Seligman and Csikszentmihalyi, 2000). Tracy Tylka and Nichole Wood-Barcalow (2015) have focused on body appreciation rather than body dissatisfaction. This approach is proving extremely fruitful and is enabling understanding of how some individuals manage to maintain body satisfaction in societies where the ideal is slender/muscular and their bodies do not correspond to this ideal. Tylka and Wood-Barcalow (2015) argue that if body image interventions reduce symptoms of negative body image without enhancing positive body image they may merely enable people to tolerate their bodies, whereas enabling people to appreciate and celebrate their bodies may make interventions more effective, and may enable maintenance of those gains.

Tracy Tylka (2011) argues that positive body image comprises having a favourable opinion of the body irrespective of its actual appearance, acceptance of the body, respect for the body and rejection of media imagery to protect the body. Positive body image has been shown to be multifaceted, holistic, stable yet malleable in interventions, protective, linked to self-perceived body acceptance by others and shaped by social identities (Tylka and Wood-Barcalow, 2015). Tracy Tylka (2012) suggests that positive body image permits individuals to appreciate the uniqueness and functionality of their bodies, to emphasize body assets and minimize imperfections so that they "feel beautiful, comfortable, confident and happy with their body" (p. 658), and that these factors act as schemata which enable people high in body appreciation to interpret incoming information in a body-protective manner. Studies that focus on the impacts of media models on women's body image have supported the protective role of body appreciation when women view idealized media models (e.g. Andrew et al., 2015; Halliwell, 2013).

Tylka and Wood-Barcalow (2015) argue that women with positive body image praise their bodies for what they are able to do, what they represent and their unique features, focusing on assets rather than flaws, and being comfortable in their bodies even if they do not conform with sociocultural ideals. Tylka (2012) suggests that interventions promoting body functionality, embodiment and body acceptance would be likely to improve body image, and Tylka and Wood-Barcalow (2015) suggest that principles from strength-based disciplines such as humanist psychology (e.g. unconditional acceptance) and Buddhist principles such as self-compassion might be likely to promote positive body image.

Training in self-compassion has also been found to improve body image. Self-compassion has been defined in various different ways, but broadly entails treating oneself in a caring and empathic way. Kristin Neff (2003) defines three interconnected elements of self-compassion: self-kindness, common humanity, and mindfulness. In a recent study Ellen Albertson and colleagues (2015) have shown that a three-week period of self-compassion significantly reduced body dissatisfaction and body shame in a multi-generational group of US women relative to wait-list controls. The authors suggest that self-compassion may be an effective way to improve body image in adult women. Most impressive perhaps is the fact that these improvements were maintained when the same women were assessed three months later, so benefits do not seem to be limited to the time period shortly after the intervention.

Work on body functionality (focusing on everything the body can do rather than how it looks) has also shown that focusing on aspects such as health, physical capacities, senses and creative endeavours, rather than viewing the body as an object, can promote body appreciation and reduce body dissatisfaction. Jessica Alleva and colleagues (2015) have also shown that focusing on body functionality can promote positive body image. In this study, eighty-one women with negative body image were allocated at random to the *Expand Your Horizon* programme (designed to improve body image through training women to focus on the function of their bodies using structured writing assignments) or a control condition. The authors measured appearance satisfaction, body appreciation, self-objectification and functionality satisfaction before, directly after, and one week after the intervention. They found that women in the *Expand Your Horizon* condition increased their body appreciation, appearance satisfaction and functionality satisfaction, and decreased their self-objectification relative to controls. This study supports suggestions that focusing on body function can reduce negative body image.

In 2013 we ran a study where we designed an intervention around the three pillars of body functionality, embodiment and appreciation (Grogan et al., 2014). The intervention was drawn from the discipline of dance movement psychotherapy (Payne, 2006). The dance movement psychotherapy session that we used attempted to facilitate an exploration of body image which focused on feeling, understanding and appreciating the body (Johnson, 2007). Our initial aim was to investigate how dance movement psychotherapy was experienced by participants in relation to their subjective experiences of body image (how it impacted on their body perception, evaluation, and feelings relating to the body).

Thirteen young people aged 17 years old took part in the study; six were male and seven were female. All were volunteers selected through a further education college in the UK, and all were white except for one young woman who identified as Asian. In focus groups and interviews after one session of dance movement psychotherapy, participants reported that they felt that the session had helped them to become more aware of certain body parts, which in turn helped them to appreciate them more and feel more positive about them.

Participants said that they felt much freer to be who they chose, and that the session had reduced the importance they placed on other people's opinions and attitudes towards their bodies. For instance, one of the young men said:

I think this has really helped me to understand that it's not about what other people think, this is who I am, this is what I want.

The session seemed to enable participants to feel more positive and accepting of their bodies. Results need to be replicated with longer sessions, more sessions, and with larger groups of young men and young women in and out of school in exercise and non-exercise environments. However, in general this study shows that this kind of session has promise as a means of promoting positive body image for young women and men.

The results support work showing that Swedish adolescent girls and boys with positive body image tend to focus on body function and fitness (Frisen and Holmqvist, 2010), and that Canadian and Australian adolescents who were proud of their bodies tended to value their unique features rather than trying to emulate mainstream cultural ideals (McHugh et al., 2014; see also Halliwell, 2015). Results also support work suggesting that adult women who exercise for functional, health and enjoyment reasons tend to report higher body appreciation (Homan and Tylka, 2014), and that activities such as belly dance promote positive body image (Tiggemann et al., 2014b).

General conclusions

This book presents an account of current research on body image in men, women, and children. It has been necessarily selective. Most of the research that is cited comes from the realm of psychology, since most empirical work on body image has been carried out by psychologists. Where possible, data from other social sciences have been presented. The result is a comprehensive, wide-ranging, but necessarily partial review of the variety of influences on men's and women's body image, and the behavioural effects of these influences.

The people most at risk of body dissatisfaction are those who belong to identified at-risk groups (white heterosexual women and gay men), those who have low self-esteem, and those who have internalized the thin/muscular ideal. Media representations of the slender ideal (slender and muscular for men) may lead to unfavourable social comparisons, and may result in dissatisfaction, particularly in women who have internalized societal ideals and men low in muscularity satisfaction. Interview work suggests that women in particular are critical of media portrayal of the "ideal body", and want to see more realistic images of women in the media. Media role models may differ depending on the age of the viewer, with viewers making active choices as to comparison groups.

Older women are not more dissatisfied with their bodies than young women in general, in spite of media preferences for very young models, probably because they choose age-relevant targets for body image comparisons, though women who have a lower "felt age" are more likely to compare themselves against fashion model ideals. There is some evidence that older men are less satisfied with their size/adiposity than younger men. Children from age 8 years present similar discourses of body shape, and similar levels of body concern, to adults. It seems that body dissatisfaction is the common experience of many people raised in Western cultures.

Based on what we know about men's and women's body image, we can conclude that the way forward in terms of developing positive body image must be a reduction in the objectification of the body (both male and female) and the development of body ideals based on function as well as aesthetics. In particular, acceptance in mainstream Western cultures of the wide variety of body shapes and sizes that represent the normal range, and the destigmatization of overweight in Western cultures, may help to reduce dissatisfaction.

Cultural factors are important in determining people's experience of their bodies, and current evidence from subcultural groups that do not stigmatize obesity suggests that acceptance of diversity may be expected to lead to a reduction in body dissatisfaction. Belonging to a subcultural group that supports alternative body images may enable women to resist social pressures to be slender, and studies suggest that identifying with groups with ideals that vary from the mainstream can buffer people against negative body image (e.g. Grogan et al., 2004; Schooler and Daniels, 2014). There is evidence that women who bodybuild at "Physique" level, attaining a highly muscled body, are supported by the bodybuilding community (other bodybuilders and competition judges), enabling these women to feel physically and mentally strong and raising their self-esteem and self-confidence.

Women who forge alternative body ideals seem to be most satisfied with the way that they look. Women who have had mastectomy as a treatment for breast cancer and who reject mainstream ideals, seeing their changed bodies and scars positively as "war wounds", seem to have a more positive body image (Grogan and Mechan, 2016). Various authors have argued that some lesbian subcultures de-emphasize the slim beauty ideal and have a broader range of acceptable body types, and reviews have concluded that lesbians tend to be marginally more satisfied than heterosexual women (e.g. Morrison et al., 2004). Black women also tend to be more satisfied with their bodies than white women, and it has been argued that they are supported through African-American and Afro-Caribbean cultures that have more flexible and less thin body-shape ideals for women than white subcultures (see Chapter 6).

A recurrent theme in the body image literature is the importance of gender in determining body satisfaction. Irrespective of age, ethnicity and class, women (in general) are less satisfied with their bodies than are men. Clearly, future work needs to do more to clarify this gender imbalance, and to present potential solutions for improving women's body image. Naomi Wolf (1991) argued that women needed to reclaim the ways that "beauty" for women is represented in the popular media and in the culture as a whole:

> Costumes and disguises will be light-hearted and fun when women are granted rock-solid identities. Clothing that highlights women's sexuality will be casual wear when women's sexuality is under our own control. ... Women will be able thoughtlessly to adorn ourselves with pretty objects when there is no question that we are not objects. Women will be

free of the beauty myth when we can choose to use our faces and our clothes as simply one form of self-expression out of a full range of others.
(Wolf, 1991: 273–4)

Writing in *Cosmopolitan* magazine in 2016, Naomi Wolf says that she feels that things have moved on significantly since the 1990s, and that compared to 1991 "we are in a golden age of choice involving fashion and the body" (p. 60). However, others are less optimistic. Sheila Jeffreys (2015) presents a much more negative view than Wolf, suggesting that beauty practices have become even more damaging to women in the twenty-first century, with more restrictive rules (such as the expectation that women will depilate as a matter of course) and the significant rise of cosmetic surgery and "non-surgical" invasive treatments such as botox and vampire facials (the use of Platelet-Rich Plasma, where blood is extracted from arms and injected into faces; Rose, 2014):

> Women entering the public world, *Beauty and Mysogyny* argues, are expected to self-objectify and enact harmful beauty practices on their bodies if they are to avoid rebuke.
>
> (Jeffreys, 2015: 1)

Self-objectification and social comparison can be detrimental to body image, and Western culture (through the media in particular) encourages competition between women in relation to their bodies. In our interviews with women and girls (Chapters 3 and 6), we have found that women compared their bodies explicitly with those of other women (models, actresses, friends and family members) and often found their bodies wanting, leading to lowered body satisfaction. Furthermore, research on media effects (Chapter 5) suggests that women and girls continue to make unfavourable comparisons against the slender bodies of media fashion models and actresses. The recent move toward the objectification of the male body was discussed in Chapter 4. It cannot be in the interests of women if cultural objectification of the body is expanded to include men's bodies as well as women's. Objectification of the body needs to be challenged whether the targets are women or men. This is particularly the case for young gay men, whose bodies are generally more objectified than those of heterosexual men, in association with higher levels of appearance concern.

Despite a large amount of new work on body image in the twenty-first century, there remain areas which require a better understanding. We still need to know more about the development of body dissatisfaction, especially in children under 8 years of age. We also need more research to investigate whether the cultural homogenization in body satisfaction, in relation to social class and ethnic groups, is a valid and reliable trend. More research with non-white, non-middle-class groups would help to answer this question. Although we now understand much more about older men's body image, there is still a lot to do in this area. We also need to know more about the associations between social media and body image.

196

Tylka and Wood-Barcalow (2015) and others have made great strides in understanding positive body image, but we still need to know more about how to promote positive body image; particularly in boys and men. We now understand much more about the intersections between gender, ethnicity, age and sexuality in relation to body image, but the impacts of complex social identities on body image still require more research.

Body image in people with physical disabilities is still not well understood, though it has been suggested that people with physical disabilities may be resistant to some of the weight and shape concerns that affect the wider community (e.g. Ben-Tovim and Walker, 1995). Eleni-Marina Ashikali and Helga Dittmar (2010) have shown that blind women may be more satisfied with their bodies and may diet less than sighted women. More extensive work on body image in people who are disabled will develop our understanding of embodiment, body dissatisfaction, thin-ideal internalization and social comparisons in men and women in general as well as in people who are disabled.

The twenty-first century is doubtless a time of increased interest in body image. Scientific developments in fields such as cosmetic surgery (Jeffreys, 2015) and pharmacology (Hall, Grogan and Gough, in press) have given people in Western cultures the potential to change the ways that their bodies look. The representation of a narrow range of body shapes in the media leaves viewers in no doubt as to how they are expected to look, and ideals are becoming culturally homogeneous. The diet and cosmetic surgery industries benefit from this dissatisfaction by offering apparent solutions that can be bought by the body-dissatisfied consumer.

In the long term, it will be important to reduce cultural objectification of the body and to shift body aesthetics to encompass a variety of body shapes and sizes, and various activists within the fashion world, as well as academics, are trying to exert social change (Chapter 5). In the short term, interventions to improve self-esteem and self-efficacy, and to reduce the internalization of thin/muscular ideals, social comparison and self-objectification, may be useful. The relatively new focus on body appreciation has already shifted the ways that we think about body image in the twenty-first century, away from pathology and body dissatisfaction and towards positive body image. Encouraging satisfaction with body types that differ from the prevailing aesthetic, celebrating uniqueness and focusing on what bodies can do rather than how they look, may result in improved quality of life for a significant proportion of the population, and particularly for women.

Summary

- The social relativity of body satisfaction has been demonstrated by illustrating how satisfaction varies by social group; the same body shape may be perceived more or less positively depending on the gender and social group of the person doing the perceiving. Being white and being heterosexual are likely to predict body dissatisfaction in women. Men are likely to be more satisfied in general, although gay and older men may be expected to be most dissatisfied.

197

- The average woman could be expected to have dieted to try to lose weight, and the average man is probably not highly motivated to diet or exercise even if he perceives a mismatch between current body image and ideal body image. If he does change his behaviour, he will probably exercise.
- Low self-esteem, internalization of the thin ideal, social comparison, self-objectification and low self-efficacy predict body dissatisfaction. Media literacy interventions are promising for use with adolescents, as are CBT, feminist approaches and exercise interventions with adults.
- There is a move towards positive body image and away from a focus on body dissatisfaction, and linked interventions are promising.
- Cultural changes in the acceptability of a variety of body types for both men and women, and a focus away from body objectification, would be likely to improve body satisfaction for both women and men.

Bibliography

Ahern, A.L. and Hetherington, M.M. (2006) 'The thin ideal and body image: An experimental study of implicit attitudes', *Psychology of Addictive Behaviours*, 20 (3), 338–42.

Albertson, E.R., Neff, K.D. and Dill-Shackleford, K.E. (2015) 'Self-compassion and body dissatisfaction in women: A randomized controlled trial of a brief meditation intervention', *Mindfulness*, 6 (3), 444–54.

Alleva, J.M., Martijn, C., Van Breukelen, G.J.P., Jansen, A. and Karos, K. (2015) '*Expand Your Horizon:* A programme that improves body image and reduces self-objectification by training women to focus on body functionality', *Body Image*, 15, 81–9.

Andrew, R.J., Tiggemann, M. and Clark, L.S. (2015) 'The protective role of body appreciation against media-induced body dissatisfaction', *Body Image*, 15, 98–104.

Ashikali, E.-M. and Dittmar, H. (2010) 'Body image and restrained eating in blind and sighted women: A preliminary study', *Body Image*, 7 (2), 172–5.

Avsec, A. (2006) 'Gender differences in the structure of self-concept: Are the self-conceptions about physical attractiveness really more important for women's self-esteem?' *Studia Psychologica*, 48 (1), 31–43.

Ben-Tovim, D. and Walker, K. (1991) 'Women's body attitudes: A review of measurement techniques', *International Journal of Eating Disorders*, 10 (2), 155–67.

Blashill, A., Williams, A., Grogan, S. and Clark-Carter, D. (2015) 'Negative appearance evaluation is associated with skin cancer risk behaviors among American men and women', *Health Psychology*, 34 (1), 93–6.

Bordo, S. (2003) *Unbearable weight: Feminism, Western culture, and the body* (10th anniversary edition), Berkeley, CA: University of California Press.

Burgess, G., Grogan, S. and Burwitz, L. (2006) 'Effects of a 6-week aerobic dance intervention on body image and physical self-perceptions in adolescent girls', *Body Image*, 3 (1), 57–67.

Calogero, R.M, Pina, A. and Sutton, R.M. (2014) 'Cutting words: Priming self-objectification increases women's intention not pursue cosmetic surgery', *Psychology of Women Quarterly*, 38 (2), 197–207.

Campbell, A. and Hausenblas, H.A. (2009) 'Effects of exercise interventions on body image: A meta-analysis', *Journal of Health Psychology*, 14 (6), 780–93.

Cash, T.F. (2012) 'Cognitive behavioural perspectives on body image', in T.F. Cash (Ed.), *Encyclopedia of body image and human appearance* (pp. 334–42), London: Elsevier.

Cash, T.F. and Hrabosky, J.I. (2004) 'The effects of psycho-education and self-monitoring in a cognitive-behavioral program for body-image improvement', *Eating Disorders*, 11 (4), 255–70.

Cash, T.F. and Strachan, M.T. (2002) 'Cognitive-behavioral approaches to changing body image', in T.F. Cash and T. Pruzinsky (Eds), *Body image. A handbook of theory, research, and clinical practice* (pp. 478–86), New York: Guilford Press.

Connors, J. and Casey, P. (2006) 'Sex, body-esteem and self-esteem', *Psychological Reports*, 98 (3), 699–704.

Coughlin, J.W. and Kalodner, C. (2006) 'Media literacy as a prevention intervention for college women at low- or high-risk for eating disorders', *Body Image*, 3 (1), 35–43.

Engeln-Maddox, R. (2005) 'Cognitive responses to idealized media images of women: The relationship of social comparison and critical processing to body image disturbance in college women', *Journal of Social and Clinical Psychology*, 24 (8), 1114–38.

Franko, D.L., Fuller-Tyszkiewicz, M., Rodgers, R.F., Holmqvist Gattario, K., Frisén, A., Diedrichs, P., Ricciardelli, L., Yager, Z., Smolak, L., Thompson-Brenner, H. and Shingleton, R. (2015) 'Internalization as a mediator of the relationship between conformity to masculine norms and body image attitudes and behaviors among young men in Sweden, US, UK, and Australia', *Body Image*, 15, 54–60.

Frederickson, B.L. and Roberts, T. (1997) 'Objectification theory: Towards understanding women's lived experience and mental health risks', *Psychology of Women Quarterly*, 21 (2), 173–206.

Freedman, R. (1990) 'Cognitive-behavioral perspectives on body image change', in T. Cash and T. Pruzinsky (Eds), *Body images: Development, deviance and change* (pp. 272–95), New York: Guilford Press.

Frisen, A. and Holmqvist, K. (2010) 'What characterises early adolescents with a positive body image? A qualitative investigation of Swedish girls and boys', *Body Image*, 7 (3), 205–12.

Grabe, S., Ward, L. and Hyde, J.S. (2008) 'The role of the media in body image concerns among women: A meta-analysis of experimental and correlational studies', *Psychological Bulletin*, 134 (3), 460–6.

Grippo and Hill (2008) 'Self-objectification, habitual body monitoring, and body dissatisfaction in older European American women: Exploring age and feminism as moderators', *Body Image*, 5 (2), 173–82.

Grogan, S. (in press) 'Appearance and smoking', in Hall, M., Grogan, S. and Gough, B. (Eds), *Chemically modified bodies: The use of diverse substances for appearance enhancement*, London: Palgrave Macmillan.

Grogan, S. and Mechan, J. (2016) 'Body image after mastectomy: A thematic analysis of younger women's written accounts', *Journal of Health Psychology* [E-pub ahead of print: DOI 10.1177/1359105316630137].

Grogan, S., Evans, R., Wright, S. and Hunter, G. (2004) 'Femininity and muscularity: Accounts of seven women bodybuilders', *Journal of Gender Studies*, 13 (1), 49–63.

Grogan, S., Shepherd, S., Evans, R., Wright, S. and Hunter, G. (2006) 'Experiences of anabolic steroid use: Interviews with men and women steroid users', *Journal of Health Psychology*, 11 (6), 849–60.

Grogan, S., Williams, A., Kilgariff, S., Bunce, J., Heyland, S.J., Padilla, T., Woodhouse, C., Cowap, L. and Davies, W. (2014) 'Dance and body image: Young people's experiences of a dance movement psychotherapy session', *Qualitative Research in Sport, Exercise and Health*, 6 (2), 261–77.

Hall, M., Grogan, S. and Gough, B. (2015) 'Bodybuilders' accounts of synthol use: The construction of lay expertise', *Journal of Health Psychology* [E-print ahead of publication: DOI: 10.1177/1359105314568579].

Hall, M., Grogan, S. and Gough, B. (in press) *Chemically modified bodies. The use of diverse substances for appearance enhancement*, London: Palgrave.

Halliwell, E. (2013) 'The impact of thin idealized media images on body satisfaction: Does body appreciation protect women from negative effects?' *Body Image*, 10 (4), 509–14.

Halliwell, E. (2015) 'Future directions for positive body image research', *Body Image*, 14, 177–89.

Halliwell, E. and Dittmar, H. (2005) 'The role of self-improvement and self-evaluation motives in social comparisons with idealised female bodies in the media', *Body Image: An International Journal of Research*, 2, 249–62.

Halliwell, E., Harcourt, D. and Easun, A. (2011) 'Body dissatisfaction: Can a short media literacy message reduce negative media exposure effects amongst adolescent girls?' *British Journal of Health Psychology*, 16 (2), 396–403.

Heinberg, L., Thompson, J.K. and Stormer, S. (1995) 'Development and validation of the Sociocultural Attitudes Toward Appearance Questionnaire', *International Journal of Eating Disorders*, 17 (1), 81–9.

Homan, K.J. and Tylka, T.L. (2014) 'Appearance-based exercise motivation moderates the relationship between exercise frequency and positive body image', *Body Image*, 11 (2), 101–8.

Huon, G. (1994) 'Towards the prevention of dieting-induced disorders: Modifying negative food- and body-related attitudes', *International Journal of Eating Disorders*, 16 (4), 395–9.

Irving, L.M. and Berel, S.R. (2001) 'Comparison of media-literacy programs to strengthen college women's resistance to media images', *Psychology of Women Quarterly*, 25 (3), 103–11.

Jarry, J.L. and Beraldi, K. (2004) 'Characteristics and effectiveness of stand-alone body image treatments: A review of the empirical literature', *Body Image*, 1 (3), 319–33.

Jarry, J.L. and Ip, K. (2005) 'The effectiveness of stand-alone cognitive-behavioural therapy for body image: A meta-analysis', *Body Image*, 2 (4), 317–33.

Jeffreys, S. (2015) *Beauty and mysogyny: Harmful cultural practices in the West* (2nd edition), London: Routledge.

Johnson, M. (2007) *The meaning of the body*, Chicago: University of Chicago Press.

Jones, D.C. (2004) 'Body image in adolescent girls and boys: A longitudinal study', *Developmental Psychology*, 40 (5), 823–35.

King, T.K., Matacin, M., White, K. and Marcus, B.H. (2005) 'A prospective examination of body image and smoking cessation in women', *Body Image*, 2 (1), 19–28.

Kozar, J.M. and Damhorst, M.L. (2009) 'Comparison of the ideal and real body as women age: Relationships to age identity, body satisfaction and importance, and attention to models in advertising', *Clothing and Textiles Research Journal*, 27 (3), 197–210.

Levine, M.P. and Piran, N. (2004) 'The role of body image in the prevention of eating disorders', *Body Image*, 1 (1), 57–70.

Martin-Ginis, K.A. and Bassett, R.L. (2012) 'Exercise: Effects on body image', in T.F. Cash (Ed.) *Encyclopedia of body image and human appearance* (pp. 412–17), London: Elsevier.

Martin-Ginis, K.A., Eng, J.J., Arbour, K.P., Hartman, J.W. and Phillips, S.M. (2005) 'Mind over muscle? Sex differences in the relationship between body image change and subjective and objective physical changes following a 12-week strength training program', *Body Image*, 2 (4), 363–72.

McHugh, T.L., Coppola, A.M. and Sabiston, C.M. (2014) '"I'm thankful for being Native and my body is part of that": The body pride experiences of young Aboriginal women in Canada', *Body Image*, 11 (3), 318–27.

McKinley, N.M. (2011) 'Feminist perspectives on body image', in T.F. Cash and L. Smolak (Eds), *Body image: A handbook of science, practice and prevention*, 2nd edition (pp. 48–65), New York: Guilford.

Morrison, M.A., Morrison, T.G. and Sager, C.-L. (2004) 'Does body satisfaction differ between gay men and lesbian women and heterosexual men and women?' *Body Image*, 1 (2), 127–38.

Murnen, S.K. and Seabrook, R. (2012) 'Feminist perspectives on body image and physical appearance', in T.F. Cash (Ed.), *Encyclopedia of body image and human appearance* (pp. 438–43), London: Elsevier.

Murnen, S.K. and Smolak, L. (2009) 'Are feminist women protected from body image problems? A meta-analytic review of relevant research', *Sex Roles*, 60 (3), 186–97.

Neff, K.D. (2003) 'Self-compassion: An alternative conceptualization of a healthy attitude toward oneself', *Self and Identity*, 2 (1), 85–102.

Neumark-Sztainer, D., Paxton, S.J., Hannon, P.J., Haines, J. and Story, M. (2006) 'Does body satisfaction matter? Five-year longitudinal associations between body satisfaction and health behaviours in adolescent females and males', *Journal of Adolescent Health*, 39 (2), 244–51.

O'Dea, J. (2004) 'Evidence for a self-esteem approach in the prevention of body image and eating problems among children and adolescents', *Eating Disorders*, 12 (3), 225–41.

O'Dea, J. (2007) *Everybody's different: A positive approach to teaching about health, puberty, body image, nutrition, self-esteem and obesity prevention*, Camberwell, Australia: Australian Council for Educational Research Limited.

O'Dea, J. (2012) 'Body image and self-esteem', in T.F. Cash (Ed.), *Encyclopedia of body image and human appearance* (pp. 141–7), London: Elsevier.

O'Dea, J.A. and Abraham, S. (2000) 'Improving the body image, eating attitudes and behaviors of young male and female adolescents: A new educational approach that focuses on self-esteem', *International Journal of Eating Disorders*, 28 (1), 43–57.

Orbach, S. (2010) *Bodies*, London: Profile Books Ltd.

Payne, H. (2006) 'Introduction: Embodiment in Action', in H. Payne (Ed.), *Dance Movement Therapy: Theory, Research and Practice* (pp. 1–17), London: Routledge.

Paxton, S.J., Neumark-Sztainer, D., Hannon, P.J. and Eisenberg, M.E. (2006) 'Body dissatisfaction prospectively predicts depressive mood and low self-esteem in adolescent girls and boys', *Journal of Clinical Child and Adolescent Psychology*, 35 (4), 539–49.

Peterson, R.D, Grippo, K.P. and Tantleff-Dunn, S. (2008) 'Empowerment and powerlessness: A closer look at the relationship between feminism, body image and eating disturbance', *Sex Roles*, 58 (9), 639–48.

Peterson, R.D., Tantleff-Dunn, S. and Bedwell, J.S. (2006) 'The effects of exposure to feminist ideology on women's body image', *Body Image*, 3 (3), 237–46.

Piran, N., Jasper, K. and Pinhas, L. (2004) 'Feminist therapy and eating disorders', in J.K. Thompson (Ed.), *Handbook of eating disorders and obesity*, Hoboken, NJ: Wiley.

Pope, H.G., Phillips, K.A. and Olivardia, R. (2000) *The Adonis complex: The secret crisis of male body obsession*, New York: Free Press.

Pridgeon, L. and Grogan, S. (2012) 'Understanding exercise adherence and dropout: An interpretative phenomenological analysis of men and women's accounts of gym attendance and non-attendance', *Qualitative Research in Sport, Exercise and Health*, 4 (3), 382–99.

Reel, J., Greenleaf, C., Bakker, W.K. et al. (2007) 'Relations of body concerns and exercise behavior: A meta-analysis', *Psychological Reports*, 101 (3), 927–42.

Ridolphi, D.R. and Vander Wal, J.S. (2008) 'Eating disorders awareness week: The effectiveness of a one-time body image dissatisfaction prevention session', *Eating Disorders*, 16 (5), 428–43.

Rose, D. (2014) *What is a vampire facial?* Available online at: www.telegraph.co.uk/beauty/skin/what-is-a-vampire-facial/ [accessed 4 August 2014].

Schooler, D. and Daniels, E.A. (2014) '"I am not a skinny toothpick and proud of it": Latina adolescents' ethnic identity and responses to mainstream media images', *Body Image*, 11 (1), 11–18.

Seligman, M.E.P. and Csikszentmihalyi, M. (2000) 'Positive psychology: An introduction', *American Psychologist*, 55 (1), 5–14.

Slevec, J. and Tiggemann, M. (2011) 'Media exposure, body dissatisfaction, and disordered eating in middle-aged women: A test of the sociocultural model of disordered eating', *Psychology of Women Quarterly*, 35 (4), 617–27.

Springer, E.A., Winzelberg, A.J., Perkins, R. and Taylor, C.B. (1999) 'Effects of a body image curriculum for college students on improved body image', *International Journal of Eating Disorders*, 26 (1), 13–20.

Steese, S., Dollette, M., Phillips, W., Hossfeld, E., Matthews, G. and Taormina, G. (2006) 'Understanding Girls' Circle as an intervention on perceived social support, body image, self efficacy, locus of control, and self-esteem', *Adolescence*, 41 (161), 55–64.

Stice, E. and Shaw, H. (2004) 'Eating disorder prevention programs: A meta-analytic review', *Psychological Bulletin*, 130 (2), 206–27.

Tiggemann, M. (2005) 'Body dissatisfaction and adolescent self-esteem: Prospective findings', *Body Image*, 2 (2), 129–36.

Tiggemann, M., Slater, A. and Smyth, V. (2014a) 'Retouch free: The effect of labelling media images as not digitally altered on women's body dissatisfaction', *Body Image*, 11 (1), 85–8.

Tiggemann, M., Coutts, E. and Clark, L. (2014b) 'Belly dance as an embodying activity?: A test of the embodiment model of positive body image', *Sex Roles*, 71 (5), 197–207.

Tiggemann, M., Martins, Y. and Kirkbride, A.B. (2007) 'Oh to be lean and muscular: Body image ideals in gay and heterosexual men', *Psychology of Men and Masculinity*, 8 (1), 15–24.

Tylka, T.L. (2011) 'Positive psychology perspectives on body image', in T. Cash and L. Smolak (Eds) *Body image: A handbook of science, practice and prevention*, 2nd edition (pp. 56–67), New York: Guilford.

Tylka, T.L. (2012) 'Positive psychology perspectives on body image', in T.F. Cash (Ed.), *Encyclopedia of body image and human appearance* (pp. 657–63), London: Elsevier.

Tylka, T. and Wood-Barcalow, N. (2015) 'A positive complement', *Body Image*, 14, 115–17.

van den Berg, P., Thompson, J.K., Brandon, K.O. and Coovert, M. (2002) 'The Tripartite Influence model of body image and eating disturbance: A covariance structure modeling investigation testing the mediational role of appearance comparison', *Journal of Psychosomatic Research*, 53, 1007–20.

von Soest, T., Kvalem, I.L., Skolleborg, K.C. and Roald, H.E. (2006) 'Psychosocial factors predicting the motivation to undergo cosmetic surgery', *Plastic and Reconstructive Surgery*, 117 (1), 51–62.

Want, S. (2009) 'Meta-analytic moderators of experimental exposure to media portrayals of women on female appearance satisfaction: Social comparisons as automatic processes', *Body Image*, 6 (4), 257–69.

Webster, J. and Tiggemann, M. (2003) 'The relationship between women's body satisfaction and self-image across the life span: The role of cognitive control', *Journal of Genetic Psychology*, 164 (2), 241–52.

Wilksch, S.M. and Wade, T.D. (2009) 'Reduction of shape and weight concern in young adolescents: A 30-month controlled evaluation of a media literacy program', *Journal of the American Academy of Child and Adolescent Psychiatry*, 48 (6), 652–61.

Wolf, N. (1991) *The beauty myth: How images of beauty are used against women*, New York: William Morrow.

Wolf, N. (2016) 'Would your life be better blonde?' *Cosmopolitan*, February, 56–60.

Yamamiya, Y., Cash, T.F., Melnyk, S.E., Posavak, H.D. and Posavac, S.S. (2005) 'Women's exposure to thin-and-beautiful media images: Body image effects of media-ideal internalisation and impact-reduction interventions', *Body Image*, 2 (1), 74–80.

INDEX